Another Good Dog

Another Good Dog

One Family and Fifty Foster Dogs

CARA SUE ACHTERBERG

PEGASUS BOOKS
NEW YORK LONDON

ANOTHER GOOD DOG

Pegasus Books Ltd.
148 W 37th Street, 13th Floor
New York, NY 10018

First Pegasus Books cloth edition August 2018

Interior design by Maria Fernandez

ISBN: 978-1-68177-793-1

10 9 8 7 6 5 4 3 2

Printed in the United States of America

Distributed by W. W. Norton & Company, Inc.

For all the dogs who never make it out the front door of the shelter.
For all the shelter employees who have to make the hard decisions.
And for all the dog-hearted people who are working tirelessly
to change the situation.

Contents

Another Good Dog

ONE

We Can Foster Dogs?

I guess it says something about our marriage that my husband didn't argue when I told him we had to drive forty minutes to a bowling alley parking lot just off the Baltimore Beltway at midnight to pick up a beagle from South Carolina.

It was five degrees on the car's thermometer when we pulled off the Beltway.

"How do we know who they are?" asked Nick as we drove past the bright neon entrance.

I scanned the parking lot. "There," I pointed. Multiple SUVs with motors running were parked next to a streetlamp where a small group of people gathered around one open trunk. We parked a few spaces away and watched as the group of mostly women chatted while handing out dog crates, bags of bedding and food, even cookies, oblivious to the cold. I watched them for another minute and then said, "I'm going to go meet them."

"I'll wait here," said Nick. Neither of us is very social. We would almost always rather stay home with a deck of cards and a bottle of wine than be forced to talk to strangers, even strangers we know. But this was my gig, so I pulled on my mittens and my friendly face, and opened the door.

I approached the group tentatively and asked about a crate. "Oh, you're the new foster," said one woman. "Big crate, right? You like big dogs?"

I nodded. I was under the impression that the dog I was picking up would be my foster and I was more of the *fosterer*, but I would soon learn that dog rescue has a lingo all its own. I'm a foster, and the dog I'm caring for is my foster.

When Nick saw me struggling with the large crate, he jumped out of the car and hurried over to help. The assembled crate barely fit in the back of our Honda Pilot. I lined it with a mattress pad and an old blanket I'd brought. I'd never crated a dog before, but the rescue had recommended using a crate. I worried it would remind the dog of the cage she'd just left. At the same time, I wasn't ready to sacrifice my carpet to an un-housebroken dog. What if this dog didn't like me or my kids or my dog, Gracie? Once I thought about it, a crate seemed like a good idea.

After we assembled the crate, Nick got back in the warm car, but I wandered over to chat with some of the experienced fosters. I learned that two pregnant mama dogs were on this transport and that several of the families were there to retrieve multiple dogs. *More than one at a time?* Two of the other Pennsylvania foster moms talked about their experience with state inspections. They'd both fostered over twenty-five dogs in one year which made them qualify as a kennel and required the inspections. I couldn't imagine doing this twenty-five times. I found it heartening that, to a person, everyone was friendly and kind. They were happy to be there and excited to meet their new foster dogs, even on a night as bitter cold as this.

My fingers had just about solidified when a white rental van zipped into the parking lot. I followed the others and we formed a semicircle around the back of the van. As soon as the smiling driver, Gina, opened the doors, excited barking echoed across the parking lot. The dogs were in crates stacked one on top of the other and secured with bungee cords. I could not imagine driving twelve hours, or even ten minutes, with that kind of ruckus. Clearly Gina was made of stronger stock than me; either that or she was deaf. She began opening the crates, calling each dog's name, and waiting for its foster to retrieve it.

It was just like my favorite children's book, *Go, Dog. Go!,* as nearly twenty dogs, big and small, cute and not-so-cute, in every shape and color, were off-loaded and handed over to their foster. The carriers were pulled apart and stacked back in the van. It was an impressive operation made even more so in the brutal elements.

Nick appeared by my side. "Which one is ours?" he asked.

Galina, our foster dog, was in a shoebox-sized crate. I crouched down and looked through the grate at her sweet face. She was about the size of a large Chihuahua and shaking like a leaf. I didn't know how big a beagle was supposed to be, but I thought she'd be bigger than this.

We pulled her out of her crate and Nick ran her around the parking lot, while Erika, the young woman who seemed to be in charge, explained the meds in the bag she handed me. The cranberry pills would prevent urinary tract infections (UTIs) common in shelter dogs because they hold their pee for so long in transport and out of nervousness. There were also heart worm preventatives, vitamins, probiotics, coconut oil, and flea-and-tick preventative, plus a few goodies—treats, food samples, and a chew bone. She handed me an official folder with Galina's name on it. "When the records are uploaded, print them out and put them in this." I nodded as if I knew what she was talking about and carried it all back to the car where Nick was putting Galina in her crate.

Galina flitted from one side of the crate to the other, watching as we drove, the whites of her eyes flashing. Although it was warm in the car, she was shaking. When I put my hand through the crate wire, she placed her head beneath it and stopped moving, allowing me to pet her. We drove like this until my arm began to cramp from the awkward angle and I pulled it out of the crate.

"We have a foster dog," I said, smiling at Nick.

"She sure is little," he replied. I'd told the foster coordinator from Operation Paws for Homes (OPH) that we wanted to foster large dogs, since that's all we'd ever had, but there weren't any available on this transport. OPH is an all-breed rescue, taking dogs from high-kill shelters in the South and bringing them northward to foster homes in Virginia, Maryland, D.C., and Pennsylvania, where they can be adopted into forever homes. They bring up dogs of every size and breed, even heartworm-positive dogs, pregnant dogs, and litters. I liked the inclusivity of their policies; the idea that any dog (or person) is worth more than another has always irritated my soul.

We were just getting off the Beltway onto I-83, the highway that would take us back to Pennsylvania, when Galina finally sat down. Her head sagged nearly to the floor of the cage in exhaustion, eyes closed, but still she didn't lay down. She swayed as we made the turn onto I-83.

That's when it happened. And while there's never a good time, these things never seem to happen on a pretty afternoon when you're not in a hurry. They always happen late at night, on the interstate, when it's five degrees and you've just picked up a beagle from a bowling alley parking lot. There was a loud *thunk* and then a waffling sound. Nick pulled the car to the shoulder. We'd blown a tire. It was well after midnight now and the temperature had dropped a few more degrees.

"Now what?" I asked, glancing at Galina who was back to pacing the cage.

"I change it."

"Should I help you?"

"I got it. Stay here with the dog." One of the things I've always appreciated about my husband is he can fix pretty much anything. I, on the other hand, am not the least bit mechanically inclined. When Nick and I met, I was using a butter knife to adjust the volume on my stereo because the button had popped off and I didn't know how to replace it. I've always been a person who will make do. I get that from my mom who grew up dirt-poor in the coal mining hills of Pennsylvania. I still watch Nick build furniture and shelves, rewire entire rooms, and install appliances, and wonder how I would have survived adulthood without him. I'm not a helpless woman; I'm sure I would have figured something out. I'd probably be using my cutlery for all manner of tools and tricks.

I waited as Nick jacked up the back of the car and removed the flat. I look out at the cold, clear night and I thought, *I am the luckiest woman in the world to be married to a man who can change a tire in frigid temperatures on the side of a highway at midnight after driving me to a bowling alley parking lot to meet some equally crazy people to retrieve a tiny beagle and a very large crate. And to not curse while doing it.*

We arrived home near one in the morning, and offered Galina water and a quick bite to eat before showing her to her accommodations. It had been a long night for us, and even longer for Galina, but she had made it safely from rural South Carolina to our living room. As I watched her cower and shake in her crate, I wondered if I was crazy to have gotten us into this.

I knelt down in front of her crate and put my hand out. She regarded it and then backed away from me. Fostering a dog seemed like such a good idea a few weeks ago, but now it was really happening. Here was Galina in my living room and so far, she didn't seem too happy about it.

"Your life only gets better from here," I told her before shutting off the lights and going to bed. "Promise."

All three of our teenagers were excited about our first foster dog, but I lay in bed that night and wondered—how would we give this little dog away when the time came? And what if it didn't come? What if no one wanted her?

When I told people we were going to foster rescue dogs, they looked at me like I had three heads, and asked, "Why?"

I fumbled around with a noble answer about wanting to help dogs who needed a home, but that wasn't the real reason. The real reason was more complicated and it started with the painful, ever-present fact that I missed Lucy. Lucy had been my dog for the past seventeen years. She'd run with me every morning at dawn, trained with me for a marathon, and protected me against aggressive dogs, friendly good ole boys, and even the occasional possum. She matched me stride for stride with her long foxhound legs.

Lucy had perfect manners—she never peed in the house, stole food off the counter, or chased the cats. She was gentle, beautiful, playful, and when the occasion called for it, fierce. For better or for worse, she killed the groundhog that put holes in our pasture, the bunnies that ravaged my garden, and the possums that simply freaked me out. She threatened anyone who threatened us, but backed down as soon as we asked. Lucy put up with every manner of indignity helping to raise our three kids: suffering through multiple costume changes, tea parties, "dog shows," endless games of fetch, and taking a lot of heat for popping an untold number of soccer balls.

About six years ago, we brought home a puppy as what Nick called, "the backup dog." But Lucy needed no backup, which was a good thing as the new puppy proved untrainable. We named the puppy Gracie. She was a hound dog like Lucy, but her relatives must have been the kind of hound dogs who lounged on the front porch while their owners drank moonshine rather than the ones who hunted and tracked. We've never determined whether Gracie's refusal to come when called, perform any kind of trick, or cooperate in any way was because she was dumber than a doornail or smarter than all of us. On a regular basis, she ran through her invisible fence to roll in horse manure or steal the barn cat's food, always staying out of reach when we tried to catch her. Inevitably, she would show up the next morning sitting just on the far side of her invisible fence line, tired, smelly, and hungry. Someone (not me) would take pity on her, remove her collar and lead her back to the house.

When Lucy died in the fall, she left a gaping hole in our collective heart. I'd been running alone for the past year as her age had finally caught up with her. She'd wait patiently at the bottom of the drive when I left for my run and hobble happily up the drive with me to the house

ANOTHER GOOD DOG

upon my return. One night her breathing became erratic and she paced the house looking disoriented and scared. We tried to calm her, all of us taking turns sitting with her. She died that night in her sleep. It was a peaceful passing after a long good life. We were blessed, but at the time I thought—*never again*. That hurt way too much.

I couldn't imagine replacing her, so we went back to being a one-dog family. It was time for the backup dog to step up. Only she didn't. Instead, with Lucy gone, Gracie began going in and out of the house incessantly, staying outside for mere minutes before scratching at the door to come in, only to beg to go back out soon after. It was if she'd lost something and was certain it was outside until she was outside, and then she was sure it was inside.

She began chewing on her back and legs for no apparent reason. She didn't have fleas. There was no rash or injury. We tried changing her diet, to no avail. When she was inside, and not begging to go out, she followed me around, parking herself behind my chair when I wrote, interrupting me with her snores and farts. She chased the cats, bit the FedEx delivery man, and escaped the invisible fence on a near daily basis.

I'd thought I would wait to adopt another dog, wait until I didn't miss Lucy so much and wouldn't compare every potential dog to her. But months had passed, and I only missed Lucy more. Gracie's behavior wasn't helping. Finally, it dawned on me. Gracie missed Lucy too. With no example or company, she'd gone slightly feral, driving us all nuts. Maybe it was time to find a friend for Gracie. And maybe a new dog would ease the hurt in my heart.

Lucy had been my very first dog. We'd had family dogs when I was growing up, but she was the first one I'd picked out and brought home as an adult. How would I find another dog like Lucy? Nick and I adopted her from a shelter when our oldest son Brady was a toddler. I can't even remember what made us decide to get a dog. Maybe we were practicing for adding another child (we had Addie a year after we adopted Lucy). Brady wasn't with us when we went to the shelter. I think visiting the shelters may have actually been a date. (We're exciting like that.)

We walked up the cement aisle and looked through the metal fences at all the dogs. One dog caught my eye—a small hound cowering in the back of her kennel. A note on her kennel said that she was already adopted. My heart sank, and we moved along visiting with the other dogs. We passed a few older dogs, big dogs with matted coats and life-weary eyes. There were dogs that lunged at the fence as we passed, running frantically up and down their pens. Several obese tiny dogs huddled together on a blanket. This was before the era of pit bulls dominating the shelters as they do these days.

Nick liked a couple lab-like dogs, but they seemed a bit too enthusiastic to my mind. I knew I'd be the one spending the most time with this dog we brought home. I was working full-time then, but had a flexible job that allowed me to work from home on the days we didn't have daycare for Brady. I pictured these big dogs knocking over Brady and clearing the coffee table with their tails. We lived in a 1,100-square-foot house. We had no room for a seventy-five-pound dog.

"What do you think?" asked Nick.

I shook my head. "I really like that hound. I wish she wasn't adopted already."

We walked back to look at the hound again, and I put my hand against the fence. She thumped her tail and ducked her head. Then she slowly crept toward me. She was six months old and about thirty-five pounds. She licked my hand and I looked in those liquid brown eyes. I wanted her.

Nick decided to go ask about her. That's something I've always loved and hated about my husband—he's never afraid to ask, and he doesn't necessarily take no for an answer. It's probably the reason we're married. I was involved with someone else when we met. In fact, my heart was set on this other man; I was just waiting for him to make a real commitment. This didn't stop Nick from pursuing me. Three months later we were dating and four months after that he asked me to marry him. The man is determined and persistent and maybe a tad bit impatient.

He returned with an application for us to fill out. He said that the person who was supposed to adopt the dog had only one more day to show up. If he didn't, we could adopt her. And, the shelter worker told Nick, if she wasn't adopted tomorrow, the dog's time would be up. So we filled out the application and waited, and the next day we drove back to the shelter and brought Lucy home. I remember looking at the enormous incinerator on the far side of the parking lot as we walked in. I found it hard to believe that they would put a puppy as sweet and beautiful as Lucy in it if we hadn't come back today. Nick said, "They just say that to pressure you," but I had my doubts. I mean, there was the incinerator. It wasn't pretend—they used it for *something*.

We pulled out of that parking lot with our precious new puppy, and I never looked back. We lived in that town for five more years and never once visited the shelter again, but every time I drove past I looked to see if there was smoke coming out of the incinerator.

That was seventeen years ago. Shelters have changed quite a bit, but not nearly enough. There are still kill shelters, but now at least, there are many rescues and no-kill shelters too. We toured the local Animal Rescue, a no-kill shelter just a few miles from our house. Most of the dogs had been there for quite some time. We took our youngest son, Ian, who was twelve at the time, with us and found one dog that seemed pretty nice. And by pretty nice, I mean he didn't lunge at Ian like he intended to kill as several had; he wagged his tail, and he had all his limbs.

We walked the dog around their property. I tried to picture him as ours. He was sweet, but nervous, and clearly wanted to go back with the other dogs. His manners were fine, but he seemed uninterested in us. Maybe I would have felt differently if there had been an incinerator in the parking lot, but we put him back. He was a nice dog; someone would certainly adopt him.

We looked on website after website at dog after dog after dog. It was pretty clear that Nick would be happy with any dog. He just liked dogs. Any of them would be fine for him. This was going to be my call, my decision. We filled out lengthy applications and enlisted our friends to be references. But none of the dogs measured up. None felt right. I'd watch Gracie roll on my couch, leaving a trail of white hair and the faint scent of horse manure, and think—*we have to be pickier this time. We can't adopt just any dog.*

I emailed about several dogs only to be told they were already adopted. I began to wonder if the shelters were leaving pictures of the best dogs up on their site to entice people into applying. The old bait and switch, as it were.

Finally, I found a dog that seemed like a good fit. He was a young border collie at a shelter in Maryland, about a forty-minute drive from us. We were told we couldn't meet him until we'd been approved, so I filled out yet another application and listed references. Over a lengthy phone interview, I answered questions about our income, family members, habits, dog knowledge, and how we would care for this dog if we were approved.

It hadn't been nearly as complicated when we'd adopted Gracie only five years before. She'd come through a rescue. It had only been a matter of a few emails before we drove to her foster home and picked her up.

A few days later I got an email telling me that there was no need for a home visit. I had not been approved. *What?* We'd had Lucy for seventeen years and Gracie for six now. Wasn't that evidence enough that we could provide a good, safe home for any dog? No, I was told; our invisible fence was not a safe situation for dogs. When I explained to my friends why we weren't adopting the border collie, they told me to apply for a different dog but not mention the fence. It wasn't as if anyone would see it if they came for a home visit. After all, it was *invisible*.

I considered this option, but in the end lying or not lying wasn't the point. There was nothing wrong with keeping a dog in an invisible fence. Let's see—the options are incinerate the dog because we can't afford to shelter it any longer, or let someone adopt it and keep it in an invisible fence? Which is worse? *AGH.* The policy was stupid, and I told the shelter contact that in a lengthy email. I never heard from her again.

Right around that time, I saw a post on a local Facebook group I'd joined for pet owners and animal aficionados. It was a plea for foster homes for rescue dogs. I imagined we'd never be approved to foster a dog, what with our dangerous invisible fence and all, so I scrolled right past.

The next day I saw a post from a local friend about her foster dog. She was a beautiful Treeing Walker Coonhound. I messaged Karen right away and asked about the dog. She said this dog was very skittish and shy and needed time. We decided to wait and see how it did at Karen's house.

Maybe it was because I was spending so much time on shelter and rescue sites, but the idea of fostering kept coming up. Every time I turned on the computer there was another mention of fostering. "Maybe we could foster dogs," I said to Nick. "Essentially give them a try out, and keep the one that's best."

"You'd never be able to give a dog back," warned Nick. "We'd end up with twenty dogs."

When another hound dog appeared with an outfit called Operation Paws for Homes, I commented on the post, casually. "We might be able to foster this dog," I wrote.

Immediately I got a message back with a link to an application. *What the heck*, I thought. *They'll never approve me with my invisible fence.* I filled out the form, clearly stating our dangerous fence. I got an email back that same day asking when could I talk. Maybe they had only skimmed my application. Maybe they hadn't noticed my big bad fence.

The next day I spoke with Mindy, from OPH. She didn't say anything about my fence. She was more concerned with Gracie and her lack of heartworm meds. I explained about Gracie's inability to swallow pills and how we'd tried for years to give her the expensive pills but most months we found them later under her dog bed. She said they'd have to consider this and she'd get back to me. Meanwhile, I wondered what the big deal was about heartworm, so I looked it up. "Holy shit," I said to Nick. "We have to get those pills into Gracie somehow." But then I read further and realized that there was also a topical heartworm medicine. I contacted my friend and neighbor who also happens to be our vet and asked him about it. "We don't carry it, but I'll write you a script," he said.

I emailed Mindy back. "No worries. We found a way to get heart-worm meds in Gracie."

And that was that. We were now officially fosters for Operation Paws for Homes.

"Operation Paws for Homes?" asked Nick. "That's kind of dorky sounding." I made a face and then informed him that I'd been reading about rescues and OPH was very professional and moved a lot of dogs. "That's good; I wouldn't want us to take in some oddball dog and be stuck with it for years," he said. I looked at Gracie, but said nothing.

Many of the rescues I'd read about were loaded with passion, but lacked organization and resources. I learned later how much rescue work is done on "a wing and a prayer," and can only admire the self-sacrificing work done by so many, but if I was going to drag my family into this with me, I needed an organization with a real budget and a real plan. The people I talked to at OPH were passionate and professional, an important combination.

OPH also valued natural, healthy dog care—doling out coconut oil to help build up the foster dog's immune system and cranberry extract to avert UTIs, feeding grain-free dog food, and dosing with probiotics.

"They're weirdos, like me," I said when I told the kids about the probiotics and grain-free food. They nodded knowingly. They'd spent the last eight years fighting my efforts to feed them more vegetables and less processed food, turning their noses up at my homemade yogurt. When I refused to subscribe to cable television or buy soda, they claimed I was stunting them socially. They rolled their eyes when I brought home a grain-grinder and invited local beekeepers to move their hives in. They were much more enthusiastic about Mom's "dog thing" than Mom's "organic thing."

The next day, we were emailed a list of dogs headed our way on a transport that very weekend!

I looked through the options. I wanted to pick a good dog for our first foster. Fifteen-year-old Addie wanted a small dog—*purse-sized*. Twelve-year-old Ian, wanted *a really, really big dog*. When I asked my oldest son Brady, a senior in high school, what kind he wanted, he shrugged his shoulders. He was already mentally checking out of this inn, so he said any dog was fine. I chose Galina, the sweet little beagle with floppy ears and freckles who was now sleeping in our living room.

Galina was an odd name, a regular occurrence in dog rescue. One dog we'd considered adopting the month before was named Cornbread, and another Burrito. I wondered if the names were chosen according to what the rescue worker had for lunch that day. I thought Galina was a city in Texas, but I googled it and discovered it was the name of a wedding dress designer. So maybe the rescue worker was reading *Brides* magazine on her lunch break.

The next morning when I opened Galina's crate, she regarded me warily from the back corner. I brought her some food and watched as she wolfed it down quickly. Then she took a tentative step toward me. "See? I'm not so bad," I said. I reached for her, and she braced herself but didn't move. I clipped a leash on and she followed me outside. As the day wore on, she warmed up slowly. At first, remaining in her crate, but eventually wandering out to meet Gracie. In a few hours, she was exploring the house, crawling under the chairs in the kitchen in search of crumbs, and happily eating every treat I offered.

Galina's first weekend with us was quite similar to having a visit from a busy toddler. She was adorable and made us speak in high pitched baby voices, but every time she was left unattended (and sometimes when she wasn't), she put something she shouldn't in her mouth. "Gross," I laughed as she made off with Ian's smelly soccer socks he'd left balled up beside the front door. Ever since he could walk, Ian had his hand or foot on a ball of some kind. He loved to play the game, any game, simply for the sheer joy of it. His sports gear littered our home. That weekend Galina gnawed on his baseball glove, chewed through the elastic on his shin guards, and popped a tiny souvenir football he'd won at the beach. She couldn't resist the delicious scents of sweat, salt, and dirt.

I pulled a paper with the high school course selection list from her mouth. "Do you need this?" I asked Addie, holding out the wrinkled, sodden sheet. She paused, her hands poised above the piano keyboard, scowled at me and shook her head, before returning to her music. She had no patience for my interruptions or this new dog. Most days, Addie filled our home with music. She practiced for hours, pouring her emotions into the music. She'd always been an intense child. Even the doctor said so when at one day old she looked him in the eye and tracked his finger as he moved it back and forth. "She's very *intense*," he remarked. I remember lying in my hospital bed and wondering if that was a good thing or a bad thing.

Turns out it's both. Having such an intense approach to life resulted in many tears and much yelling in her younger years. As a teenager, her highs are high and lows are low, and she always has an opinion that strains the fabric of our conservative small town. But when Addie pours all that intensity into her music, the result is stunning. Again and again, I listen to her sing or play and am left marveling at her gift and wondering where it will take her. Making a living in the arts is no small feat, but I am learning to accept her dream. When she talks about majoring in musical theater in college, her eyes light up with excitement, and each time I counter with, "But what else would you study?" her face drops and my heart knows I should have stayed quiet.

When Galina found a bottle of vitamins, she made music of her own, racing through the living room, the pills rattling in the plastic jar. I chased after her already imagining how I would explain to OPH that my foster had overdosed on children's vitamins. That night when she chewed the side off the ottoman, I was almost grateful. The ugly vinyl ottoman had been an impulse buy and looked every bit as cheap as it was. Nick hauled it to the garbage and I vowed to keep a better eye on Galina.

On the counter at the orthodontists' office where I've taken all three kids for braces, there is a shadow box containing a mangled, half-eaten retainer with a sign that says, "Dogs love retainers!" Every time I've seen it, I've thought, what kind of person would let their dog chew up a retainer? Now I knew—the kind of person who brought home a strange beagle in the dark of night and didn't keep tabs on it.

By the end of the weekend, Galina seemed to like us more, but she still shrank from my touch. As I petted her, she froze, waiting for me to finish. It didn't make sense that she shied from our attention, especially because she followed me from room to room, wagging her tail as I talked to her. *What was her story?* Galina arrived with no history. I scanned the handful of documents that came with her. No clues to her origin, only information on her health when pulled from the shelter. It seemed that people who work in the shelters don't have time to document each dog's story, they're too busy trying to keep them alive. We'd have to deduce Galina's history by her behaviors.

One Tuesday morning, Ian called shortly after he'd arrived at the middle school. He'd forgotten his drumsticks and practice pad, could I bring them? It was rare that Ian forgot anything. Brady and Addie had both been diagnosed with ADD at some point in their elementary years. They forgot instruments, lunches, and homework on a regular basis, but Ian was different. He had his father's sense of responsibility, laying out his clothes the night before, reminding me about his orthodontist's appointment, and was always dressed and ready thirty minutes before it was time to leave for practice. So when he called that morning asking if I could bring his drumsticks, I groaned and questioned whether it was necessary, but ultimately agreed to bring them to the school office before band period.

I decided to take Galina with me on the drive to school. She hadn't been in a car since her arrival. As we drove, she peered out the window, occasionally letting out a quiet hound mutter when she saw something of interest. After leaving the drumsticks in the office for Ian, I hurried back to the car. Galina was sitting in the driver's seat, paws on the steering wheel, watching out the window for me. As I approached she spun two circles, tail wagging, and then retreated to the backseat.

"See? You do like me!" I said, when I got in the car. She lay down on the seat and regarded me with her sad hound dog eyes as if to say, "For now."

A few days later, we woke to eight inches of fresh snow. When I took Galina outside, she launched enthusiastically off the porch only to be immediately swallowed up in the deep powder. Her surprised expression made it clear she'd never seen snow before. With a quick shake of her head to free her long ears, she accepted the situation and in moments was leaping along like a dolphin across the yard. Ian chased after her with his sled.

The day was everything a snow day was supposed to be—sledding, shoveling, and hot chocolate. In the evening we all curled up on the couch in the living room to watch a movie. When I flicked on the TV, Galina stared at it intently. She climbed up on the back of the couch, never taking her eyes off the screen, and sat through the entire movie, seemingly enjoying it as much as we did.

This being Pennsylvania, the kids were back in school the very next day. We referred to this area as Pennsyltucky, partly because of the terrain, but mostly because of the attitudes and the plentiful 4x4 vehicles. Perched just four miles above the Mason-Dixon line, our exit is a frequent pit stop for people making their way from Baltimore or D.C. northward, as it boasts pretty much every fast-food restaurant in existence including a Cracker Barrel, whose parking lot is jammed at all hours. The original town is half a mile west of the exit and consists of one stoplight, a family-owned grocery store, and plethora of antiques shops. There's a Walmart next to the interstate that serves as the town center; you can't stop in to buy a roll of paper towels without running into someone you know.

"How's the dog-thing going?" asked a friend as we stood in line to check out.

"I like it," I told her.

"What kind of dog do you have?"

"She's a beagle. Well, mostly beagle. She's kind of small."

"Like a pocket beagle?"

"Is there such a thing?"

"Yeah, I saw them in the paper. They weren't cheap."

I went home and informed my family that Galina was actually a pocket beagle. Nick looked at me skeptically.

"Where'd Galina come from?" asked Ian as she sat in his lap while he worked on homework at the kitchen table.

"South Carolina."

"Didn't anyone down there want her?"

"She was on the euthanasia list."

Ian put down his pencil. He looked at Galina in his lap. "They were going to kill her?"

I nodded and unloaded the groceries. "They kill lots of dogs."

"Like how many?"

"The shelter where she came from has to euthanize more dogs than they adopt out."

"I'm glad she's here," he said and went back to his work. I was too. But in the big scheme of things, we'd only saved one beagle. There were countless others who never made it out of the shelter. I didn't want to think about it. I couldn't imagine having to be the person who decided which dogs lived and which dogs died.

Gracie watched Galina warily that first week, keeping her distance. But one morning I caught the two of them playing a game of tag in the living room. I'd come running when I heard Gracie's snarls, but as I watched, they chased each other back and forth around the couch and coffee table. Galina looked like she was smiling and Gracie's mouth hung open in delight. Eventually they lay down side by side on the carpet in a sunny spot. We were all in love with her, it seemed, even Gracie.

One night as I was walking Galina, waiting for her to focus and take care of business, there was a commotion in the driveway. Because of the snow and ice, the hay truck couldn't get up the hill to our barn, so the hay was unloaded on the driveway instead. Nick began loading bales in and on our SUV to haul up to the barn. Galina was very interested in this activity, so I took her up the hill to watch.

I looped her leash around a post in the barn and helped stack the bales. Galina watched patiently, until a few chickens wandered into the barn probably looking to see if there was a second seating for dinner.

"What are these delightful creatures?" Galina yapped, in a high-pitched bark we hadn't heard her use before. A voice that clearly said, "I have found my people and they are chickens!"

She threw herself into the task of reaching the chickens, using every ounce of her tiny beagle self to strain against her leash, her bark cut short by the pressure on her neck. When we finished unloading the hay, I allowed her to herd the chickens into a corner, the leash restricting her from actually touching them. (I was pretty sure she was interested in more than just playing with them.)

Eventually I dragged her away, but as we walked down the hill, she assumed a certain swagger and couldn't avert her gaze from the barn full of feathered bliss. Our little beagle was coming into her own, it seemed.

A month had passed and she remained in our care. I checked her page on the rescue website regularly to update the pictures and see if she had any adoption applications. She was ready to find her forever home. Why wasn't anyone choosing her?

I worried we were getting spoiled by our first foster dog. Maybe the next one wouldn't be as much fun or as smart. "Next one?" everyone wondered when I mentioned it. How could I explain that, yes, we had started this venture looking for our next dog, but as I grew to love Galina, I realized that there were more like her, thousands more, who would never make it out of the shelters.

One night, Nick and I were watching college basketball. He was on the couch, and I was sitting on the floor in front of the couch working on a puzzle with one hand and stroking Galina's back with the other. She let out a drowsy whimper and rolled over for me to rub her tummy.

"You like doing this, don't you?" Nick asked. I knew he was talking about fostering dogs. All our conversations revolved around the topic lately.

"How could we not save more Galinas? There are so many other good dogs who deserve a second chance and will never get one. The least we can do is foster a few more. Maybe then we'll adopt one."

"Right," he said, but the way he said it wasn't cynical, it was accepting. He knew me. We'd been married almost twenty years.

He'd listened to my opinions and dreams and schemes, sometimes questioning, but rarely doubting. He might not be as convinced as I that we needed to rescue more dogs, but we were partners in this life, and if rescuing dogs was something I was determined to do, I knew he'd help me do it.

Finally, we received word that Galina had an approved adopter! I read the email and discovered the adopter had been following the blog I'd begun writing about our foster adventures. She already loved Galina and was excited to adopt the "floppy-eared princess." The emails flew back and forth. I answered questions and made plans for them to meet her.

The day before Galina was to leave, I sat with her on the futon in my office, rubbing her ears and trying not to be teary. I wanted to say my goodbye now. I didn't want to cry in front of the adopters. I'd always known she was leaving, but I hadn't been able to picture it until a date was set.

Every day that Galina was here, she had made me laugh. Her presence had been a wonderful distraction from all that was plaguing my mind and my heart. That winter my dream of being a novelist was finally coming true, but it wasn't anything like I pictured it. There was so much work between the time I finally wrote The End, and when that book could be held in a stranger's hand at the bookstore. For so many years I wrote and queried agents and publishers, receiving rejection after rejection. I took that frustration and channeled it into writing more. Eventually, I got used to the rejection notices and even stopped saving them—hitting delete the moment I saw the word "regret."

When I finally got a publication contract, I thought, *This is it. I made it.* But I hadn't and I haven't. Being a writer is rewarding in many, many ways, but definitely not financially. I was coming to terms with the fact that I'd put literally thousands of hours into reaching this point and in the end, it would feel great to say I'd been published, but it didn't change the fact that we had three college educations to pay for, and my income wouldn't even pay for the books they'd need to study at the school we couldn't afford.

It was March now, and Brady still hadn't decided on a college. He had full scholarship offers to several big schools in the South and Southwest, but they were enormous universities that made these offers based solely on the fact that Brady was a National Merit Scholar. These schools were like small cities. They were known for football and partying rather than academics. One of them was currently in the news because of racial unrest and what looked like institutional bigotry. I couldn't imagine my kid who grew up in our one stoplight town, played D&D on the weekends, and regularly lost his wallet and shoes, thriving or even surviving in a Big Ten atmosphere. Besides that, they didn't have the program he wanted to study—creative writing. "You'd have to major in English. What would be the point?" I asked. "And you'd probably need a bike to ride to classes," I threatened. Brady hadn't been on a bike since he'd crashed one into a tree on a camping trip four years before.*

"But it's free," he said. Which was a great point.

The school he really liked had offered him a decent scholarship. But to pay for the rest, Brady would have to take out a loan. He'd graduate nearly $100,000 in debt, which I knew all too well would be darn near impossible to pay off with his creative writing degree. The other option would be for Nick and me to pick up the difference. This would be equivalent to us buying a luxury car we never got to drive every year for four years. And then we'd have to find a genie in a bottle to pay for Addie's college and hope that something changed or our government finally reined in the exorbitant price of college by the time Ian graduated high school in five years. Brady knew this too, so he was ready to try the free ride at the big school rather than go into debt or ask us to pay for

---

* Living on the steep side of a hollow in the hills of Pennsylvania does not lend itself to bike riding. Add to that the windy, narrow, shoulder-less roads in our town. Sadly, none of my kids are very proficient or confident on a bicycle. The only chance they have to ride is when we cart their bikes along on vacation each summer, and two summers before Brady had crashed his bike into a tree. He hadn't been on one since.

the school where he wanted to be. We were in a tight spot. I wished I'd spent the last ten years working at one of the fast-food restaurants out by the interstate instead of squirreled away in my office writing stories.

My heart was torn. I wanted my son to have the college experience I had. I wanted him to have four years following his passion and meeting friends he would keep for life, but at what cost?

I went to move the laundry from the washer to the dryer and Galina followed me, a little beagle shadow. As I passed through the living room, I tried not to notice the layer of dust on the furniture or the dog hair coating our carpet. Years ago, after Addie was born, I'd decided to quit my job and stay home full-time. We let the house-cleaning service go and I took up the job. I'm no Martha Stewart and my cleaning attitude has always been keep it clean enough to be healthy. That means there might be a few messes, but there isn't mold growing anywhere.

After Ian was born, I began doing freelance writing for regional papers and a few magazines while I secretly worked on a novel. Cleaning became even less of a priority. Now that I had a real publishing contract and a book deal, I had to write. It wasn't just to keep my mind engaged so I didn't go crazy from struggling with the directions for Legos or trying to match up the Polly Pocket shoes and purses. It was a job. A low-paying job, but a job nonetheless. Cleaning the house had devolved into shoving things in baskets and occasionally running the vacuum cleaner. If a houseguest loomed or I had to host book club, I would dust, clean a bathroom, and keep the lights dim or hold our meeting on the porch. Between my writing, Galina's trail of destruction, and three teenagers disinclined to follow a chore chart their mother was unlikely to follow through on, the mess in the house was bad. Seriously bad. And it stressed me out.

Galina had been a wonderful distraction from all of that—the dead-lines, the decisions, the mess. Even now, with tears on my face at the thought of goodbye, I could laugh remembering the time she dragged a stuffed elephant from Ian's room that was so big she couldn't see where she was going so she wandered in circles bumping into the door frame, or the time I'd pulled off my sweatshirt and she'd attempted to carry it off, but instead it caused her to trip repeatedly as I chased her down.

I called my OPH coordinator and got the scoop on the adoption contract. It was long. OPH's contracts were meant to protect the dog for life. This was a good thing. This was a good organization. I trusted them, and I trusted their process, so I knew the people coming for Galina would be more than qualified to take her home.

Despite my present sadness, I was excited to meet Galina's new family. I hoped they'd change her silly name. Maybe Princess Sugar Paws or Sweetie the Sock-Eater. Okay, maybe not those names, but a forever name for her forever home.

The adoption was supposed to take place Saturday, but Friday afternoon I got an email that said Galina's adopters had chosen another dog. At first I was relieved, and then I felt guilty that I was relieved, and then sad for Galina. And sad for us, too, since we'd all been coming to terms with saying goodbye and now we'd have to do it all over again when the next adopter appeared.

Later that same evening, Nick, Brady, and I drove two hours to Susquehanna University, the school that Brady wanted to attend, for a presentation on their honors program. As the presentation dragged on, I checked my phone and saw that Galina had a new approved adopter! *Could we meet her tomorrow?* Lump in throat, I sent a quick note to the potential adopter.

I knew they would be the perfect parents for Galina when in response to my honest warning about Galina's chewing habits, the adopter wrote, "We know about the chewing. Our previous beagle mix chewed through our home. I don't own a pair of flip-flops without teeth marks in them!"

The new adopters arrived Saturday morning with Galina's new furbrother, Gimli, a Chihuahua about the same size as Galina with crazy Taco Bell–dog ears. The couple worried Gimli would be protective and aggressive with Galina, but she won him over in mere minutes. *That's my girl,* I thought. Galina warmed up to her adopters even faster. When she met new people, Galina would generally hang back, shy and unsure, until she got to know them. Not with these two. It was almost like she recognized them. *Hey, it's Mom and Dad!* She trotted happily along beside her new dad when I gave him her leash.

Before they left, Ian selected one of Galina's stuffed animals from the pile in her crate and her favorite sock that had not yet been completely unraveled and gave them to her new family.

After she was gone, I kept thinking of things I should have told them. Sometimes when you walked her, she'd duck from loud cars and then spring after them when they passed. I did remember to warn them that she loved to eviscerate toilet paper rolls.

All that day, as I sorted what was left of her toys between salvageable or not, I held in the tears. That night I watched basketball with no little snuggle muffin to make it worth my while. At bedtime, there were no late-night dog-chasing-dog shenanigans. No laps around the living room; Gracie went to bed uneventfully.

The next day was no easier. I missed the happy little whimpers Galina made when I opened her crate in the morning as she crawled out like a soldier under fire to lay as a little fur ball of ecstasy at my feet—so happy to see me, she couldn't even stand up. Gracie began napping in the abandoned crate.

A few days later, we got our first report. Strider, the dog formerly known as Galina, was happy as a little clam in her new digs with her forever family. Her new mommy sent a video of her rolling in the leaves of her new yard and dragging her furbrother, Gimli, by his leash down a tiled hallway. Galina looked happy. She'd found her forever family. She'd made it out of that shelter where she could have died. Where she very likely *would* have died. I still had a lump in my throat at the thought of her, but no tears because I realized her leaving meant we could now save another dog.

Nick watched the video over my shoulder. "Look what you did," he said.

"Look what *we* did," I corrected him.

TWO

A Foster Puppy!

With Galina launched, we pored over the listing of the next batch of dogs coming up on transport. Among the many options I spotted a brown-and-white puppy with folded-over ears. "Look!" I exclaimed, calling Nick and Ian to come look at the website. "She's as cute as Gracie was when she was little!"*

"You want another Gracie?" asked Nick.

"She's not another Gracie, she's another Gracie-as-a-puppy. Don't you remember how adorable she was?" I figured this adorable puppy would stay with us for two weeks, and then she'd get adopted

---

* Not that Gracie isn't still cute—in fact, that is probably her saving grace, so to speak.

lickety-split, before I was tasked with attempting to train her. To be fair to Gracie, her lack of manners was as much my fault as hers. When we'd brought her home, I'd been the busy mom of three active kids, working several part-time jobs, attempting to write a novel, and grow all our food. I had no business adopting a puppy. I certainly hadn't put in the time to train her.

"We'll take Wheat Penny," I emailed Mindy, my foster coordinator. And then we all got very excited—*a puppy*! How much fun will that be?

Mindy emailed back. "Great! I've attached the Puppy Guidelines."

Wait? There are Puppy Guidelines?

As I read the puppy foster guidelines from OPH, a small panic set in. Sheesh! This wasn't going to be easy. When I explained to Nick that we would have to keep Wheat Penny quarantined inside our house and she wouldn't even be able to go outside to pee, he was worried. When I told him she had to stay in an area of the house that we could potentially treat with bleach, he blanched.* When I told him this might go on for as long as nine days, he asked, "What's the return policy? Couldn't we put this one back and chose a different one—preferably a dog?"

"They have these rules for a reason," I told him. "It'll be fine."

I spoke those words, but in fact I feared this experience might derail our entire foster career before it was off the ground. Because puppies coming from unknown origins with questionable vaccination histories can carry dangerous and hard-to-kill viruses, OPH took the Puppy Guidelines very seriously.

Silly name, resemblance to Gracie, and crazy quarantine requirements aside, Wheat Penny was an adorable seven-month-old, fifteen-pound beagle/spaniel mix, and we were all excited to meet her. We would set her up in our guest bathroom (tile floor) for her quarantine period. A friend gave us puppy pads, and I lined the tub with blankets as a cozy little bedroom for her. I asked a few questions to clarify the seriousness of the quarantine rules, and was informed by OPH's medical coordinator, Jen, that they weren't at all "bendy." She also told me that

---

* Pun intended.

CARA SUE ACHTERBERG

because Wheat Penny was an older puppy, it was entirely possible that she'd already had a few vaccinations. Jen gave me her word that as soon as she had that information, she'd spring Wheat Penny. (Fingers crossed, candles lit, juju sent.)

The transport was again a late evening drop. This time Nick wouldn't be able to accompany me as he was returning from a business trip that night. No problem. I could do this solo. I'd set up the crate again in the back of our Honda Pilot. What were the odds of another flat tire?

Friday afternoon, Brady returned from school and reported that the Honda was making a weird sound.

"What kind of sound?" I asked.

"A not-good flopping sound."

I checked the tires. They looked fine. I took the car for a spin. Definitely a not-good-flopping sound. Now what? The Pilot was our only car large enough to hold the dog crate. Wheat Penny looked small in the pictures, but I wasn't convinced she would fit in our cat carrier and didn't really want to jam her into it after her long ride up from South Carolina. Instead, I recruited Addie to come with me for the pickup. She could hold Wheat Penny on her lap for the ride home.

Addie was enthusiastic about the adventure. "We're picking up a puppy late at night in the parking lot of a bowling alley?" she asked, eyebrows raised and a smile spreading across her face. She donned all black clothing for the trip and planned to Snapchat (*what?*) the entire thing.

We arrived at the parking lot and I told Addie we had to wait for an unmarked white van to arrive, she grinned. "Seriously?"

It was about sixty degrees warmer for this transport than the last, but the scene was much the same. Friendly strangers gathered around an SUV where more friendly strangers handed out dog food, treats, toys, and towels. I made small talk while Addie remained in the car and took more pictures reporting our activities on Snapchat.

When the van doors opened, Wheat Penny's joyful little face was the first I saw, and Gina, who had once again driven the transport van, quickly unloaded her for me. Wheat Penny didn't have a collar, just a band like the ones you get at a music festival or bar that show you're

26

old enough to drink. I put the collar on her that I'd brought (which could have circled her tiny neck twice) and carried her to the car. She was a squirming bundle of happiness, attempting to leap out of my arms toward every person we passed as we made our way across the dark parking lot. Per the puppy guidelines no one was allowed to touch her but us and she wasn't allowed to touch the ground. Addie walked beside me and took pictures and narrated our progress to Snapchat-land.

I settled* Wheat Penny on Addie's lap where she proceeded to squirm, chew Addie's fingers or phone, and/or lick Addie's face for the entire thirty-minute drive home. By the time we reached home, Addie was no longer Snapchatting. "Stop it!" she told Wheat Penny who shivered with excitement and attempted to climb over Addie's shoulder. "Make her stop!" she told me as Wheat Penny chewed on her arm and pawed at her hair.

Nick was home when we arrived and helped me move Wheat Penny into her new digs in the bathroom. Addie vanished.

"She is ridiculously cute," he admitted.

"I know," I said and smiled, watching her do laps around the tiny bathroom space, pausing occasionally to cover us in puppy kisses.

Wheat Penny was the puppy you saw on greeting cards. She wasn't the least bit hound-like, but more closely resembled a miniature golden retriever, if there was such a breed. She was loose-hipped, happy, with four white socks, a soft golden coat, and ears that flopped in different directions.

When Wheat Penny was released from quarantine a few days later, she happily took over our house. Her puppy prowess was remarkable. There was nothing she wouldn't chew (including the cats), and the housetraining was sketchy at best. She developed a penchant for pooping in the kids' bedrooms and was consequently banished to the kitchen after I spent a morning scrubbing poop stains that had been tracked from one bedroom through the hall on an otherwise unaware foot.

---

* As much as it's possible to settle a seven-month-old puppy who has just been released from an entire day spent in a small crate.

27

I did find a job for Wheat Penny. She was excellent at reveille. Each morning when the appointed hour came and went and no teenagers emerged from their rooms to get ready for school, I knocked on each bedroom door, and upon hearing nothing, opened the door and released Wheat Penny. She would stand frozen, ears perked and muscles tensed, as she scanned the room. The moment the unsuspecting teenage victim made the mistake of rolling over or moaning some lovely greeting like, "Go away," she leapt on her victim in a flash, licking, pawing, nuzzling. There was no way to sleep through a Wheat Penny alarm.

Another excellent ability she had was that of carpet and corner cleaner. No popcorn kernel, bread crumb, or errant piece of pasta was left behind. She tried very hard to secure the position of assistant dishwasher, climbing into the dishwasher to lick the plates.

But one of her most amazing talents we called "shock and awe." She would creep into the living room and launch herself over the side of the couch into the face of unsuspecting readers and TV viewers. She did this at full speed and took great pleasure in surprising her victims.

Once she mastered house training, we released her to explore the house. Ian followed her and reported back, "She's really good at the lava game."* Wheat Penny could spring across four- and five-foot spans to avoid touching the carpet, and always aspired to the highest perch in any room.

"No dogs on the furniture," called Nick from where he was working on the computer in the next room.

I chased her into the kitchen. I looked around to see where she'd gone, completely missing the fact that she was sitting in the center of the kitchen table, chewing on a pencil. She looked up at me, cocked her head to the side in that classic-puppy pose, and the pencil fell from her lips before she launched herself off the table to clamor for my attention.

Gracie was not impressed with Wheat Penny, even if they did make a nice matching set. On my blog, I posted a picture of Gracie as a puppy

---

* The Lava Game is the age-old game of moving about the house *on top* of the furniture—jumping from coffee table to couch to end table to ottoman and never touching the "lava" (floor).

beside a photo of Wheat Penny. They could have been siblings. The cats never hesitated to smack Wheat Penny when she came within reach, but even their hostility did not deter her exuberance.

After the rough introduction, Addie fell completely in love with Wheat Penny, taking endless pictures and scratching Wheat Penny behind the ears, crooning, "Who's the cutest puppy ever? Who? You are!"

Even Ian, who grew very tired of Wheat Penny's overtures, couldn't hold his hard line for long. Whenever he sat down to eat, she circled his chair, occasionally jumping in his lap or nipping at his feet or licking his toes (if they were available). He ate almost constantly, as he was playing baseball, soccer, and throwing shot put and discus on the middle school track and field team that spring. Usually he grumbled and put her in her crate before taking his plate to the table, but it wasn't long before he was speaking in the baby-language we all adopted around her.

As expected, Wheat Penny had an approved adopter in less than a week. After all the ups and downs of Galina's adoption, we weren't expecting Wheat Penny to be swooped out from under us in mere days! She couldn't leave immediately though, because the Puppy Guidelines dictated that she had to remain in the foster home for two weeks before she could be adopted.*

I fielded plenty of emails from her excited adopter who referred to her as "Wheat Berry" and me as "Clara." Wheat Penny's impending adoption changed the status of our little darling. No longer was she a potential long-term guest, now she was more like a visiting grandchild. We indulged her, allowing her on the couch for wrestling, tummy scratches, and ear kisses.

When her adopter arrived to meet her that Saturday, she was instantly smitten. She told me she'd already been interviewing dog-walkers so that Wheat Berry wouldn't be alone all day long while she worked. It appeared that Wheat Penny had found her sugar mama.

---

* OPH requires a two-week hold on puppies, to be certain they are healthy and don't break with parvo, an extremely dangerous and contagious virus. Parvo risk is also a reason for the quarantine.

After the visit with her adopter, I met my friend, Mer, for a hike. I brought Wheat Penny along to entertain her ten-year-old daughter, Shannon, who had been petitioning for a new puppy.* "Don't worry, she's already adopted," I told Mer before Shannon could even ask. I gave Shannon the leash, and Mer and I followed the two of them up the trail.

Mer also had a college-bound son. We commiserated about the crazy cost of college and our boys' seemingly unrealistic dreams. We'd been friends since our own college days, and roommates briefly after college, so she was someone I could trust with my fears about our finances and the reality of making a living as a writer. We didn't solve our problems, but if felt good to air them. We were both baffled how so many people were sending kids to colleges that cost upwards of $50,000 a year. When we had our babies three weeks apart eighteen years ago, college was expensive but the in-state tuition costs had more than tripled since then.

We arrived back at the parking lot and Shannon reluctantly turned over Wheat Penny's leash. "Guess we'll be dog shopping soon," said Mer, with a roll of her eyes. "Thanks."

The next day I ran into a friend at the grocery store. She'd read on my blog about the damage Galina had done to our ottoman, and about Wheat Penny's "poop hallway" incident and she asked if I was still glad we were doing this. I told her I was. One of the best things about fostering was something I hadn't anticipated. When my kids became teenagers there was less and less we could together as a family.† We laughed and complained about Wheat Penny and still reminisced about Galina. Fostering might have been my idea, but it was something we were doing together as a family. Brady would graduate in less than two months, so family time was especially sacred. If uniting against (or in favor of) a destructive, adorable puppy was something that put us in the same room laughing together, I'd take it.

With Wheat Penny/Berry's imminent departure, I couldn't resist a plea that came across the OPH wires to foster a dog being returned by

---

* Nick said this was like taking crack to an addict.

† Without a credit card or a beach house.

her adopter.* Carla was a Treeing Walker Coonhound† being returned after four years for numerous reasons, none of which had to do with Carla in particular and all of which had to do with a large coonhound living in a suburban home with three children under the age of six (and one on the way).

I took one look at Carla on the website and had to have her. She was my dream dog. When we moved to our present home, we had daily visits from our neighbor's gorgeous Treeing Walker Coonhound named Trailer. I loved Trailer's long ears and beautiful, deep bay. I loved his goofiness and his amazing nose and his unrelenting friendliness. I was lonely those first few years—missing my old friends and struggling to find friends in a community that was more insular and conservative than the one I'd left. Many days Trailer's visits were the highlight of my day. His deep hound bay would echo across the hollow announcing his arrival. The kids and I would hurry outside and he'd greet us with unbounded enthusiasm and his big goofy smile. His presence kept the foxes away from our chicken pen and scattered our cats.

That first Thanksgiving, Trailer stole the turkey carcass my mom left on the porch.‡ When I asked the neighbors where they got him, they said they bought him at a gun show. I couldn't imagine me and my Quaker husband heading off to a gun show, and I had serious qualms about buying a purebred dog, so I figured my Treeing Walker would have to be Trailer. Luckily, our neighbors shared him happily. Trailer died a few years ago, and I've missed him ever since.§

---

* Per OPH adoption contract, if an adopter decides they can no longer keep a dog they've adopted through OPH, they must return the dog to the first available foster home.

† Treeing Walker Coonhounds do not walk up trees. They're bred to chase and tree racoons and get the walker part of their name because they are descended from walker coonhounds.

‡ She takes home our turkey carcass every year and returns it in the form of turkey noodle soup.

§ Not to mention a month or so after he was gone, a fox became a regular visitor stealing our chickens one by one.

When Carla's sweet face appeared on my computer screen, I yelled to Nick, "Look at this dog!" He was a fan of Trailer, too, so it took no convincing to get him on board. I'd said all along, "One dog at a time," but if I stuck to my guns, I couldn't take Carla. As it turned out, Carla was the gateway drug. For the very first time, we had *three* dogs in the house.

THREE

Hooked

Carla arrived a few days before Wheat Penny left. She weighed seventy-five pounds and stood nearly as tall as the counter. Her beautiful tricolor coat was short and smooth. She had thoughtful eyes and gorgeous, silky, long ears and a large, busy hound dog nose.

The email explaining why they were returning her after four years said, "Carla is just existing here, she's not living." Basically, she was an enormous hound dog trying to be a suburban pet in a busy household that increasingly had no time for her. I couldn't resent the owners for surrendering her. I was sure it wasn't an easy decision. Carla deserved a better life and they knew that. It's very tempting to get angry about much regarding dog rescue, but anger doesn't help. I was quickly learning that if we wanted to help the dogs, we had to look past the people.

Carla had picked up a few nice suburban dog habits. Unlike your typical coonhound, Carla had wonderful manners. She waited patiently while I prepared her dinner, she walked nicely on a leash rarely pulling, and she was polite with the other dogs.

On our walk that first Saturday morning, she froze in her tracks at the sound of a neighbor's rooster. I coaxed her along and she followed me, scanning the treetops for the danger. *What self-respecting coonhound was afraid of a rooster?* Perhaps, one raised on a street with a neighborhood association. We rounded the bend and came upon another neighbor's rusted out Chevy sitting on blocks, she shied from it warily, but couldn't take her eyes off it.* I'd been watching this particular car melt into the hillside for years. The vinyl roof was nearly gone now and weeds grew through the windows, but there was a fresh sign in the window, NOT 4 SALE.

When we got home, I took Carla with me up the hill to the barn. I opened the gate to let the horses out of the paddock and they took off across the pasture at a gallop. Carla yelped and practically dragged me off my feet in her fright. "No horses either?" I asked. Next, we fed the chickens. She circled the chicken pen, nose to the ground. We'd lost more chickens to foxes again, and Nick had recently lined the pen with boulders. I checked for any evidence of attempted break-ins. The chickens fussed at Carla as we passed and she barked back at them. "There you go," I said. "You tell 'em!"

Back in the house, I put Carla in her crate. She seemed to like her crate, but when she wagged her tail it thumped the sides creating a noise so loud you had to wait for her to stop to hear the person sitting next to you. Brady was eating cereal at the table. He watched her tail-wagging, and said, "That looks like it hurts."

The biggest thing about Carla was that she was big. She took up a lot of space. I loved the solidness of her. She reminded me of Trailer and was nearly as big as he had been. The night before she'd peed on the

---

* Maybe somewhere in the recesses of her heart, she sensed her granddaddy roamed the countryside riding shotgun in a car like that.

living room carpet, and let me just say that when a seventy-five-pound dog pees, it can fill a bucket. That had been a serious cleanup job and I wasn't anxious to repeat it, so we would utilize the crate until she adjusted to her new surroundings. To be fair, Lucy had peed on that carpet often her last year when she struggled with incontinence. We'd shampooed the heck out of it, but my guess was that dogs could still smell the pee, even if we couldn't.

After breakfast, I left to volunteer in the OPH booth at a festival in York—Green in the City.* I brought Wheat Penny along even though she was already spoken for; I knew her cuteness would be a draw, and I was certain she would rock the kissing booth where visitors could receive a puppy kiss for a donation. Wheat Penny did not disappoint; she was so exhausted after her morning of happily slobbering faces, fingers, and strollers, that when I pulled her out of the booth and attempted to set her on her feet, she collapsed to the ground instead. I carried her to the car and she snoozed the whole drive home.

I enjoyed having three dogs for the weekend, but it was a full-time job. What with keeping shoes out of Wheat Penny's mouth, taking Carla out for frequent walks, and admonishing Gracie to "stop being such a bully," very few chores were ticked off my list. Still, I loved the whole weekend and it made me wish I worked full-time at a doggie day care.

The biggest problem with three dogs was that I only had two hands, so inevitably someone was always missing out. It was the same issue with three kids. Ever since Ian was born, I'd felt scattered and unorganized as a parent. I was outnumbered. What I hoped, though, was that instead of feeling neglected, the fact that my kids had to share their parents' affection and attention with two siblings had made them more self-reliant.

At the OPH booth, I listened to other fosters talk of their households of four and five dogs and thought—*maybe that will be us someday*. But

---

* Green in the City celebrates all the earth-friendly efforts being made in York (our closest "city"—about fifteen miles north of us) and the surrounding county. It attracts all manner of hippies and soft-souled people so I never miss it.

somehow I doubted it. We might have physical room for that many dogs, but I wasn't sure I had emotional or mental room for that many.

On Monday, I said goodbye to Wheat Penny. It was easier this time, maybe because of Carla's presence or maybe because puppies are a lot of work. That morning, I'd had to fish a dried cat turd out of her mouth, and I thought, "That's the last time I'll have to do that!" Just after lunch, Wheat Penny (now Ladki—Hindi for "lady") left for the high life as a spoiled only child of a young, single executive. I couldn't help but think Wheat Penny had a wind at her back. And I was glad for her.

With Wheat Penny gone, Carla seemed to deflate. I wondered if she had only just realized that she wasn't going home. She began to sleep all the time and we rarely heard her beautiful hound bay. After a few days of this, I decided that she was mourning. She missed her family. To be fair, she was a hound, and forlorn is the default expression on most hound faces, but the appetite we were warned about was not in evidence. She barely ate her meals and refused all treats. She never attempted to counter-surf (although she had the height and reputation to excel in this sport). When I was sad I didn't eat either, so I understood. I gave her space and plenty of petting, but let her be sad.

Near the end of the week, she began to "talk" more. She made a few hound mutters when she first woke up and then one afternoon she stood on the deck barking at the woods, letting her beautiful hound bay echo across the hollow. From that day forward, the soundtrack of our days included coonhound bays and barks and mutters and whines. Maybe she'd decided we were worth protecting or maybe she had simply found her voice.

I took her for a run and was delighted to discover that she was an excellent and inspiring running partner. We did the fastest 3½ miles I'd done in months. She was focused, never stopping for her personal business, and only a few times tugging toward an errant squirrel. I hoped her forever family would include at least one runner, and maybe a fisherman.

On our way home, we passed close to the creek that snakes up the hollow following the road. Carla pulled toward it, so I allowed her to pick her way down to the water's edge. She hesitated only a moment, and then plunged in. Deer Creek is not a big or deep creek, but Carla waded out as far as the leash would allow and it was up to her chest. She splashed with her front paws until she was thoroughly soaked and then put her mouth in the water and drank deeply. She looked across to the other side of the creek and back at me.

"No way, girl, we're not going that way," I told her and tugged on the leash. She obediently followed me back to the road, but her step was lighter as we headed home.

At a party that week, after sharing news of our latest foster dog, several people confessed to me how much they wished they could foster, but didn't think they could stand to give up a dog. "I'd end up with a whole houseful," joked one friend. I'd thought a lot about that. After all, that was why we'd fostered in the first place. We could have been happy with Galina or Wheat Penny or Carla, but then what? We just go back to ignoring the fact that so many dogs just like Carla were being euthanized every day?* A few tears? I could handle that if it meant I could save another good dog. No, I wasn't ready to stop yet. We could offer our home as a sanctuary for a few more dogs, even if sometimes it left a lump in my throat.

What was really making me rethink the foster idea, though, was Carla. She was almost exactly the dog I'd been looking for before we started fostering, the one we spent all those hours visiting shelters in search of. But I didn't want to *foster fail*† just yet. It was very tempting to hold on to Carla. I knew we could make her happy here, but I was also certain that there was a forever home out there waiting for her. Someone else was looking for a dog just like Carla.

Carla and I got in the routine of running several mornings a week. She was an enthusiastic companion. As she emerged from her time of

---

* The ASPCA put the figure at 1.2 million in 2015, while a study from the University of Mississippi State College of Veterinary Medicine put the number closer to 780,000 in 2016. Either number is a shame on our nation.

† Foster lingo for a foster who adopts her foster dog.

mourning, her energy increased. She continued to challenge me to run faster than my well-worn knees would have liked.* On steeper parts of my regular run when I might normally be tempted to slow to a walk, I couldn't bear to ask it of Carla and pushed on through, sometimes letting her steady pull propel me forward.

There was a time when men in trucks would slow and note my progress, sometimes even chatting me up. Those days were past now and the only man in a truck who stopped to chat me up on my runs was my hay-guy, Kevin, and we usually just talked about hay. With Carla by my side, pretty much every pickup truck and mud-splattered four-wheel drive slowed as it passed me. I knew they weren't checking out the middle-aged woman on my end of the leash, they were ogling the gorgeous coonhound on the other end.

In terms of coonhounds, Carla was supermodel-pretty. She looked good when she arrived with us, but the coconut oil and probiotics had given her coat a glossy sheen, while the steady exercise had toned up her top line. She stood taller now, the sadness that was weighing her down beginning to lift. She was beautiful. I understood why those good ole boys were gawking. I stared at her too.

She was talking more too. Sometimes I knew what she was trying to say, but several times a day, she just seemed to need to sing. When that happened, I let her out on the deck and she barked for a good ten minutes or so. It echoed down the hollow and bounced off the hill across the creek. It was good that we lived on a rural street. No one minded. But I could understand that in close quarters she might fray a few nerves.

One night, we finished up dinner and Carla joined us on the deck. After checking to be certain we'd cleaned up every bite, she positioned herself at the edge of the deck, her nose poked out over the railing toward the woods across the valley. She began her song.

"What do you think she's saying?" I asked Nick.

He watched her. "Probably nothing important, she's like the local twitter feed for dogs on our hollow."

---

* I use the term "run" loosely; it was more like a "jog."

"I wonder if she's calling for her old owners, telling them to come get her."

He shrugged. "She seems happy here."

I rolled my eyes at him. He'd been dropping plenty of hints about keeping Carla.

"We aren't keeping her."

"So you say."

Gracie wandered outside and watched Carla silently for few minutes. Then she sighed and lay down behind her, perhaps in hound solidarity, or maybe she was thinking of Lucy.

The next Saturday I took Carla to our local Pet Valu for an OPH adoption event. She behaved beautifully, allowing everyone to pet her and accepting all treats offered. Small children were drawn to her and one little boy hugged her so long his mom had to pry him off. The next day I took her to a soccer game where she watched enthusiastically, barking along every time the crowds cheered. When she sat on the ground beside me in my folding chair, her head was level with mine. I fingered her velvety ears as we watched Ian's team struggle.

They'd had a tough season, losing every game. Ian was frustrated, but not discouraged. Each week he'd explain how they could have won if they'd just done one thing differently. I loved that my son was such an optimist. That day as we walked off the field after a particularly painful loss, Ian smiled. "I could hear Carla cheering for me!"

Day by day, Carla was healing. Her appetite returned with gusto. I discovered she knew how to sit and lie down for treats. One afternoon, I took her and Gracie for a walk down the hollow to the creek so Carla could splash. On the trip home, she bounded about like a puppy, nearly slipping her collar and towing me across the grass. A pickup truck rolled by and the guy inside smiled and yelled, "Looks like the dogs are walking you!" They surely were, but watching Carla bound around happily, I was glad for it.

A very wise horse-whisperer friend of mine, a cowboy named Brad who lives just over the hill from us, once told me that when training any animal, you need to set them up to succeed. You had to make the *right* choice the *easy* choice. Brad showed me how to apply this concept when he helped me with my four-year-old quarter horse, True. At four, most horses have at least been broken, if not schooled, but True was neither, having spent his last few years babysitting yearling colts.* With Brad's help I finally managed to ride True and stay on his back most days. I learned to think ahead and did my best to set True up to succeed—making sure the right option was the easy one.

I found that the same methods applied nicely to teenage children. For example, if a person sorts their laundry into the hampers in the laundry room, their laundry is done in a timely manner. If that person instead leaves their dirty clothes to molder on the floor of their room, they will soon be wearing the stuff on the bottom of their drawers that they got last Christmas and never intended to wear. No need to yell or scream about putting laundry in the laundry room. Instead make the right choice the easy one. It didn't take long to see that it was also an excellent strategy with Carla.

Carla had earned the nickname Goldilocks at our house because she liked to try out all the chairs, sofas, and beds in search of the best spot. We'd allowed both Galina and Wheat Penny on the furniture, but with Carla, Nick insisted we return to our house rule—*no pets on the furniture.* I hadn't always been a proponent of this rule. It was an allowance I gave when we first moved in together. I loved to snuggle with little furry creatures, but Nick had this little teeny, tiny, annoying habit of being allergic to animal fur. In possibly the most definitive demonstration of his love for me, he had suffered through the adjustment of living in close proximity to multiple furry creatures for almost twenty years.

When I first met Nick, I had a cat named Shamu who slept every night snuggled against my belly. There was much I adored about

---

* It should be noted that a free horse is never a *free* horse.

Nicholas (and still do). In fact, there was so much I adored that when my animal-allergic guy moved in, I kicked Shamu out of my bed. You can imagine how she felt about this. But I was in love and didn't consider the capacity of her anger.

That first evening that she slept in her new cat bed, she got up during the night and pooped in Nick's shoes. Cats are nothing if not clear about their feelings. There is none of the whining or pining of a dog. Cats take action.

When we picked out Lucy at the shelter and brought her home, Nick was firm—*no dogs on the furniture*. Through Gracie and three more cats, the rule had more or less remained in place.

Sweet little Galina wormed her way onto the couch while Gracie watched in jealous shock. And Wheat Penny had been on the furniture from the moment she arrived. But both of those precious pups were lap-sized babes. Carla was decidedly *not* lap-sized.

Training her to stay off the furniture became an ongoing task, but applying Brad's rule helped. Another neighbor loaned me a dog bed with a PVC pipe frame which at least gave the illusion of being off the floor—kind of like a dog hammock. I loaded it with blankets and a soft comforter to make it extra inviting. Carla tested it out gingerly and spent one afternoon napping on it, always thumping her tail when I came in to check that she was still on her bed. *Problem solved*, I thought. But just in case, I explained to everyone that they needed to keep their bedroom doors closed and I positioned empty boxes on the couch and futon.

The next day, I finished a new post for the blog about Carla's big weekend at the adoption event and the soccer game, and then went to check that she was on her bed where I'd left her and hadn't pushed the boxes aside to climb on the couch (as she'd tried to the night before). She was nowhere to be found. I searched the first floor—no Carla. I went upstairs and checked that yes, all three kids had remembered to close their doors. Where was she?

It's pretty hard to lose a seventy-five-pound coonhound indoors. Gracie was tailing me on my search, like a younger sibling trying to point out that *she* wasn't on the furniture. I was just starting down the stairs when I realized my own bedroom door was ajar. And there was Carla sprawled out on our queen-sized bed, with her head on Nick's pillow.

"Carla!" I cried.

She didn't even lift her head, only thumped her tail, but I was pretty sure I saw a smirk. I dragged her off the bed and closed the door and she slunk back downstairs and lay beside her PVC bed, a doleful look on her face.

Finally, the perfect adopters (and I mean perfect like I'd made them up myself) were approved to adopt Carla. I had a lovely conversation with her future adopting mama. We made plans for the family to meet and adopt Carla on Thursday. Hooray! So, as if I hadn't already learned this lesson from Galina's adoption, I assumed Carla was leaving and made the bold move of agreeing to take a new dog from Saturday's transport.

Symphony was adorable—short black and white fur with a big black patch over each eye and a broad smile. She was listed as border collie, but she more closely resembled a large Boston terrier. She even came with a story—a street dog picked up by paramedics and living at the firehouse in Greenville, South Carolina. She reminded me of the dog on *The Little Rascals*, and looked to be the perfect size playmate for Gracie. Carla was too big, Wheat Penny was too small, but Symphony looked just right. All was well with our dog world. Wednesday night, I took Carla for one last swim in the creek and we said our goodbyes.

And then Thursday morning I received an email from the potential adopters saying there had been a drastic shift in their situation. The husband had lost his high-paying job early that morning, arriving at his office to discover security guards clearing out his things. They would sadly be unable to adopt Carla at this time. *Whoosh!*

In a panic, I checked Carla's page on the OPH site. There was only one other application and that one didn't look like a good fit. The potential adopters were elderly and lived in the city. I glanced at Carla, creeping around the living room, sniffing the boxes on the couch and

---

* That was the rug being pulled out from under my carefully laid plans.

chairs. I scanned my calendar, wondering how I was going to have time for two foster dogs when I had an important deadline looming for my second book.

I called Nick and told him what happened.

"Guess we have to keep her," he said.

Ian's reaction was similar when he arrived home from school.

"What's Carla doing here?" he asked.

"Her adopters bailed."

"Yay! That's a sign. It means we should keep her," he told me as he scratched her head and combed the cabinets for snacks.

What to do about Symphony? I couldn't renege on my plans to foster her. She'd already been spayed, vaccinated, and microchipped in preparation for her transport on Saturday. Besides, foster dogs had too many abandonments in their lives already; I wouldn't be another. I could do this. Somehow.

For her part, Carla stepped up her behavior, sleeping on her own bed (most of the time) and running like a champ with me in the mornings, steadily improving my times. It was almost as if she was petitioning to stay. In the morning instead of circling me in the kitchen as had been her habit, she waited patiently at the bottom of the stairs for the kids to get up. She obviously knew who was working on her campaign and who was looking for an exit strategy.

The dog I picked up on Saturday morning was much smaller than we anticipated. Forty pounds sounded big, but Symphony packed it on a sturdy little frame. She was nervous, unsure, and peed pretty much every few minutes everywhere she went as if she were marking her territory.* She growled at Gracie and threatened the cats. She pulled on the leash when I walked her and escaped out of the house twice (she was a door opener which meant she was no dumb cookie). She refused her dinner, was silent, wary, watching us. I never saw her sit down—not once—the whole day. She walked from room to room keeping track

---

* It was also possible she had a urinary tract infection from the long time spent in a crate for travel from South Carolina.

43

of everyone. Although she looked more like a Boston terrier than a border collie, it seemed likely there was some kind of herding dog in there somewhere.

The first night I went to bed exhausted from taking Symphony outside to pee every fifteen minutes, walking Carla, supervising all the interactions between the dogs, and cleaning up after Symphony's accidents. I lay in bed thinking, *I can't do this. What have I gotten myself into? Two foster dogs are too much for me. How the heck do other fosters have three and four dogs? They must be nuts. I must be nuts. This is the last dog. Ever.*

Twenty-four hours later Symphony was a new dog. A happy, friendly, sweet little girl. She slept contently in her crate surrounded by the collection of shoes that she had piled beneath her. She played with Gracie, gobbled her food in mere seconds, and was delightfully more or less housebroken. She wanted very much to play with the cats, but they were not the least bit receptive to her overtures. Crash did play one short game of chase which ended when he climbed to the tippy top of the big pine tree in the front yard.

The kids loved Symphony and laughed at her funny smiley face. We renamed her "Stitch" because her resemblance to the cartoon character was so strong. Symphony didn't suit her; she wasn't a fancy dog. She was an I'll-be-your-faithful-friend-to-the-end kind of dog.

She proved to be a merry soul and excellent company. The week flew by. I walked Carla and Symphony together and this worked beautifully as they had some kind of one-up thing going in terms of claiming territory. First one peed, then the other peed on top of it. Back and forth. It made for quick potty walks. They got along wonderfully, wrestling in the kitchen and lying side by side to watch television in the evening. Stitch spent her days collecting items to hoard in her crate and Carla continued to prowl the premises in search of a soft place to sleep.

I felt distinctly more in control of the dogs than the kids. They were all busy with their lives—Ian with sports, Addie with the spring musical, and Brady enjoying the last moments of high school. Increasingly, I felt like I needed to make an appointment to talk to them.

Mornings seemed to be my best opportunity. And yet I always regretted sending them out the door once again, annoyed with their mother.

After arguing with Addie about the pile of things she left on the counter, the notice we'd gotten about a failing grade, and her inability to follow the no-food-in-your-bedroom rule, I cringed as the door slammed behind the kids heading out to school. Yes, they were quite definitely out of my control. Okay, maybe I never had control in the first place, but I sure thought I had it. Now I felt like a passenger in a car being driven much too fast over the kind of hills that make your stomach drop. My opinion was not one they welcomed, and on a good day it was barely tolerated. When had that happened? We used to bake cookies together, go on hikes in the woods, and read books at bedtime snuggled side by side. They used to smile when they saw me arrive to pick them up from practice.

Maybe this was one of the reasons I liked fostering dogs so much. I could decide what they ate and how they spent their time, two things I had decidedly less control over anymore with my kids. Plus, the dogs were always happy for my attention.

It's not like I didn't know this was coming. Nick and I joked about when our kids would be teenagers, right up until the point where they actually became teenagers, and now we stumbled through our days of empty cupboards, stinky laundry, unset alarm clocks, music we didn't understand, and the daily reminder that we knew NOTHING and all I could think was—how did *this* happen?

Stitch and Carla swirled around me as the car disappeared down the driveway with all three of my kids inside. The middle school and the high school stood side by side, so conveniently they could all ride to school together. On the days Ian decided to ride the bus, I was always oddly relieved, figuring I was splitting the risk. I watched the clock nervously until it struck 8:00 A.M.* The kitchen looked like a war zone—papers, dishes, wrappers, jackets, and books everywhere I looked. Jelly dripping down the side of the jar and over the edge of

---

* I figured the police would have called by eight if they were killed in a fiery wreck on their way to school.

the counter. The peanut butter knife was stuck to the newspaper left open to the comics. I followed a bread-crumb-like trail of dirty socks out of the kitchen through the living room and up the stairs, gathering them as I went and depositing them in the laundry room. The light was on in the bathroom and a radio blasted from a back bedroom. I couldn't lay a finger on the point at which the kids stopped doing all the things I worked so hard to teach them when they were small. Things like turning off their lights, placing cast-off clothing in hampers, and hanging up their wet towels.

I don't recall the day when they stopped smiling at Gracie and me when we opened their door to wake them up in the morning. Now they yelled, "*I KNOW!*" in a voice that clearly placed me on the rung between being lectured by a hall monitor and a new flare-up of acne.* And what happened to the earnest children who wanted to save the earth and ran through the house turning off lights? I was certain I had raised nicer, more considerate kids than this.

Okay, God's honest truth, they'd never been so great at utilizing the hampers, preferring to leave piles of clothing on the floor until I threatened never to do their laundry again or they suddenly realized they needed that uniform piece or favorite shirt. They'd long ago given up helping out in the kitchen, but I could still picture my smiling three-year-old darling carrying his dishes to the sink.

Maybe I was feeling that way because I'd gone apple picking with a borrowed three-year-old the day before. His excitement at our adventure was refreshing. We had a sword fight with the plastic weapons he'd brought along, and then his mom and I filled three baskets and the bottom of his stroller with apples. As I stirred homemade applesauce that afternoon, I told my kids about my fun day picking apples with Roran. They smiled kindly without even turning down their music as if I were some sad, desperate street person asking for a handout.

---

* But not the dog. No, Gracie can sit in the center of the floor and scratch incessantly, causing her collar tags to jingle much louder than my sweet voice saying, "Honey, it's time to get up." If there was some way to send Gracie in instead of me, I would, but she prefers to ride as my backup.

I really did miss those kids—the ones who thought I was cool and played Go Fish for hours. I missed the kids who would sing "The Wheels on the Bus" and make up silly new verses. I even missed the kids who had tantrums in the grocery store. (Well, maybe not those kids.)

Now I had to beg them to tell me about their days, stay at the dinner table longer than ten minutes, or go apple picking with me. I took Carla and Stitch for a walk and lamented that I hadn't taught my kids enough and now it was too late. Now they couldn't hear me. I wished they ate kale and sweet potatoes. I wished they turned their clothing right-side out before they put it in the hamper. I wished they were better at calling their grandparents, writing thank-you notes, and opening the doors for others. I wished I could get them to feed the animals, help in the garden or stack wood without threatening and then overpaying their minimal labor.

I'd had all these ideas about the kind of parent I would be, but in the heat of the moment, I'd mostly just winged it. I thought I had plenty of time to teach them all the things I wanted them to know and do, but the finish line snuck up on me. It was apparent on a daily basis that my control over them, if I ever had any, was tenuous at best.

I wondered what happened to the thousands of moments that passed by unnoticed in the last eighteen years. Many older parents tried to warn me that it would go by fast. I would nod and agree, but I didn't get it. I truly didn't. I sometimes find myself uttering the same words to young parents in the throes of potty training or homework slips, and know with complete certainty they won't believe me.

I rounded up all the shoes and returned them to their places. I wiped down the counter and cleaned the jelly off the floor. I loaded the dishwasher and listened to its faithful hum. I restored the kitchen to order in preparation for their return, promising myself that when they did, I would try to pay better attention to these moments we still had.

The next Saturday, I left Carla on the deck to do her daily singing and took Stitch with me to plant potatoes. We have just under six acres on our hillside farm. We've installed terraced gardens everywhere possible and I try to grow most of our produce, canning and freezing to make them last through the winter. Stitch sat beside me as I planted the potato hills until she spied the barn cat creeping across the grass. When the cat slipped under the shed nearby, Stitch raced to the shed and circled it, whining. Then she began digging. Instead of stopping what I was doing and dealing with her, I tried to finish the last row. In those few minutes she went from a black and white dog to a black and brown dog. She and Carla were due at an adoption event in another hour, so I recruited Ian to help me bathe Stitch with the hose. This turned out to be a serious wrestling match that left all three of us soaked. When I toweled off Stitch, though—wow! She was a knockout. Her white spots were blindingly white and she was even prettier. I fitted her with a bright red harness for the event and she looked like a million bucks.

The event was about forty-five minutes away at a pet store in a large shopping center. It was a gorgeous day and OPH was set up on the sidewalk. Stitch was perfectly mannered at the event—happy to lick anyone who approached. Another volunteer held her so I could stay with Carla, who was anxious. She paced the sidewalk watching the cars come and go, barking. Loudly. This was good and bad. It certainly drew attention to OPH. People did a double take when they heard the distinctive hound bay, but at the same time I imagined anyone who was considering adopting her thought, "Oh my God, can you imagine that noise in our house?"

Carla finally wore herself out with the barking and then ate herself sick with the treats offered by friendly kids who asked her to sit and shake, or just fed the treats to her because they could and she was so grateful. Finally, she collapsed and in very un-Carla-like fashion, laid out on the hard cement for a nap.

Driving home, I thought, *maybe two foster dogs isn't too many.* Carla and Stitch made it look easy, but I knew we wouldn't be a three-dog family for long. Stitch was popular at the event and clearly someone would want this wonderful dog.

The end of April was nearing and Brady would have to make his college decision. Or, more rightly, *we* would have to make a decision. Whenever we brought it up, he put in his earbuds or fled the room. Finally, I trapped him in his room one afternoon and asked him what he wanted to do.

"You have to decide," I told him. "The deadline is this week."

"I don't know," he said. "I wish I'd done more. I tried so hard to do all the right things." The heartbreak in his voice brought tears to my eyes.

"You did do all the right things. You did everything," I assured him.

"I'll just go to Texas."

"I don't want you to go to Texas," I told him. The University of Texas in Dallas had offered him a full ride and a stipend. Obviously, they were in need of some academic talent. They'd made the same offer to all National Merit Scholars. But their programs didn't include creative writing. Brady could only study English.

"I don't know what else to do. It's too much money to go anywhere else."

In that moment, I felt like I had failed him as a parent, when in fact, our system had failed him more. He was right. He had done everything he was supposed to do. He'd gotten good grades, blew away the SATs, even getting the National Merit finalist status. He took AP courses and scored 5's. He traveled to Central America to do service work, and volunteered with us at a community lunch for the homeless. He was on the Quiz Bowl team at school and president of the Creative Writing Club. He played tennis for the high school and soccer in a recreational league. He'd even written a novel and self-published it for an independent study class. He wrote for the local paper and had entered and won literary contests. When I was a kid, if I'd done half of that, I would have gone to any school I wanted to and not gone into debt to do it. Instead, Kenyon, his first-choice school, had wait-listed him. Three other schools had accepted him and made scholarship offers that amounted to about one third of their hefty price tags. Only one school, Susquehanna University, had offered more than half, but it still left a big chunk of expense on the table for someone to pick up. Brady or us. I felt like someone changed the rules mid-game. I was angry and there was nowhere to direct that anger. It wasn't Brady's fault. We made too much money to qualify for aid, but too little to afford most colleges.

I sat down on his bed next to him. "Where do you really want to go?" I asked.

He looked at me for a moment and then said, "Susquehanna."

"Okay, then, we'll make it work."

The relief on his face was worth every last dollar that we would have to come up with for the next four years. Later, Nick and I talked and agreed. We'd find a way.

As the days passed with Stitch, her real personality blossomed. I was her chosen person, but she kept careful note of the whereabouts of everyone in the house. Rarely did she lie down unless we were all in the same room. Nick and I had offices on opposite ends of the first floor, so when he worked from home a few days the next week, she spent her time in the room between us, keeping herself busy checking in on us while simultaneously accumulating a new cache of belongings in her crate. I'd cleaned it out one morning in search of Ian's calculator and discovered not only the calculator, but Addie's band gloves, everyone's shoes, and my Kindle.*

Maybe the hoarding habit was picked up after living on the streets. Shoes were her favorite items, but she didn't chew them like Galina, she simply gathered them. In general, I applauded this activity because it saved me from nagging the kids to put their shoes away. At lunch time, I noticed that on top of the shoes, she had placed all the dog toys—not just hers and Carla's, but Gracie's too. Gracie must have slept through the entire theft. She wasn't one to let her flattened fox go without a

---

* Which still sports a tooth mark and a spiderweb crack thanks to Stitch—but it works!

fight. After lunch, Stitch added a few abandoned socks, a set of magic markers, Ian's graphing notebook, and a pair of earbuds.

Later in the afternoon, I went to the kitchen to make a cup of tea. The writing was sticking and I hoped caffeine might help. I noticed Stitch's crate had been cleaned out. There were only the blankets, none of her loot. Nick and I were the only ones home, so I knew it wasn't a child with a sudden case of I've-got-to-clean.* I looked in the living room and found Carla's bed piled high with Stitch's stash. She'd even added two pairs of snow pants she'd pulled out of the Goodwill box in the hallway. Carla lay next to the bed, snoring, completely oblivious to the squatter who had taken over her space.

Stitch watched as I put everything away, her head following my movements like a ping-pong match. She waited until I'd gone back to work and then began loading up her crate again. A short time later, I heard a strange dragging sound. I emerged from my office to catch her toting an entire bag of dogfood to her crate. Stitch was nothing if not entertaining.

On a rare evening home without any kids that week, Nick and I hung out on our screened-in porch with the dogs. Carla sat with me on the love seat as I sipped my wine, and Stitch was stretched out on the chaise lounge, while Gracie chewed on a stuffed animal nearby. "I love hanging out with my girls," I told Nick.

"I know," he said, and I braced myself for a lecture about animals on the furniture, but instead he pulled out his phone and took a picture of me and the dogs. Maybe everybody was changing.

The next day on the way to soccer practice, with dogs seated on either side of him, Ian said, "I think we should keep fostering dogs, but just keep them all."

I smiled. "Not a bad plan," I told him.

---

* Not that my kids EVER had this little-known condition.

Late that night, I got the email telling me Stitch had an approved adopter. Her potential adopter wondered if she could come meet her the next day, as she was only twenty minutes away. I knew she'd take her home if it seemed like a good match, so I told everyone to say goodbye before they left that morning.

"But what if they don't like her?" asked Ian.

"What's not to like?" I said.

"True that," said Brady.

As predicted her adopter thought she was perfect for her family. I was happy for Stitch. Maybe it was because it happened so quickly, or maybe it was because Stitch was one dog I wouldn't worry about, but the lump in my throat was a little easier to swallow this time around. Stitch was a great dog who had found a great family. Her new mom emailed me that night and said they loved her and had decided to keep the nickname we gave her, *Stitch*.

Meanwhile, it seemed Carla would be here indefinitely. No one was applying to adopt her. I took her for a walk around the pasture, watching her sniffing her way from fence post to fence post and decided that it was fine if she stayed here as long as it took. I wanted her to find her perfect home like Stitch had. She would be harder to place, but no matter what, this next move needed to be her last. A dog can only have her heart broken so many times.

FOUR

Babysitting

ick and I went away for a weekend in Virginia wine country. My
parents stayed with the kids while we were gone. The kids didn't
truly need babysitters, but they did need referees, cooks, and occasional chauffeurs. The kids had been warned—*Grammy and Pop Pop are
NOT allowed to walk Carla.* I explained to them that they would have
to put down the earbuds, close the laptop, and get their butts out of bed
and walk Carla while we were gone because even though Carla was well
mannered and sweet, she was also a seventy-five-pound coonhound and
not always conscious that there was someone else on the other end of the
leash if a squirrel or a cat happened by. Her bigness could be dangerous.

I was reasonably certain my kids would step up. They loved Carla
and they loved their grandparents. But I still worried. Not about my

coonhound—but about my parents' affection for that coonhound. I worried my mom would have her usual attitude—*I can take care of this*, and rather than asking the kids to walk Carla, she'd just do it herself.

Despite my concerns, everyone survived the weekend with no injuries to report, and we came home to begin the most chaotic month of our year. Brady was graduating, Ian was playing two sports which were headed into playoff season, Addie had just finished one show and had auditioned for a new show that began rehearsing that week, and it was the time of year when the garden tended to go from neat little rows of baby plants to out-of-control weed-infested jungle in less than an hour. Nick had been preoccupied as of late, too, spending hours online lusting after used tractors and scheming about all the things he could do with that new tractor once he had it. Throw on top of all that three horses in need of a spring tune-up, the graduation party yet to be planned, and the beach camping trip to follow. The deadline for my next novel was a week or so away, the house was a wreck, and the relatives would arrive momentarily.

While we'd been gone, Carla had more than a few accidents in the house, barked incessantly, and was simply underfoot. My mother wasn't happy. "When are you going to get rid of that dog?" she asked. I defended Carla—her schedule was disrupted, she wasn't getting exercise, no one was paying attention to her needs, but secretly I was frustrated! This dog was housebroken. She'd been so good up until now! *What happened?*

Knowing this situation could happen again (when we were gone for the beach camping trip in a few weeks), we needed a better solution. Carla couldn't come with us; I'd have enough to do keeping track of my own and other people's teenagers. Carla was not a house dog. Or at least she wasn't a house dog if someone didn't take her for a four-mile run every morning. I didn't know our house sitter well, but I was pretty sure she wasn't a runner.

Carla had been here almost two months and there were no applications for her. It was time to start treating her as our dog even if she wasn't *our* dog. We would train Carla to stay within the invisible fence.

I made it clear to the lobbying interests that it didn't mean that we would foster fail. It simply meant we were preparing for a summer of Carla—just in case!

For some reason that has never been that clear to me, *invisible fence* is a dirty word among some dog lovers. In fact, one of the reasons we ended up fostering was because the shelter that had the one dog I was prepared to adopt had denied us based on my confession that we owned an invisible fence.*

I have no problem with an invisible fence. Our property is too hilly, rocky, and weird-shaped for a traditional dog fence. Never mind that we don't have the thousands of dollars to install one. If we put up the one we could afford instead of the invisible fence we have, it would have been a twelve-foot-by-twelve-foot cage. Instead we installed an invisible fence that has an ice-cream-cone-shaped ¾ acre+ space for the dogs to roam. It runs under the enormous pine branches, avoids the driveway, and includes the raspberry and asparagus patches.

Lucy spent seventeen years within the bounds of an invisible fence— happily. She loved to run. And I loved to watch her run. She happily patrolled our yard, safely raced the UPS truck up the driveway, and shooed off any rabbits that threatened our garden. And if the detractors of the invincible fence were worried about it hurting a dog—well, they should come witness Gracie bound right through it without even flinching.

Our weekend away had made it obvious that Carla was not the kind of dog who should spend her days inside. She was a coonhound, after all. Letting her roam freely in the invisible fence space made sense. She and Gracie could finally play the way two big dogs should, instead of the abbreviated bouts they had inside that always ended with furniture upturned and someone yelling, "Settle down!"

We put up the little white flags, tested the extra collar and started training Carla. Now she sat on the porch cowering, terrified of the

---

* Everyone told me I should lie if I wanted to adopt a dog, but I couldn't bring myself to do it. See what truth-telling gets you? Instead of one dog, I've now had fifty.

beeping sound the collar emitted when she wandered too close to the flags. We turned the fence down as low as it went and she'd never felt anything worse than a static shock, but she was not leaving the porch, no way, no how.

My guilt ate at me, but I told myself she was smart and would figure it out. I just had to be patient and remember that Lucy did the exact same thing each time we moved and installed a fence (three times in her lifetime). She would venture out and embrace her newfound freedom, eventually.

Feeling overly confident in my ability to manage my world, I agreed to babysit two other foster dogs over the long Memorial Day weekend. I had the garden mostly under control, Carla was figuring out the invisible fence, the manuscript was right on schedule, the graduation party was more or less planned,* and I'd decided that cleaning the house wouldn't be a solo effort.

After surviving ten days of three dogs, I was confident we could handle four, especially on a gorgeous weekend with no actual plans, just lots of ideas. Kylie and Hitch† came to stay for the holiday weekend while their foster parents went camping.

Kylie was over-the-top excited to be here, but I soon learned that Kylie was over-the-top excited to be anywhere, meet anyone, or do anything. She was one overly enthusiastic two-year-old foxhound mix. She was mostly white with a few brown patches, about Gracie's size, and had a tremendous hunting drive.

Hitch was a small, dachshund-shaped dog. He was black with a white bib, and he shrank from my hand when I reached for him. Hitch's foster, Erika, explained that Hitch was very timid and "hand shy." If he got loose he would run from you.

---

* Brady told me to "just buy food" and leave the rest to him.

† Sounds very much like a movie title, doesn't it?

The first few hours went fine. I walked both dogs around the yard.* Carla was not impressed with either dog and spent the afternoon lounging on the porch, occasionally lifting her head to watch the antics of Kylie when she spotted a BUG! or a BIRD!! or a CAT! or a OMG—A SQUIRREL!!!!

Because Kylie was so demanding of my attention and arm strength, I decided to take Hitch out on his own. The little guy was excellent company. He had perfect manners on the leash and was happy to go wherever I wanted to go, so we toured the gardens and yanked a few weeds. It was a beautiful afternoon, and I made my way to one of the Adirondack chairs at the top of our hill. Nick and I liked to sit in these chairs in the early evening to do what we called, "surveying the manor," which means relax with a glass of wine or a beer from a distance far enough away from the house that we can escape the chaos. We sit in our chairs watching the bats dart across the pasture in search of bugs, making their wild zigzag flights from the barn to the woods. We discuss our present life and imagine our future. We talk about the kids, the gardens, our work, and, of late, the dogs. Sometimes we just sit quietly and pretend we are only guests at this quirky out-of-the-way B&B.

Hitch laid down beside me and we watched the birds try to figure out a way through the net that covered the blueberries. He seemed to be relaxing, but when I reached down to scratch his ears, he leaned as far away as the leash would allow, his eyes filled with fear. *Poor little guy.* I couldn't imagine what circumstances of life brought him to this point. We sat in the sunshine for a bit, side by side, but me keeping my scary hands to myself, and then it was time to get back to work, so we headed to the house.

As we approached the door, Hitch balked. He was wearing a nonslip collar so when he stopped and I pulled, the collar didn't slip over his tiny head. Rather than pick him up (since he was afraid of my touch), I pulled a little stronger on the leash and stepped into the house. Hitch

---

* Basically, Kylie walked both Hitch and me around the yard in a dog-human-dog train.

didn't move and I tugged again, this time the collar snapped and Hitch took off like a shot up the hill away from the house.

Bizarrely, the nylon nonslip attachment had simply broken off. Hitch weighed all of ten, maybe twelve pounds, so it wasn't his brute strength or size that snapped it. I didn't have the time to wonder about it. I grabbed Kylie, figuring Hitch knew her, and we took off up the hill after him. I could hear Erika saying how hard it was to catch him in a fenced yard. Now, I'd have to catch him in southern York County, unless he made it to Maryland, since that was the direction he was running. I was already picturing me and the rest of the search party out with our flashlights that night tromping through the surrounding fields. And then tomorrow the Girl Scouts would organize search teams and maybe bring us bottled water . . .

Dreading making the call, but knowing I had to, I dialed Erika. She didn't know me very well, so her first thought was probably, "Why did I leave my little dog with this idiot?" To her credit, she didn't say that, she said something like, "He won't go far, he wants to be with you. I'm sure he's scared. Just try to get him to follow Kylie."

We spotted Hitch at the top of the pasture just on the other side of the fence. As Erika predicted, he ran gleefully toward us, tail wagging. Erika stayed on the phone and talked to me as we walked back to the house with Hitch running big looping circles around us, and Kylie practically levitating on the end of the leash in her joy at the adventure.

Following Erika's advice, I led Kylie into the house, leaving the door open for Hitch to follow. We kept walking without looking back and I hid around the corner in the hall, leaving Kylie in view. Hitch appeared in the doorway for a moment and then backed out and dashed away. I took Kylie back outside. Gracie joined us on this run and for once she didn't snarl at the new dogs, just played along with our game of Please-Follow-the-Leader. Carla, who was lounging under the crabapple tree, couldn't be dragged into our drama and just thumped her tail as we passed. After several tries, Hitch finally followed Kylie and Gracie inside and I quickly closed the door.

When the kids got home from school, I told them about my afternoon's adventure and said, UNDER NO CIRCUMSTANCES were they to let this dog out of his crate. Then I went to the store and bought a small blue harness for Hitch.

Later, I was in the kitchen preparing food for our impromptu cookout that evening. Nick was picking up his new-to-me tractor that afternoon and we'd invited the family that helped haul it plus a few other friends to come for a cookout. Because I knew I'd have to keep Hitch in his crate all evening, I'd put up the baby gate to block the doorway and brought him in the kitchen with me so he could have an hour of freedom. He sat nearby and watched my preparations, always moving quickly out of the way when I approached.

Brady appeared in the kitchen to inform me that he was going out for the evening to meet friends at the Comic Shop for something called a "draft." I nodded as if I knew what that was. Being eighteen and already accepted to college and about to graduate, hanging out with the family wasn't a priority for him. I remember being eighteen too, and so I didn't hold it against him. I couldn't get away from home fast enough. I was still thinking about the summer I graduated as Brady headed out the door. "What time will you be home?" I asked, realizing too late that as Brady paused to answer my question, he'd left the door wide open. Hitch shot out the door in a blink and took off up the hill.

This was not on my agenda. I had people arriving in thirty minutes, shrimp to marinate, a kitchen to tidy, dishes to find, veggies to cut up. I did not have chasing down a slippery, crazy-shy dog on my agenda. And yet, it is the tyranny of the urgent that dictates our days, isn't it?

I spent the next forty-five minutes trailing Hitch while trying to maintain control of Kylie. Of course, the moment we almost had him back in the house was when a van full of kids pulled in the driveway and off he went again. I asked all our guests to hide in the kitchen* and

---

* Not just stay in the kitchen, but seriously HIDE—no sounds, no moving. I didn't want anything to spook my little friend.

led Kylie and Gracie back out to lure Hitch in. After two or three* tries, he finally followed us inside. After that, the evening went off without a hitch.† Everyone enjoyed playing with all the dogs, even Hitch, and it was a fun night.

Actually, it was a fun weekend. We took our little guests on several adventures and Carla discovered they both liked playing in the stream with her. Gracie watched their antics with disdain from the shore. Hitch turned out to be a major-league snuggler and everyone got a little time with him, even Carla.

I wasn't sure I'd be ready for four dogs again any time soon, but the weekend did teach me a few lessons.

It's a GREAT idea to have an ID tag on your foster dog with your address and cell phone number. As I followed Hitch over hill and dale, and occasionally lost sight of him, it was no small comfort to know that Erika had tags on both dogs.

I have wonderful, flexible family and friends who don't think I'm nuts to invite all these dogs into our lives.‡ Our party and our weekend went great even with two extra dogs and a few unexpected hikes thrown in.

Dogs just want to be loved and they are more forgiving than most people. Hitch had obviously been treated badly by humans in the past, yet it only took him a few hours to begin to trust us. Even when he was running away and terrified, he kept looking back over his shoulder to be sure we were nearby, and anytime I was out of sight, he stopped and circled back to me. He wanted to trust me.

And finally, four dogs is WAY too many for me. The weekend turned out alright, but I'm pretty sure if Erika hadn't come back for them I might have lost my mind and the compassion of my family by Wednesday.

---

*   Or maybe ten.

†   So to speak.

‡   Or if they think so, they at least don't say it out loud.

In some ways Brady was already gone. Even the hours when he was here, he was somewhere else—earbuds in listening to music I didn't understand, texting with people I didn't know, reading books I'd never heard of, and surfing websites certainly not meant for parents. I was proud of the fact that he was so independent and obviously ready to be out our door. Yet, my heart broke at the thought of him being gone.

I watched him walk across the stage that week, accept his diploma, grin for the cameras, toss his hat in the air. He celebrated for two days straight—eating every manner of junk food, laughing, throwing fris-bees, solidifying memories to take with him when he goes. More than likely, that was the last he would see of some of those people, but he won't feel that truth until decades from now.

It seems like only moments ago, he couldn't remember to hand in homework and lost his shoes and jacket on a regular basis. Learning to drive stressed us both and I wondered if he'd ever be able to find his way without me or his father in the seat beside him. And now he came and went, driving to school, the tennis courts, and following the GPS to a friend's house on a lonely, dark back road. Undoubtedly, he made a few wrong turns, but he figured it out eventually.

He will negotiate the world in much the same way, like the rest of us. I can't imagine the day when he won't barrel down the stairs noisily, tease Gracie, chat with the latest foster dog, and leave the open milk container on the counter and his socks on the porch.

His leaving was just one more example of the pain of parenting no one warns you about. The other stuff—sleeping through the night, potty training, starting kindergarten—there are entire books warning you about these trials, but no one points out that one day this person who has taken up residence in your heart 24/7/365 for eighteen years is going to leave. And it will hurt like nothing you can imagine. There was no metaphor for this pain that was already casting its shadow on my heart even though I still had three months—*three months!*—before he left. I thought the dogs leaving one after the other had been preparing me, but I was realizing that it wasn't the same. At all.

The end of the school year came and went, and Carla did not leave. Despite the fact that I knew there would be plenty of tears when she left, I wanted her to go. The longer she lingered here becoming entrenched in our lives, the harder it would be on her when she finally left. More than that, the longer Carla was here, the fewer dogs we could help save. We'd had Carla for nearly two months. There were weekly, sometimes daily, emails asking for foster homes for so many deserving dogs that I'd taken to deleting the emails without even looking at them. It hurt too much not to be able to help. It made me want to turn my horse pasture into a dog pasture.

In two months my first novel would be published. Some days this seemed surreal. When you want something for so very long, once it finally happens inevitably it can never measure up to your dream. In my most insecure moments, I wondered if it was all a hoax. I couldn't imagine anyone paying money for a story I made up on my mornings running through our hollow and my afternoons with my laptop.

Books have always been sacred to me. Just the sight of a stack of books sitting on my bedside table waiting to be read makes me giddy. My Amazon wish list is pages long—my mother complains that it is all books. But those books were *real* books written by *real* authors. What if my book was horrible? What if people read it and thought—*Boy, who is she kidding? I can't believe anyone published that!* Or what if, worse yet, no one read it? It felt a little like that dream of being caught out in public in your underwear. My heart and talent or lack thereof, exposed for everyone to see. I grew anxious and snappy, food stuck in my throat and when handed one glass of wine, it usually led to four. I found it difficult to concentrate on even the simplest task.

When my first review came in from an advance reader and it was positive, I finally began to relax. Maybe the world would like it. Sure, I knew not every review would be as shining as that first one, but at least one person who'd never met me and had nothing invested in my book had liked it! Maybe, just maybe, I was a real writer too.

June began and already I was tired of kids home all day doing nothing unless I prodded them into it. I took away the screens to get their attention, and then they spent the hours growling at me before resentfully picking up a book or drumsticks, and sometimes even a bicycle. Dishes grew on the counter like mushrooms in the dark corners of our barn. No one knew where they came from. Food disappeared from cabinets, laundry multiplied, the recliner was left forever in the open position. Even when it was quiet, it was never really quiet. It was hard for me to think and my writing came to a standstill. The rhythms of the house were off and my brain grew fuzzy every time I sat down at the keyboard.

Carla sensed this. That morning she had missed her run so that I could meet with the horse/house sitter to go over the notes of caring for not only Gracie, the cats, horses, and chickens, but Carla too. The sitter listened politely to me explaining everything and followed me through all the gardens that would need to be watered if there was no rain. She nodded as I talked, but I'm pretty certain she was really thinking, *You are crazy lady. Bonkers. Nuts. I just hope your check doesn't bounce.*

Later, I struggled at my keyboard, distracted by Carla on the back deck barking at Brady and a pack of teenage friends who were huddled over a strategy game of some sort, oblivious to her barking. Finally she was quiet, but a moment later the pizza delivery guy roared up the driveway and she began barking in earnest again. Who had ordered pizza at 2:00 P.M.?

I sighed and shut down my laptop. I tidied my desk. We were leaving the next day. I wouldn't be back to my writing for a week. Time to pack. I called to Carla, but had to drag her away from the boys; after all, there was pizza. I took her upstairs with me to finish packing. She walked toward our bed, but I pointed at the pile of dirty clothes on the floor and she settled there instead, sighing her unhappiness. It would be a tough week for her while we were gone. She would be one more worry for me while I attempted to relax on the vacation that seemed like such a good idea six months ago. I loved to camp and I loved the beach, why not do both? And then why not invite any kids who wanted to come? It would be fun.

It *would* be fun. Once we were there. It was getting there that was tricky. Nick listened to me list all my worries about Gracie and Carla, the cats and horses (I wasn't worried about the chickens, they could eat bugs), and then he asked, "You do remember they aren't people in little furry suits?"

FIVE

The Dangers of
Winnie-the-Pooh

Our vacation turned out to be anything but a vacation. Camping for many people does not constitute a vacation, but for me, sleeping outside, roasting marshmallows, disconnecting from technology, and being with friends has always been my favorite vacation. In fact, we'd been camping every summer with these same families for at least ten years. It had rained on us a few times and more than once someone's kid had a meltdown, but the fun certainly made up for the unfun.

Not this time.

This time we settled into side by side campsites, tucked into a grove of pines within hiking distance of the beach. There was even a paved bike path for the kids to use. The bathhouse was close, but not too close. What's not to love?

How about the excruciating heat? Or the suffocating humidity? Or the nearly nonexistent land breeze which brought with it biting flies? Seeking relief on the shoreline resulted in several blistering sunburns. Add to this the worst torture of all—teenagers deprived of Wi-Fi. *And we were paying for this?*

By midweek, we were all miserable at our hot, fly-ridden, sandy campsite so we decided to take a ride on the ferry that connected our beach in Delaware to Cape May, New Jersey. We had no intentions of going into Cape May, we simply wanted to sit on a boat for a few hours. We were in desperate need of air-conditioning, Internet, and food prepared by someone other than us. Once aboard, the kids gathered in the air-conditioned lounge, ordered junk food, and gorged on free Wi-Fi. The adults enjoyed frozen cocktails and the fresh breeze on deck.

Rum drink in hand and kids nowhere to be seen, I took advantage of the free Wi-Fi to check email. I could blame it on the alcohol or the heat or the momentary high of escaping the campground, but when the pictures of four adorable puppies appeared, I knew I had to have them.

"Oh my gosh!" I squealed to my friend Amy. "Look at these puppies!"

The puppies were named after Pooh characters—Pooh, Kanga, Piglet, and Rabbit. Amy decided she wanted Piglet.

"I want them all," I told her.

I didn't ask Nick. I didn't consider the seventy-five-pound coonhound at home. I didn't work through the logistics of where we would keep four puppies. I just acted. I remembered the fun of Wheat Penny—her puppy breath and her silliness and the way she made all of us laugh. I was miserable at the moment and puppies seemed like the perfect solution. I had to have them. Before I could stop myself, I had emailed Mindy, "I WANT THEM!"

Then I went in search of Nick and found him on another deck enjoying a cold beer watching the seagulls chase our wake.

"Nice, huh?" I said.

He put his arm around me and said, "I love boats."

"They're pretty nice."

"Let's get a boat someday."

"Okay."

He took a long drink of his beer. I poked the ice in my cup with my straw, looking for more rum drink, and casually said, "So, OPH just posted pictures of four puppies that need a foster."

"What about Carla?"

"She'll be adopted any day now, I'm sure."

He smirked, sipped his beer, but didn't say anything, so I pulled up the pictures on my phone. "Aren't they adorable? And they're named after *Winnie-the-Pooh* characters!"

"All puppies are adorable," he said, but he did scan through the pictures.

"So, it's okay with you if I do this?" I asked.

He rolled his eyes and said, "As if I have a choice."

"Good, 'cause they arrive next week!"

The kids were over the moon excited about fostering the puppies. I'd promised them we would foster *a* puppy this summer, so why not four? I found Amy and we toasted to my four adorable puppies.

I got everyone's word that they would help with the puppies, and hoped that their word would be better than it had been in the past. I distinctly remembered similar vows in regards to the gecko, beta fish, and bird that led to prolonged reminders on my part and eventual abdication on theirs. Sadly, all the small critters in cages lived short, tortured lives in our care. Everything would be different with the puppies, though, they promised!*

The first thing we had to do in preparation for the puppies was rename them. With over 4,800 dogs in the system, their *Winnie-the-Pooh* names were taken long ago.† I was sad when I heard this news because we have always been a Pooh family. The baby nursery was

---

* Cue the pretty music and birds singing.

† OPH never repeated a name in their database.

decorated Pooh, the first videotapes (dating myself here), CDs, books, and even computer games were all Pooh. I sang the song, "Christopher Robin" to my little cherubs when I tucked them in every night. Brady's middle name was Christopher after you-know-who, which was a compromise because I seriously considered naming him Christopher Robin.[*]

We were still on our beach camping trip when I learned we had to rename the pups, so I posed the question to my dear friends while sitting around a table in our favorite brewery.[†] We'd escaped the squalor of our campground once again in search of alcohol and air-conditioning, so everyone was in a happy mood. We considered using the names of the beers we were sampling, but decided that no one would want to adopt Noble Rot or Hellhound. After very little deliberation, we chose Jillie Bean, Lug Nut, Marzle, and Chick Pea.

Jillie Bean was the childhood nickname for one of the kids traveling with us. Lug Nut was the name of a dog a friend used to have.[‡] Marzle was the main character in a novel written by my would-be Christopher Robin during his junior year in high school, and Chick Pea simply sounded cute. All the names made more sense if you had a little beer buzz going.

On our first morning back from vacation, Carla and I went for a slow run (more of an amble). For once, she wasn't leading the way and there was no sprinting or any kind of bounding. The humidity got us both. I thought she might like a dip in the creek but when we got there, the weeds were high and her ear got caught in some stickers, so she backed away, retreating to the road.

I was glad to be home. Glad to be finished with a week full of raging temperatures, swarming flies, blistering sunburn, and kids tormented

---

[*]   I told him about his almost-name while were on this vacation, and he said, "That would've been pretty cool."

[†]   Dogfish Head brewery in Rehoboth Beach, Delaware.

[‡]   Sadly, Lug Nut's eventual adopter didn't keep the name.

by a lack of Wi-Fi. Suffice it to say, it hadn't been the most idyllic vacation. I was pretty certain none of us would be camping at the beach again anytime soon.*

We were only two days until puppy touchdown, when Mindy emailed to say that there were two Pooh puppy siblings whose planned adoption had fallen through. Would we be willing to take two more? Eeyore and Roo needed a foster home too.

Uh . . .

I tried to remember her words after she told me I'd been approved to foster four months prior. She'd said something like, "Now, always know that you can say no. I might sound desperate or pushy, but it's okay to tell me no."

Hmmmm . . . uh . . . I dialed Nick at work.

"What's two more puppies when you have four already?" he said. I knew I'd married him for a reason.

Carla watched us prepare the mudroom for puppies with very little interest. She was just happy to have us home and happy to be back to her regular runs.

Addie had an important performance on the same night as we were to pick up the puppies, so Nick drove to Millersville to hear her perform and Ian went with me to get our puppies. I hated to miss Addie's concert, but that was only the beginning of the sacrifices to be made in the name of fostering puppies.†

Ian and I arrived at the bowling alley parking lot with a large crate filled with towels. I'd explained to Ian that, per the Puppy Guidelines, he and I were the only ones allowed to touch our puppies as we moved them from the transport van to the car.‡

---

* Or in this lifetime.

† A calm, quiet, non-stinky house would be another.

‡ Because these puppies have yet to be fully vaccinated, OPH takes serious precautions against the puppies being exposed to potential viruses. There's also the risk that the puppies are carrying a contagious virus like parvo themselves. The quarantine is all-encompassing and serious.

"What if people want to pet them?" he asked, looking at the large group of OPH volunteers gathered in the parking lot.

"They will, but you can't let them."

He nodded. Ian is a nice kid, but he's also a rule-follower, so he was probably the best person for this job.

When Gina opened the van door, the puppies were peering out of their crate. I could see the two light-colored puppies, Jillie Bean and Marzle. They were unbearably cute and everyone around me squealed. Gina told me to start moving them. Even she wasn't allowed to handle them.

Ian and I shuttled the puppies one and two at a time, dodging the outstretched arms of people who could not resist them even though they probably knew puppy protocol as well as I did. Once they were loaded, I got a cooler full of vaccines, bags of wormers, collars, toys, probiotics, vitamins, and cranberry pills. Ian stayed with the puppies in the car.

On the drive home, we listened to their sweet noises and talked excitably about *our* puppies. It felt a little bit like Christmas morning. When we were home, we installed them in their pen and stayed up way past our bedtime watching them and figuring out who was who.

The next morning, I hurried Carla along on her morning pee stroll, anxious to get back to the puppies. So far, she'd had no interest in them, but Gracie had wandered by the pen and snarled a few times. They only wagged their tails and jumped at the sides of the pen, happy to meet her.

All that week, it felt like my only job was caring for puppies. Much like the first few weeks home with a newborn from the hospital, my days, thoughts, work, and heart were consumed by my babes. After everyone was cleaned up, watered, fed, snuggled, and the pen poop-free, I would slink off to my laptop, but it was impossible to focus. The random noises, shrieks, and barks mixed with the metal rattling as they crashed into the sides of the pen sounded like the soundtrack to *How to Train Your Dragon*. Facebook was one thing, but a roomful of puppies? So much for meeting any deadlines.

It was time to write up the pups for their OPH adoption page. They'd already generated a lot of interest,* but as I knew them better now, I set to work writing their individual bios. I thought it would be hard, but in much the same way as my own children displayed characteristics and oddities as newborns and toddlers that have carried right on through to their teens, I was confident I could lay out the basics of each pup's personality.

Boz was the runt, smaller than the others with the black and tan markings of a hound. His head looked a little big for his body and his massive paws said maybe he wouldn't always be a runt. He had a hound dog's countenance, which made him look sad and forlorn and adorable—all irresistible traits in a puppy.

Jillie Bean was already listed as *adoption pending*,† and her potential adopters emailed to set up a time to meet her. This was no surprise. Not only was she quintessentially cute with those liquid eyes and constantly tilted face, but she was quite simply the nicest puppy in the bunch. Not that I didn't like them all. She was just more even-keeled—happy to play, but not yanking ears or picking fights. I didn't know if her new adopters had a psychic sense or just good puppy karma, but they'd hit the lottery with their pick.

Chick Pea was my girl, the one I'd keep if I was going to keep one of these precious pups.‡ She was strikingly handsome with the coloring of a boxer—brown with black points. One of her ears was crooked and stuck out to the side while the other folded forward, a feature I found made her even more irresistible. She had long legs and I was certain she would grow into an awesome running partner. She was bright and

---

* Jillie Bean had an adopter before we'd brought her home!

† Adoption pending, or "AP," as people at OPH called it, meant that her potential adopters had applied and been approved, but had yet to meet her and decide to take her home. In other words, they got first dibs.

‡ Which I wasn't. No more puppies for me. Gracie cured me of that idea.

confident, more people-focused than puppy-focused. I hoped she'd get adopted quickly before I got too attached.

Homeboy also had an approved adopter. He had similar coloring to Chick Pea, but with lots of splashy white on his legs, chest, and even a splash on his back. He was a small, stocky pup. He wasn't pushy and hung back when the others rushed forward, yet he never hesitated to jump into each tangle. He was all puppy, but maybe a tad bit smarter than the others. When everyone else was fighting over one food bowl, he'd wander over to the other bowl and help himself. If everyone was diving for the tennis ball I'd just tossed in the cage, he'd sneak off with the plastic retainer case.*

And Lug Nut! What a gorgeous, expressive, chubby face! He reminded me of Gary Coleman's character on *Different Strokes* who always said, "What'chu talkin' 'bout, Willis?" That was his default expression—that thought. He looked almost exactly like Homeboy, only bigger. He was a solid hunk of adorable puppy. He was the only one who could take on Marzle and his endless, ferocious energy. He would make a great dog.

And then there was Marzle. Marzle was the same yellow as Jillie Bean, but with more white and a broader, bigger body. He was a dog's dog. Even when everyone else knew it was naptime and headed for the crate, he would wander the pen looking for anything available for his busy mind and mouth. He had an insatiable need for contact and play. When I was in the pen trying to clean up and I felt someone grab my pony tail, I always knew exactly which puppy it was. When I reached in to give morning pets, the open mouth I would feel encasing my pinkie, that would be Marzle. When the puppy battles reached an intensity that demanded I leave my keyboard and go settle things, I always knew which puppy I'd be yanking out of the fray.

---

* The most coveted toy in the pen. And, no, there was not a retainer inside that case when it graduated to puppy toy. (I believe that was Stitch's doing.)

Nick and I were at a fiftieth birthday party for a neighbor held at the VFW one Saturday night a week after the puppies arrived when my phone rang. I went outside to answer it, concerned it was one of the kids calling to tell me something was wrong with the puppies. It was a wrong number, but I noticed I had several Facebook messages. One was from an OPH volunteer named Jamie. She said her mom was visiting from Indiana and wanted to adopt Carla. In my sangria-induced happy state, this made no sense to me, so I closed my phone and went back to my friends and my sangria.

The next morning, I scrolled through the messages on my phone. Nick was at the counter making breakfast and I was nursing my hangover with a big cup of tea and wondering whether I had only imagined the message about Carla from the night before.

"I didn't imagine it!"

"Didn't imagine what?" he asked, turning the bacon with one hand and reading the news on his phone with the other.

"Someone wants to meet Carla!"

"When?"

Jamie's most recent message was from two hours earlier. Apparently, sangria-happy me had told her this morning would be great. I looked at the clock. "In about an hour!"

I'd always felt that Carla understood English. There were certainly times when she chose to play her dog card and feign ignorance, but most of the time she knew exactly what I was saying when I asked her to please get down off my bed or please move her large self out of the way because she was blocking the hall. When we finished our breakfast, Carla was waiting at the door to the deck. This was her signal that she was ready for her breakfast. If we didn't catch on, she'd let us know loudly that the service was lacking. We fed her on the deck and Gracie inside to keep the peace.[*]

Normally she gulped down her food and turned back to the door, wanting to be let in so that she could double-check that Gracie didn't

---

[*] Food was VERY important to Carla and not so much to Gracie.

forget to eat every morsel of her own food. But on that Sunday, she finished eating and turned and walked to the edge of the top deck and stared out across the hollow. She didn't bark, she didn't move, she just sat there like she was waiting for something (or someone). Eventually she lay down, but not in her normal dog-as-rug position, but in an upright, alert pose, watching the driveway. Waiting. It went on so long that Nick went and got the camera and took her picture.

Carol and Jamie and their family arrived right when they said they would. Carla had retired to her couch and I was outside weeding when they pulled up the driveway. I went to get Carla, but she was already at the door. I clipped on her leash and she walked out to greet them, as if she were expecting them.

Carol was delightful. She'd recently retired and hadn't had a dog since her beloved beagle died five years before. So she knew a little about hound dogs. I gave her some time alone to get to know Carla, while I chatted with her young grandson and his parents. Carol decided to walk Carla down to the end of the drive and back. I was busy introducing the cats and answering questions about the chickens, and they took off before I could stop them.

There were two problems with taking Carla for a stroll to the end of our driveway. First, not only was Carol retired, but she'd recently had knee surgery. Second, our driveway is a steep hill. When I took Carla out for her run in the morning, she was always excited and hurried down the hill. In fact, most mornings I had to give a steady whoa on the leash all the way down or risk tumbling down the hill after her. Remember those sangrias? Well, I hadn't been up for running (or much of anything else) that morning, so Carla was about four hours late for her daily run.

I watched in amazement as Carla walked slowly and carefully beside Carol all the way down. When they reached the bottom, Carol waited while Carla looked down the road longingly, but then they plodded right back up the driveway.

We talked some more and Carla remained at Carol's side. I stressed how much daily exercise Carla needed, and Carol said, "She'll be good for me. I need that too." She said ever since she'd retired, it was easy to stay home in her jammies all day, but she knew she should get out. Carla would be the incentive.

The whole time we talked, I felt teary. I knew this was right. The magic had finally happened. Carla was a perfect fit for Carol. She'd be loved and adored and useful too. She'd help Carol as much as Carol would help her.

Carol planned to drive back to Indiana later that week. I warned her that Carla liked to look over your shoulder and drool as you drove. Carol just smiled and patted her new dog. She was ready for Carla and all her Carla-ness.

Many times puppy visitors asked, "How can you get anything done? I'd just stand here and watch them all day."

Honest truth—sometimes I did. It was very easy for me to while away a good hour just watching the puppies wrestle or throwing tennis balls in the pen. When a storyline stuck, I'd pick up a puppy and carry it to the church pew on our back porch breathe in the puppy breath and almost always find my answer. Two weeks went by in a blur and all six puppies had approved adopters eager to take them home.

With their quarantine lifted at the nine-day mark, we hooked up our puppy pen with our neighbor's borrowed pen and created a puppy paddock in the grass. The pups loved the big, wide world and I climbed into the pen to play with them. They were thrilled to have me, chewing my laces and leaping on my back. Homeboy hung back as usual, letting the other pups have first dibs. I reached for him and cradled him like a baby for a belly rub. As I stroked his smooth belly, I realized, *Homeboy wasn't a boy*!

I'd had this puppy for two weeks. How was it possible that until today, I hadn't noticed that he didn't have a penis? I carried Homeboy/girl to the house and held her up for Nick.

"She's a girl!" I said. "I'm never gonna live this down."

He gave me a confused look. Nick liked the puppies, but he wasn't really on a first-name basis with any of them, so he most likely didn't even know how many girls and boys were in the pen.

"They told me the two extra puppies were boys!" I rationalized.

"I don't see what the big deal is," he said. "It's still a cute puppy. Does it matter?"

"Yes, it matters!" I shrieked.

I moved all the puppies back into the puppy room and sat down at my computer to compose the email in which I would confess to the powers that be at OPH that Homeboy was actually Homegirl. And then I waited for the horror, the hand-smack, at the very least, the teasing. I was certain it was coming. Instead, I got an email back from Mindy, my foster coordinator, who simply said, "LOL."

Later I heard confessions from other fosters who had similar experiences of dogs and puppies arriving, listed as one gender, but actually being the opposite. Kindly, no one mentioned that it hadn't taken them two weeks to figure it out!

I retired to the porch with a glass of wine and my embarrassment. It was still my defense that I was told this was a boy puppy. And, there is a great body of evidence supporting the fact that most of us see what we expect to see. Magicians capitalize on it and marketing people count on it. Our government expects it of us and good teachers try their darnedest to teach children to see beyond it. And yet more times than not, we still see the old woman in the image and not the beautiful girl. I'm not the only one guilty of seeing what I expect to see and not seeing the possibilities or the person (puppy).

My very progressive daughter thought it was pretty cool that I embraced the whole puppy and wasn't hung up on the physical designation of my puppy's gender. I tried to see it that way, but in the end, all I could really say, though, was—*I just never looked*. It didn't occur to me. I was too focused on SIX PUPPIES and their poop/pee/chaos/needs/kisses.

After learning that she was a girl, we tried calling her Homegirl, but Homeboy still suited. She might be a girl, but she was a tomgirl at that.

I'm sure there are plenty of you out there right now thinking: How is it possible you had this puppy in your care for two whole weeks and never noticed that he was a she? *How incompetent are you?*

Very.

But you know what? The bottom line was that I had loved these puppies the best I could. They were healthy and happy and ready to break my heart and go to their forever homes. And it really didn't matter so much to me if they were boys or girls, they were precious puppies. Every one of them.

The next week was a week of goodbyes; by Saturday morning there were only three puppies left. As the puppies ate their breakfast, I took the quiet moment to check my email and discovered that at some point during the night, Homeboy's adopter had decided he didn't want to adopt Homeboy. He'd had his heart set on a boy puppy. A girl wouldn't do.

Now what? All three were supposed to leave that day so that Nick and I could sneak off for a scheduled birthday celebration. Nick's birthday is actually in December but we'd had to repeatedly postpone his gift—a beer tour of Lancaster. I'd scheduled it for that weekend because all the puppies were supposed to be gone.

Homeboy and I watched the other pups disappear down the driveway. She'd had a few experiences all alone, but every other time she was eventually reunited with some or all of her siblings, so she didn't start crying for about an hour. Our reservation was nonrefundable and it was just one night, so there was no choice but to hand Homeboy off to the kids and head to Lancaster.

When we arrived at our hotel that Saturday there were Christmas decorations everywhere. Since Nick's birthday is three days after Christmas this seemed appropriate, but no, it wasn't clever me, it was the Christmas in July convention. The hotel was inundated with Santa look-alikes, insanely sweet and pleasant midwesterners, and harried people carrying tubs of Christmas ornaments—presumably all buyers or sellers of Christmas decorations.

Our absence left Ian in charge of Homeboy and her sadness. Reportedly, she whined so much that he was forced to carry her, hold her, walk her, and play with her that night until he couldn't keep his eyes open anymore, and then he left her with his eighteen-year-old brother who was wearing headphones. When we got home the next day, Ian greeted us with Homeboy in his arms and handed her over saying, "Now *you* can listen to her."

It's hard to lose your family, so we moved Homeboy into the kitchen so she would have more company. To keep Gracie out of the kitchen (she was still making bodily threats toward Homeboy), we propped up a sagging baby gate with Addie's mellophone case. We all enjoyed Homeboy's company for another week, before she took off for her new home in Virginia with a mommy who couldn't wait to spoil her rotten. The puppy room was empty and I felt like we'd just returned from a long messy, wonderful trip.

SIX

Foster Fail?

There was something different about our newest foster dog. And it wasn't just his eyes—one was crystal blue eye, and the other eye was extraordinarily split exactly down the middle, half brown and half blue. Frank was skinny and shy when we picked him up in the bowling alley parking lot. His coat was a dull brindle brown and white, and he weighed forty-five pounds when he should have weighed sixty. Frank was an "owner surrender," so he quickly ended up on the euthanasia list.* Most likely he was confused and a little bit stressed at the turn his life had taken.

---

* At many shelters "owner-surrenders" are not held long before being moved to the euthanasia list, as the shelter knows that no one will come looking for the dog.

When I took him to some grass to relieve himself after the long drive, he left a nasty mess of blood-tinged diarrhea that was nearly impossible to clean up. So much for not leaving a trace. I contacted OPH medical and was told as long as we didn't continue to see blood, it was relatively normal from the stress of the trip.

As we drove home, I stole looks at his sweet face watching me. There was a depth of sadness there, but overriding it was something more—hope maybe, or longing. He was looking for his person. He never took his eyes off me during the entire hour drive home, even though he must have been exhausted.

That night, I lay in bed still picturing his remarkable eyes peering back at me from the crate in the backseat. They were full of heartbreak and intelligence. Frank was no ordinary stray. *I am not going to foster fail*, I told myself. Heck, if I was gonna foster fail it would have been with Carla, not some skinny, funny-looking, boy dog with crazy eyes.

The next morning, I took Frank to the farmer's market where he charmed everyone he met. We stopped at the fancy homemade dog treat vendor so I could buy Frank a treat, but when the woman heard Frank was a rescue and saw how skinny he was, she gave us an entire bag of premium homemade treats *for free*!

I thanked her and we started toward another booth. I was looking for kale as the caterpillars had eaten all of mine. A little boy teetered toward Frank, and his mother asked if he could pet him. I smiled and said that would be fine. Frank had given me no reason to think he wouldn't be fine around little kids.

The little boy's face was level with Frank's. He took Frank's big head in his hands and rubbed his nose to Frank's. Then he put his tiny hands inside Frank's mouth to examine his teeth. "What a great dog," the mother said. "Is he yours?"*

"Kind of," I told her. *What? Where did that come from?*

---

* I would later learn that I was lucky in this instance as rubbing noses and inserting hands inside mouths is not a safe way to "meet" a dog, especially a dog with such an unknown history. OPH does outreach programs to teach children how to safely interact with dogs.

"Well, he's great," she said and took her child's hand.

A week later Frank was still deathly skinny. His head looked oddly huge atop his emaciated body. Someone hadn't taken care of this dog. But Frank? He didn't have a resentful bone in his body (and I could easily feel pretty much all of them).

I tried to cling to my convictions. I was not adopting another dog. I was only fostering. Somewhere along the line, the idea of adopting a dog to fill the hole Lucy left got overshadowed by a feverish desire to help as many dogs as possible. It wasn't time yet to stop. Nick loved Frank too. He actually said, "Just keep him and then do only puppies." That was crazy talk coming from him. The puppies' noise and smell had nearly made him move out.

But here's what I knew—it hurt when Galina left. It hurt even more when Carla and then Homeboy left. I had sleepless nights and too many tears. *Could I keep doing this?* After only a week, I knew that pain was nothing compared to how much it would hurt when Frank left. Maybe I wasn't made for this. Maybe I wasn't as strong as I thought.

But I wanted to be. I wanted to do this. Not for Galina or Homeboy or Carla or Frank, but for all the dogs to come. Because I knew, as evidenced by all the amazing dogs we'd already met, that another good dog was right around the corner. And they deserved the chance I could give them.

Frank was a Catahoula Leopard Dog, more or less. Breed assignment is not an exact science in rescue work. Catahoulas are working dogs and herders by instinct. Frank was skinny and smiley, with a tongue longer than Mick Jagger's. He followed me everywhere. His devotion so sure no leash was necessary. We walked the fence line early one morning and spotted a groundhog who had recently dug a home beneath the tree line along the pasture. *Damn groundhog.* For years, Lucy had kept groundhogs from moving in. I was tempted to let Frank chase him down as he was clearly asking to do. But the hole was outside the pasture for now. We'd see if we could live peaceably. I tossed a rock in the groundhog's general direction and he scurried into his hole. *Was Frank as good a dog as Lucy? Was it fair to compare?*

Later, as I worked at my desk, Frank lay behind me on the guest bed, watching my every move.* I clicked onto his OPH page and looked at the only picture there. It was grainy. Frank was standing in a grass-bare yard, looking cowed and anxious with the words "coming soon" printed beside him. I knew I should update his page, but instead I spent the better part of the week in a crazy debate between my head and my heart about Frank. I knew as soon as I started writing about his awesomeness on his adoption page, some wonderful person would want to adopt him and I was still trying to figure out if I was that wonderful person.

Nick was pressuring me too. He even went so far as to say, "What if I put in the application and he's my dog?"

But Frank wasn't his dog.

Frank loved *me*. When I left him for the first time, he nearly went through a window screen to follow me. I'd always said I just wanted a dog who came when he was called. Frank didn't even have a real name and he came when he was called.†

After much debate and waffling, we made the decision not to adopt Frank. We loved him, maybe too much, for which we would decidedly pay in a week or so when his wonderful new adoptive family arrived to take him home.

The biggest reason we decided against adopting had to do with Gracie, whom I maligned on a regular basis to anyone within earshot and occasionally on my blog.‡ Sure, she drove me nuts and she was everything I didn't want in a dog—disloyal, disobedient, disrespectful, and, for lack of a better word—dumb. But, we'd had her since she was a puppy. The kids loved her. This was her home. Gracie was going nowhere.§

---

* Who knew writing was such a spectator sport?

† Gracie makes a point of not even looking in my direction when I call her name.

‡ But for the record, I DO love Gracie.

§ Although I do occasionally flirt with the idea of switching pictures on the OPH website and giving Gracie away to an unsuspecting adopter. Kidding. (Mostly.)

When I explained to Nick that we couldn't keep Frank because it would make Gracie seem even more inferior, he said, "Gracie has always been the second-tier dog."

True. But for better or worse, we were committed to Gracie. And despite potential jealousy, Gracie was tolerating the foster dogs better than expected. Occasionally, they even brought out the best in her. When I was trying to teach Frank to sit, Gracie sat repeatedly for me (a skill she'd rarely before demonstrated).

Galina and Stitch had taught Gracie to eat her dinner when it was served,* before another dog ate it. Carla taught her to walk on the leash. When we were out for a run, I looped Gracie's leash over Carla's and when she attempted to dart somewhere, Carla's bulk held her. And when she lagged behind, Carla dragged her along for me.

I was hopeful that Frank would teach her to come when she was called. She was getting very good at coming when I called Frank. Whenever I yelled, "Frank, come!" both dogs barreled into the room. I didn't have to do this very often as Frank rarely let me out of his sight.

I knew another week with Frank might make us regret our decision or be happy we chose to let him go. It probably depended on whether he got his teeth on a chicken and whether Addie finally decided to give him a chance. He loved Addie and made regular overtures, licking her leg and following her around the kitchen. "Oh, gross! Get away from me dog!" she yelled, but he was undeterred in his affection. When he destroyed her favorite umbrella, she labeled him the "worst dog ever!"

Either way, the decision was made. The option was no longer an option. I would not entertain the idea of foster failing anymore. Not that foster failing was failing, I explained when pressed. It seemed to have been a great option for plenty of people. But for us, for Gracie, for right now, foster failing was not an option.

---

* Instead of leaving it to soften and collect flies before the cat claimed it and then barfed it up later.

Frank ended up staying with us for another two weeks before heading to his new home. He needed to be treated for worms.* His adopters were generous people, who hugged me when we met. They were excited to take him home, but respectful of my sad feelings. They pulled out of the driveway and I watched Frank disappear from my life. My heart hurt.

I was sure Frank's did too. I wished there was some way to explain to the dogs why they had to leave, so they didn't think I was one more person deserting them. It always helped to see the pictures adopters sent a few weeks later of a happy dog who'd long forgotten us.

On the surface, Frank's leaving was well-timed. My debut novel, *I'm Not Her,* was released that week. It was exciting and terrifying at the same time. A ten-year dream come true, but publicizing it was a whole other kind of work that was difficult for me and far outside my comfort zone. The effort seemed endless and consumed large swaths of my time. There was always something else I could do. I'd read articles by other authors sharing their five-step plan to becoming a *New York Times* bestseller and they made it sound easy. It was not. Sleep became tough; my mind was always spinning. I spoke with the social media manager and another person in marketing at my publisher and both assured me I was doing fine—blogging, being accessible, tweeting; I'd even delved in to Tumblr, although truth be told I still didn't understand it. There was so much to do that some days I was overwhelmed and simply surfed Facebook or wandered around the gardens trying to figure out where to begin.

I tried to write. I needed to begin my third novel. It was due in December and so far, all I had was an entire notebook filled with snatches of conversations, ideas, interviews with characters, and a very loosey-goosey plot idea. One of my characters was a boy with Asperger's syndrome, so I was reading books and blogs and beginning to think that all of us were on the Autism spectrum somewhere. Some of us just managed our obsessions and distractions better. Another of my

---

* Extremely common with all the rescue dogs.

characters was a hospice nurse, and I lost entire days reading first-person accounts of working in hospice. I wondered if there could be anything like hospice therapy dogs—dogs who could visit hospice patients and just hang with them, lending the comfort of their presence. Little by little the dogs were creeping into every corner of my world. As my third novel finally began to appear on the page, several of my foster dogs made cameos, including Frank.

Summer was ending and fall would bring big changes for all of us. Ian would start his last year of middle school, and play "fall ball" (lower key travel baseball) and rec soccer. Addie would begin her junior year of high school, but this year she was dividing her classes between "brick and mortar" classes (those held in the high school building) and online classes. For the first time, she was actually excited about going back to school rather than dreading it.

When she was little, Addie made friends easily and charmed her way into every situation, but as adolescence descended everything became more complicated. She didn't want to be like the other girls and she wasn't. She had always been an independent thinker, but as her world expanded, she discovered feminism and liberals and turned her intense passion to what was wrong with our world; always ready to take up the fight of the disenfranchised. I was proud of how brave and committed she was, but her unwillingness to dress or act or think like the average teen made an American high school a place she didn't exactly find welcoming. For the past two years, she'd spent her lunch periods in the library reading *Psychology Today* and writing fan fiction for *Les Misérables*. She studied French so that she could read the story in its original language. She found her place in the music and theater departments and most of her teachers appreciated how well she thought (and lived) outside the box, but I was hoping this new plan would make for a happier kid.

Brady would leave for college in two weeks. As I helped him pack his things, I found myself in tears almost daily at the thought of him leaving. How had it happened so fast? You think you have all the time in the world to raise your children and teach them all that they'll need to survive, but the day is upon you and there's so much left unsaid and undone. I was in turmoil emotionally and the chaos of our days felt relentless. I longed for my solitary days alone with the computer and the cats.

And I missed Frank. He had been such constant company those last few weeks. He'd been my bodyguard and devoted friend, never leaving my side and always happy to listen to my ramblings even when Addie slammed her door on my nagging or Brady put in his earbuds when I asked if he had packed anything.

"I'm going to get another dog," I told Nick as we sat in our chairs surveying the manor one night.

"It's kind of a crazy time right now. Sure you don't want to take a breather? What if Frank comes back?"

We'd been getting emails from Frank's adopters that things weren't going well, but I had faith that they just had to get used to each other. Frank would settle down. The adopters were such nice people—they'd even sent Addie a new umbrella to replace the one that Frank had destroyed. The tag was signed, "*Frank.*"

"Frank isn't coming back. He's the best dog. They'll figure it out," I told Nick.

"Even if he doesn't, you're so stressed right now."

"Which is exactly why I need another dog."

"You make no sense."

"This time, I'll pick a dog that will get adopted quickly. No more hanging around and getting attached."

Nick took a sip of his beer and shooed Crash off the arm of his chair. "Right."

Later, after I'd checked the transport list and emailed Mindy, I told Nick, "These ones will go quick. They're border collies!"

"*They?*—there's more than one?"

"I can't just take one of them. They're brothers or cousins or something. They were owner-surrendered together."

I pulled up the pictures of Texas and Tennessee on my phone. I knew Nick liked border collies as much as I did. "They're beautiful. They'll get adopted quickly," I told him.

"Not everyone can handle a border collie," he said.

I ignored his comment and told him about the leash divider I'd ordered online so I could walk them together.* Even if it didn't work, I figured as long as they didn't both take off at the same time, in the same direction, I'd be able to hold them. Their combined weight was barely sixty-five pounds.

And in the meantime, I'd try very hard not to lose my heart or my footing.

---

* In my teens and early twenties, I fox-hunted occasionally. I remembered the young hounds happily coupled together as they learned the ropes. I envisioned Texas and Tennessee having the same experience.

SEVEN

Heartbreak

Leaving Brady in his new dorm, two hours away, was scary. This was my kid who everyone affectionately termed an "absent-minded professor." What if he lost his key? Brady liked to take long walks, meandering for miles lost in the stories in his mind. That was fine in our little rural town, but how was that going to work here? What if he was mugged? Selinsgrove didn't seem too dangerous, but still. One of his classes was scheduled for 8:00 A.M. and it was a rare day that summer when we'd seen Brady before noon. How would he ever get up in time? I'd bought him an alarm clock, but there were no guarantees that he'd use it.

"This is the honors hall?" I asked as we made our way down the narrow hallway. I noted that the rooms on either side of his were for girls. Things sure had changed since I went to college and boys weren't allowed on the hall after 11:00 P.M. Brady's room was already crammed with his roommates' furniture, boxes, and luggage. A refrigerator was perched atop two stacked dressers. There would be three boys crammed in a dorm room meant for two because the school had accepted so many new students they'd run out of housing. I couldn't imagine how three young adults could coexist in such a tiny space, especially when I knew that one of those young adults hadn't cleaned his room in a decade, hoarded books like the Library of Congress, and wrote on a manual typewriter.

When it was time for us to leave, Brady walked us to the car. Standing under the ancient oak trees that ringed the campus, he hugged me. "Thanks for making this possible for me," he said. "I love you."

In that moment I realized we'd done okay. Somehow, some way, we'd raised a grateful, smart, loving person. He might get lost or lose his key, but he'd figure it out.

"Just like that," I said to Nick as we pulled out of the campus. "It's over."

"It's not over."

"You know what I mean."

"Yeah."

The part of Brady's life where his parents guided his days was over. For the first time in almost nineteen years, I wouldn't know where he was or what he ate or whether or not he was happy on a daily basis. Sure, we could call, but it wasn't the same. I couldn't exactly ask him for a play-by-play of all the days that I'd missed. I had to let go.

I was happy for the distraction that Texas and Tennessee brought. When we picked them up from transport, they seemed shell-shocked, creeping along beside us across the parking lot. They were beautiful border collies from the same shelter in rural southwest Virginia. Texas looked like the border collies in the pictures—black-and-white patterns played across his body. Tennessee was all black and a little larger and more solid that Texas. They were sweet boys and it was easy to love them. You couldn't find better-mannered guests.

Those first few days, they watched everyone's every move. Sadly, they cowered when any of us raised a hand above our waists, moved quickly, or picked up anything large. The dogs were in the kitchen eating their supper as Ian gathered his gear for baseball practice one afternoon. When his ride pulled in the driveway, he grabbed his bat from where it was learning in the corner, swinging it up over his shoulder. This sent both dogs scrambling across the wood floor, their nails struggling to find purchase.

"Poor pups," I told them as I lured them out from under the kitchen table after Ian left. They seemed grateful for any kindness thrown their way. Ducking their heads and sniffing at a proffered treat, like that visiting relative who was always saying, "Please don't go to any trouble . . . really, I'm fine." They crept about the house cautiously, and Texas ran into our sliding glass door numerous times. I wondered if they'd ever been in a house before.

At transport, another foster had told me about "male dog wraps," after I mentioned my concern that these boys we were picking up might mark our house as Frank had when he first arrived. She explained that the wraps were basically diapers that covered the hind end of a male dog, encasing the potential weapon.

"You need to cover up those bad boys," she said.

Brilliant! I thought. First thing the next morning, I headed to the pet store to get some male dog wraps of my own. Tennessee gave me a worried look as I strapped a pirate-patterned wrap on him. I whispered, "I'm just covering up that bad boy," and gave him a pat. It didn't take long for both dogs to understand the place to pee was outside, and we put the wraps away for the next male foster dogs.

Texas and Tennessee had only just settled in when we learned that Frank was being returned. I'd watched by email as the heartbreak unfolded for both Frank and his adopters. He could not make the adjustment to his new home. It just wasn't the right fit.

"We have to take him back," I said after I told Nick the news.

"I know," he said, with a gleam in his eye. I knew what that gleam meant.

"That doesn't mean we're keeping him."

"It doesn't mean we're not either," he said.

I wasn't looking forward to wrestling with *that* decision again. I'd thought all along that it was up to us to choose a dog, but I was beginning to wonder if it wasn't actually up to the dog to choose us. *Was Frank too attached to us? Would he be capable of adapting to another home?*

Frank was alarmed to find new dogs in the house when he arrived, and he challenged Tennessee on several occasions. Texas was happy to let him rule the roost, but Tennessee wasn't so willing to let him steal all the toys and all my attention. A few snarls later, they'd worked it out and spent the rest of the afternoon chasing each other around the kitchen, slamming into cabinets and upsetting the water bowl.

Along with a large bag of food, a collar and leash, and my mixed emotions, Frank returned with his own beautiful custom dog bed. The huge L.L. Bean bed was large enough to share with his two new best friends. The almost-adopters insisted we keep it as it was monogrammed, *Frank.* We found a spot for it in the kitchen and it gave the canine guests, and occasionally Ian, a place to relax when restricted to the kitchen. The "Frank Bed" would become the favorite spot for dozens of fosters to come.

I'd been attempting to walk Texas and Tennessee on a dual leash and for the most part it worked, but the dogs had very different personalities and as such, they didn't always want to go in the same direction at the same time. It was Texas who seemed to do most of the unsorting whenever they got tangled. He'd quietly back up, duck, or lift a paw to untangle them while Tennessee kept moving along oblivious to the messes he was creating. They were the yin and yang of border collies.

I was outside in the garden one afternoon, having left the three dogs in the house for a rest (or a wrestle as the case might be). Suddenly the door swung open—one of the dogs had figured out the lever handle. All three of them took off across the yard, ducking under the pasture fence and continuing up the hill. I watched for a stunned moment before running to the house for three leashes and taking off after them.

They only went as far as our horse pasture. I could see Frank running in large goofy circles around the horses. He knew to give them wide berth. The horses were completely unconcerned or possibly unaware as Texas and Tennessee approached them from opposite sides, crouched low in the grass. Images of one or both border collies getting their heads pummeled by Cocoa's alpha mare hooves sent me flying over the fence.

I knew I needed to get them out of the pasture, but it was fascinating to watch them work. Tennessee crept closer to the horses, his body close to the ground. He glanced back at me as if awaiting my signal. Texas approached them from the far side, his body so low that only his ears were visible in the tall grass. This was not their first rodeo. These dogs were clearly trained. When one of the horses shifted a few feet away from the others in search of better grass, Texas scuttled sideways like a crab, his eyes never leaving the horse.

Finally, I whistled and called them. Texas immediately turned and trotted calmly to me. Tennessee glanced back at the horses, and then at me as if to say, "Are you sure? Couldn't we just have one little chase?" I called again firmly and whistled and he came to me. I clipped on leashes and we headed back to the house with Frank loping along behind us.

I watched Texas and Tennessee trot along in front of me. *Real border collies!* What would Nick say if I told him I wanted to keep all three dogs?

When Frank was returned, I'd asked my foster coordinator, Mindy, to place a hold on him while I sorted out my feelings about adopting him. I didn't think my decision had changed, but I wondered if his return was a sign. I tried to imagine our lives with a dog like Frank in it. I weighed his jealousy at sharing me with the dogs who came and went in our lives, with his happiness at being in our home.

In the end, I decided that if I kept Frank I couldn't keep fostering. It wouldn't be fair to the dogs we fostered, or to Frank. It wasn't time yet. There were too many more dogs left to save. Too many being euthanized because they had no place to go. Frank could survive without us, but there were so many other dogs who couldn't. I emailed Mindy, "Change Frank back to adoptable."

The following Tuesday I had my first ever live TV interview. I woke up with my stomach in knots. *What was I thinking agreeing to this?* I wanted to be a writer, not a movie star. I read over the notes from the TV studio about not wearing loud patterns or white because "they can play tricks with the camera." I stared at my closet until I felt a panic creep in. "Just get it over with," I muttered and pulled out a black top and purple skirt. There is so much I love about being a writer, but promoting my writing is right up there with visiting the dentist or shopping for tires. A necessary torture. I can't speak for all writers, but I'd much rather write than talk. So, the idea that on this day I would have to talk ON LIVE TELEVISION was terrifying.

To calm my nerves and delay the inevitable, I spent extra time with the dogs that morning giving them an extended playtime outside because I knew they would be cooped up for a good portion of the day while I was in Harrisburg. The horses were in the barn away from the hot morning heat, and Texas cast longing glances toward the empty pasture.

Now that I knew Texas and Tennessee would come the moment I called, I never put a leash on them. The three dogs had their usual crazy runaround and tackle game for a good twenty minutes. I marveled at the speed and intensity of their chase and laughed when Tennessee reversed directions so fast his feet went out from under him and he tumbled partway down the hill. Texas seemed to be flitting about on the edges of the game that morning, occasionally whacking at his head with his paw in an odd way, like swatting at flies. I could have watched their shenanigans all day, but I needed to put on makeup and agonize over my hair before the interview, so I called the dogs and headed for the house.

Frank stayed by my side, while Texas and Tennessee swirled around us as we walked down the hill. When we reached the bottom, Texas spied my neighbor's goats and immediately assumed the low crouch of a herding border collie, creeping toward the road. I panicked for a moment, worried he would dart across the road to herd the goats; but when I whistled he immediately spun around and raced back to me. *Such a good dog.*

My interview went fine. While my pulse raced and my face flushed red, I managed to come across coherently thanks to the host who was very good at her job. When I got stuck at one point, my mind blanking, she smiled and prompted me with another question. Anyone watching would have thought my book was the best thing she'd read that year, when in reality she'd only seen a picture of the cover.* I liked her though, and felt like if it weren't for the cameras and the lights and the people watching our every move, we could have been friends. I hadn't told anyone about the show beforehand because if people I knew were watching, I'd have been even more nervous. So other than Nick there wasn't anyone to call to see how it went.

"You did fine, really. You looked great," he told me as I walked to the car. I checked my phone for messages and saw one from my neighbor, "OH MY GOD! You were on TV!" She'd been at a doctor's appointment and had seen the show in the waiting room. "I told everyone in the office that I knew you!" she told me later. There it was—my five minutes of fame. It was a relief to have it behind me.

When I got home, the dogs treated me no differently than before I'd become a TV star. I let them out of their crates and then took them out for a romp, but they tired quickly in the heat and we went back inside. Not having the heart to put them back in their crates again, I double-checked that there was no food on the counters and left all three boys gated in the kitchen to run a quick errand. I needed to get my passport photo taken so I could renew my passport for an upcoming trip.

I was gone about twenty minutes. When I arrived home, Frank and Tennessee greeted me at the door. I knew something was wrong the moment I stepped inside. There was an eerie smell, almost chemical; it made me shiver. Texas lay on the giant Frank bed with his chin on his front legs as if asleep. Only he wasn't asleep. He was too still. *He was gone.*

I screamed, and Ian and Addie came running. Texas's body still felt warm. Had he choked on something? I looked in his mouth and

---

* I left a copy for her to read at her request.

saw nothing. "NO, NO, NO, NO, NO!" I yelled as I searched for any sign of life. "This can't be happening! My beautiful boy!" I sobbed. I knelt next to Texas and stroked his still form. "This can't be happening. Please, let this be a dream." Addie and Ian stood beside me, not knowing what to do or say, but the other two dogs began wrestling as if nothing was wrong.

At that moment, Nick pulled in the driveway. Addie ran outside to tell him what was happening. He was white as he checked Texas all over, too, prying his mouth open and forcing his fingers down his throat searching for an object that wasn't there, hoping he could still save him. Neither of us could find any sign of injury or trauma. Texas was dead.

I made phone calls, spoke with several OPH officials and the medical director. No one knew what could have happened. They would send his body to the state lab for testing to rule out anything contagious he could have brought with him from Virginia. I spent the rest of that teary day hugging Tennessee and Frank, and calling people, looking for clues, trying to figure out how Texas could have just laid down and died.

"It happens," said my vet, Chris, who is also my neighbor and friend, after we'd talked through every possibility. But it still made no sense to me. He was healthy, happy. Just that day I'd noticed what a shine his coat had gotten. He ate well, had learned to love treats, played and ran and smiled his big border collie smile. I could still picture Texas creeping up on my horses, letting it go as far as I dared before calling him off. He was a beautiful dog. I told Chris about the head swatting I'd seen Texas doing that morning and he said it might have meant something or not. We couldn't know without an extensive autopsy, and OPH and the state would only test for infectious diseases. Autopsies were expensive, and I understood that resources would be better spent saving dogs.

That night when the tears finally slowed, I was angry. One of the reasons I'd gotten into fostering was because I didn't want to ever watch another dog die. Losing my beloved Lucy the year before had hurt too much. I didn't want to do it again. I'd rather suffer through a thousand goodbyes than bury another dog. And now that's exactly what I was doing. I didn't sign up for this. I was done fostering. No more.

The next morning, I walked Tennessee and Frank. They played and tussled as if Texas had never been here. I made the painful call to Texas's approved adopter, who was actually my friend Mer. Her daughter, Shannon, had fallen in love with Texas when she met him the week before and was planning to adopt him and train him for agility. Texas would have been a superstar. We cried on the phone and I cried more when we hung up, imagining Shannon's heartbreak at her mother's news.

How many tears had I shed this year over dogs? Loving them was too risky, I decided. There was no way around the inevitable grief. *Could I keep doing this? Could I continue putting my heart out there again and again?*

I couldn't get the image of Texas lying on the Frank bed out of my head. He was so still. So gone. The sick feeling in the pit of my stomach persisted and just looking at Tennessee or thinking of little Shannon brought tears. It had been almost a year since Lucy died, and here I was again. Back in this dark, painful place.

Sitting on the hill with Nick, surveying the manor the next night, we talked about it.

"Maybe you need to dial it back a bit," he suggested.

"What would that look like?"

"I don't know. Just take a break."

If Frank wasn't AP* for the family we'd met the weekend before at an adoption event, I might have very well just adopted him and been done with it.

Messages from other OPH volunteers, fosters, and staff continued to come in. Everyone shared my grief. Several people said, "Texas knew safety and love before his death. That's what we do for these dogs."

---

* AP means Adoption Pending. An adopter has been approved to adopt the dog in question. This doesn't mean they will adopt the dog, only that they have seven days to decide whether or not they will.

I wrote about Texas's death on my blog. It helped to write about it. It's how I think, how I process my emotions. Spilling my pain on the page helped take the edge off it, but how long would it follow me around? Texas most likely would have died whether he was here with us or back on the farm where he was unwanted and likely mistreated. Everyone said there was nothing we could have done to prevent it, but I couldn't help wondering, doubting. Maybe it would be best if we stopped fostering.

I looked at Tennessee and Frank lying beside me, for once content to rest. I stroked Tennessee's black fur and rubbed Frank's wide head. I loved them both. How could I not? And the risk was part of that love. It's unavoidable when you open your heart to anyone—dog *or* human.

At the edge of the woods Crash pounced on a mouse—letting it get away again and again, only to chase it down. When Frank noticed the activity and took off with Tennessee right behind, I didn't call them off. I let them put Crash in a tree and hoped the mouse would make it.

Life. Death. *Was it different for animals? Did they know something we didn't?* When it was dark, I called the dogs away from the tree and headed to the house. The Frank bed was back in its place. I'd washed it and then almost put it in the basement, but changed my mind and returned it to the kitchen. Back inside now, Frank and Tennessee piled on it.

I could still picture Texas there, but it helped to know he hadn't suffered. Chris had assured me that the fact he was lying so peacefully and there was no evidence of trauma—no blood, no foam, meant that he went quick. Dying was inevitable for all of us, so a peaceful passing was more than you could ask for. Texas was a beautiful, amazing, sweet dog. I knew by the way he cowered at loud noises and sudden movements that his life didn't start out so peaceful, but I was glad that in the end he knew safety and love and happiness. I was glad we were able to give him that, but mostly I felt blessed to have had the privilege to love, even for a short time, such a good dog.

Without Texas, Tennessee morphed into a different dog. Left to his own devices, gated in the kitchen, Tennessee managed to decimate a plastic laundry basket, destroy the zipper and strap (the two most important elements) of Addie's book bag, and gnaw the corner off one of her school-owned textbooks.

Apparently, without his playmate, he was bored. After he devoured my favorite sandals, Nick brought home a box of hard plastic tool-casings from his work.* He set the box in the kitchen with the lid opened and we pretended not to see as Tennessee snuck a few bright yellow drill casings out of the box. That box kept him busy for the better part of the weekend.†

Tennessee and Frank had approved adopters waiting to take them home, but we had one more week together, as both dogs were on hold until we got the results of tests on Texas. My emotions over their pending adoptions raged back and forth—happy for them, they deserved forever homes, but teary at the idea of saying goodbye to them, especially Frank.

A week later, all the tests came back negative, which meant we still had no real answers about Texas. My heart was so very tired of thinking about it. *Did I miss something? Could we have done something? If only I'd been home* . . . all these thoughts spun through my head when I watched Tennessee and Frank playing without Texas. I'd always hated mysteries. Living with this one frustrated me, but I had no choice but to make peace with it.

The following week we said goodbye to both Frank and Tennessee. Frank was the first to go. And the hardest. I already missed his wide soft head, always there, right next to me, pressing his nose to my hand. When we met his family for the Meet and Greet‡ at a nearby park,

---

* Nick works for a company that makes power tools and hand tools. I'm not naming names, but the plastic casings of drills and saws that he brought home were black and yellow (and they weren't Steelers promotional items).

† All the foster dogs to follow would have the same joy, and we'd find ourselves warning future adopters that their new dog might be prone to chew yellow power tools.

‡ The OPH term for when an approved foster meets the foster dogs and makes the decision to take the dog home or not.

Frank bounded out of the car and introduced himself. He and his new furbrother (a lab-shaped yellow dog named Cole with blue eyes like Frank!) liked each other immediately. Frank wandered around smiling and wagging up everyone, gobbling up the offered treats (and then casing the bag for more). As always, he gravitated to the kids, but seemed equally enamored of his new mom and dad who obviously adored him.

When they signed the contract, it was a lump-in-throat moment for me, but no tears because it was clear this was his family. He'd have a new best buddy to play with and two kids to adore. Frank would be happy and busy. The whole family had such a joyful, easy energy, any dog would be lucky to go home with them, so I was thrilled that Frank was the one. He posed for a picture, sitting happily between his two kids with a big goofy smile on his face, and then they were off.

Still, I held my breath until I got the email from his new mom the next day. He was settling in great. He and Cole had played happily for hours. *Yay for Frank, my favorite boy*, I thought as I sat with Tennessee on Frank's giant bed. We'd decided to keep the bed, partly because it was a great bed for multiple dogs to share and it reminded me of my favorite foster dog, and partly because I didn't want his new family to feel obligated to keep his name. Most adopters change the foster dogs' names, which was appropriate because it was the beginning of a new life. Frank was now Cooper.

Tennessee left amid a momentary monsoon a few days later. His family had already met him at the OPH event the week before, so they knew they wanted him. His Meet and Greet was quick. He was over-the-moon excited when they arrived, and he impressed all of us with the way he dialed back the energy when he approached their preschooler, careful not to knock her over. His dad texted me later and said that "Black Jack" (perfect name) had found his forever family. Okay, that did bring a few tears. I was happy for Tennessee, but I couldn't help but think of Texas.

I'd decided I'd take another dog, if only to distract me from Frank and Tennessee.

"Another one?" Nick asked. "I thought you were going to take a break?"

"I can't," I confessed. "I need to do this."

I didn't understand why I needed to do it, but fostering had somehow graduated from my hobby to my calling. Losing Texas sheared my heart off at the knees, but at the same time it created an urgency in me. There were too many dogs like Texas still out there. Dogs that might never know safety and love. I had to help. I owed it to Texas.

I volunteered to pick up Tweety, a foster dog who'd been in boarding the previous week.* Wanting to keep my heart from dwelling on all that I had lost, I drove to get Tweety in the still pouring rain moments after Tennessee left.

We were both drenched when we arrived back at the house. Tweety was a favorite at the boarding facility and it was easy to see why. She was friendly and affectionate—her tail never stopped wagging. One of the employees sent along a giant bone and a stuffed animal for her to keep.

She'd been in the house about an hour when an email arrived to set up her Meet and Greet for the next day. *What?* The only thing I could tell the adopters about her was that she was overweight (the first foster dog I'd met that was fat!). That was it. Other than that, she was darn near perfect. Nick said she looked like the dog they put in the dictionary to illustrate the word "dog." She reminded me of the *Far Side* dogs with her brown square body, little head, and curvy tail. She headed home to Virginia less than twenty-four hours after she'd arrived here.†

After Tweety left, we had a few days with no foster dogs. Nick asked again if I still wanted to keep doing this.

"I do," I told him. "I hate that it hurts, but I can't stop now. There are too many dogs out there."

---

* Sometimes there are dogs whose time is up at a shelter, but no foster home is available. If OPH has already made a commitment to those dogs, they will still bring them up on transport. They're then placed in a boarding facility temporarily until a foster home opens up.

† As I write this, she still holds the record as the fastest adopted foster dog we've had.

EIGHT

The Yin and Yang
of Puppies

After the intense emotions of summer, I decided what we needed was puppies. As we drove to meet the transport, Nick asked, "What kind of puppies are they?"

"They're four months old. One looks like a coonhound and one looks really weird."

"I thought they were related."

"That's never been clear."

"Hmm."

"We're also getting Melissa's puppy."

"Who's Melissa?"

"My friend who just started fostering. This is her first one, but she couldn't make transport."

"And she's getting a puppy?"

"That's what she wanted."

"Hmm."

I knew Nick was thinking I was getting in too deep and overcommitting, as I'm prone to do when I'm passionate about something, but I appreciated that he didn't say anything. He never got involved in the details of all this rescue work. He asked very few questions. Maybe he didn't want to know.

It was a gorgeous fall night when we picked up the puppies. I'd recently been asked to mentor several new fosters and I introduced myself to them. I didn't feel like I knew enough to be mentoring anybody, but I offered a few bits of advice about protecting your house, something I wished someone had clued me into when we started. "Keep the dogs somewhere contained where you can easily clean up after them. Like maybe a kitchen. You'll need a tall baby-gate if you don't have one."

"The write-up says the dog I'm getting is housebroken."

I hesitated and then went for total honesty. "Don't believe that."

"Really?"

"It's not that the dog isn't housebroken, it's just that after the stress of transport and the new house, sometimes they regress."

"Oh," said the new foster, the excited look on her face dimming.

"But maybe I'll be wrong," I told her, just as the transport van pulled into the parking lot. I probably wouldn't have believed anyone either back on the night we picked up Galina. I was too excited to think clearly or heed any warnings.

Charm and Chism indeed looked nothing alike. We put them together in our crate, and put Melissa's puppy, Connor, a big black Lab puppy in the airline crate I'd borrowed. The crates sat side by side in the folded-down backseat. As we pulled onto the Beltway, I could hear growls coming from the crate with Charm and Chism.

"Doesn't sound like they're siblings," said Nick.

"Or maybe it does."

I saw him smile in the dark. Our three kids were finally reaching the age where the fights were no longer daily or physical, which was nice, but that didn't mean there weren't fights. Now they fought about issues like who ate more than their share of the Cheez-Its, who trashed the bathroom, and who had use of the gaming computer. With Brady away at college, Addie and Ian had settled into a peaceable friendship. For years, though, they had fought ferociously. Sometimes the words that passed between them took my breath away. Would their bond emerge from childhood intact? My little brother and I are close now, but as children we battled relentlessly, just like Addie and Ian. On the other hand, I can't remember a single fight with my older brother, though there must have been a few, and these days we live on opposite sides of the country and rarely speak. Family connections are complicated. Maybe the pain inflicted would bind them together somehow.

When we got home, I moved Melissa's puppy, Connor, to a bigger crate in the kitchen and put both our puppies in the puppy pen together in the mudroom. We gave them a snack and water and then turned out the lights.

We had just gotten in bed when serious barking erupted downstairs.

"Got it," I said to Nick, who hadn't made a move. He'd always been good at sleeping through crying children and alarm clocks, so he might have been asleep already.

I opened the mudroom door to find Charm huddled in the back of the crate I'd attached to the pen and Chism positioned at the entrance to the crate in the play-with-me stance. Her front paws were stuck out in front of her, butt in the air, and tail wagging. At the sight of me, Chism began running circles around the pen, occasionally pausing to launch herself at the fence where I was standing. She was oblivious to Charm, trampling over her when she crawled out of the crate to greet me. They didn't seem like siblings or even friends.

I took Chism in the kitchen and let her run laps around the island while I snuggled Charm in my arms. Charm had the beautiful coloring of a Black and Tan Coonhound. Her mile-long legs reminded me of a newborn colt. If she grew into them, she was going to be a big girl. I fingered her floppy ears and she leaned against me, sighing. A person could easily lose their heart to this hound.

Connor watched Chism from his crate, but showed no sign of wanting to join her. I covered his crate with a blanket, so he could go back to sleep. I put Charm back in the pen and spent some time with Chism. I tossed her a tennis ball and watched as she dashed around the kitchen with no intention of bringing it back. Her gorgeous coat—a splashy pattern of gray and white and black, almost like army camouflage—would surely attract adopters. Her file said "hound mix," but she didn't seem very houndish, more like a Lab-mutt on speed. Her intensity was off the charts. Chism took up all the air in the room.

I caught her mid-flight and tried to calm her, but she squirmed out of my arms to launch herself at the cat who appeared on the other side of the sliding glass door. I watched her slam into the glass and then paw at it and I thought, *Whoever adopts this pup better know their way around a dog training manual.* She would either be the coolest dog they ever owned or the most difficult dog to ever rule their life.

It would take all night to wear off all her energy, so I caught her wriggling body and put her back in the puppy pen. Charm was dozing in the crate and lifted her head warily as I deposited Chism back in the pen. I closed the door to the crate, and put down another blanket for Chism, who picked up the blanket and began dragging it around. I dumped every dog toy I could find in the pen and shut off the light.

Melissa arrived early the next morning for Connor. Standing beside her van, she said, "Those puppy guidelines . . . are they serious?"

I laughed and said, "It won't be as bad as you think."

I was aware that I was stretching the truth a bit, but I didn't want to frighten Melissa off before she'd even started. And besides, *she* was the one who wanted to foster puppies. I was almost afraid to check in with her later that day, despite the fact that I was her default mentor for OPH. I'd given Connor a little time in the kitchen to bounce around that morning and after a good night's rest, he had almost as much energy as Chism, but was about a month older and ten pounds heavier.

In terms of fostering, Melissa was jumping in the deep end. She insisted she wanted to foster puppies, not dogs. I didn't discourage her; I figured this would be baptism by fire. Connor would either be her first and last foster, or we'd know she was a nutcase like the rest of us. You probably did have to be a little crazy to do this, but it was a good crazy.

That week I watched as Chism bullied Charm out of toys, food, and my attention, but the battles of the first night didn't repeat themselves. It appeared they had negotiated a truce of some kind. Still, I rarely left them alone together for long. They didn't snuggle together, but they didn't wrestle either. They were roommates who shared the same space but had entirely different interests.

Charm was most interested in snuggling. True to her name, she charmed everyone she met. She loved to be held and became a regular couch buddy for Ian in the rare hours that he was home. Between soccer and baseball, school work and the nonstop eating of a thirteen-year-old in a growth spurt, he rarely sat still.

Chism also loved people, but instead of sleeping in their laps, she'd rather chew on their arms or play chase. She was curious and smart and it wasn't long before she was climbing out of the pen and reaching for the lever doorknob.

One morning that first week, I was in the kitchen canning applesauce, while the puppies played. Chism spent a few minutes making bodily threats to the cats through the glass door while Charm began sifting through the basket of dog toys. In general, Chism had no use for toys, unless Charm picked one up. I watched as Charm politely selected a toy from the overflowing toy bin. Before she took three steps, Chism stole it easily and carted it over to the Frank bed where she promptly ignored it so she could bark at the cats again.

Charm selected another toy and once again Chism dashed over to take it. Charm dropped the toy and stepped back as if to say, "Oh, you wanted that? So sorry, I'll just find something else to play with." Charm then selected a tennis ball out of the toy basket, but in moments, Chism grabbed the ball out of her mouth. I took the ball from both of them and tossed it across the floor, knowing Chism would chase after it and she did. Meanwhile, Charm picked up a stuffed ladybug with crinkly wings, but the moment Chism heard the crinkling, she dropped the tennis ball and ran back for the ladybug. Charm let her have it.

"Girl, you're gonna have a rough time in the real world if you don't start standing up for yourself."

Charm cocked her head at me and then began rummaging in the toy bin again. Quite possibly, there wasn't a more agreeable puppy in the world.

The next weekend, Ian, Nick, and I drove up to Brady's college for family weekend. Because we had puppies at home, we only planned to spend the day. The pouring rain canceled all the activities the college had planned. I had been looking forward to kayaking on the Susquehanna River, even though Brady groaned when I told him I'd signed us up. Instead we took him to Target to buy sweatpants, socks, and snack food. We stopped in Dick's searching for a new pair of Crocs and had lunch at the little pub in Selinsgrove that brewed delicious beer and root beer.

I'd missed Brady so much that a few hours weren't enough, so I suggested bowling. We drove to a town a few miles away in search of the bowling alley. When we pulled into the parking lot the GPS had led us to, it was a local VFW hall. We were about to give up and take Brady back to the dorms, when Ian spotted a tiny sign that said, LANES. It was above a set of stairs that led to the basement of the building. Sure enough, there was a bowling alley down there. We were the only customers that afternoon; a vending machine provided snacks and shoe rental was only a dollar. Nothing like small-town America.

Despite the weather and despite the abbreviated visit, I was happy as we drove home. Brady was doing well. He'd found friends and was enjoying his classes, even his Chinese history class, which sounded to me like a form of torture. He hadn't lost his keys and had only slept through a few of his 8:00 A.M. classes.

"This is our exit," I said as we approached the north side of York.

"Tell me again why we're getting another dog?" asked Nick. We were following sketchy GPS directions in search of the house of another foster who had picked up our newest foster and was graciously holding her for us. Rollie was a ten-month-old shepherd/Lab mix.

"Because I'm weak," I told him. I'd seen the transport list and the repeated begging for foster homes and I'd caved. We didn't need another puppy, but I couldn't bear the thought of a puppy in a boarding kennel.

"I don't want to sit with it," said Ian from the backseat. "What if it pees on me?"

Everyone was grumpy by the time we found the house. When I knocked on the door, a chorus of dogs started up, just like at our house! I'd set off the "dog bell," as Nick called it.

When Christine let me in she immediately began explaining the dogs swirling at my feet—a personal dog, a foster, and a foster fail. Again, it was a familiar scenario. I'm always explaining my own swirling dogs to friends, neighbors, the milkman, even the UPS guy. Partly it's because for me the dogs are part of the family and thus require an introduction, and partly because I want to explain that I'm not completely nuts, there's a reason for all the dogs.

Christine led me into her kitchen through multiple baby gates to retrieve our new foster, Rollie, who was in a large crate alongside *another* large crate holding *another* foster dog. These crates took up serious real estate in their kitchen.

This was the first time I'd been in the home of another OPH foster and it was a relief to know we were not the only people who lived like this. Something you learn very quickly when fostering dogs is your home will never be the same. The dogs become the priority and home decorating gets pushed aside. Of course, one bonus is that I never have to explain why my house is a mess. *You have a dozen foster dogs? Of course your home is a mess.*

For instance, our home now features a lovely gated entrance to the kitchen.* And in the living room, where once the antique mission table resided, there is a large dog crate, tricked out with a fancy dog bed that matches the carpet. (It sits near the base of the stairs and is normally piled high with everything I'm too lazy to carry up the stairs at the moment.)

In our entrance hall, there are not just several bags of dog food (puppy, personal dog, foster dog), but also the cabinet that used to be in our mudroom but doesn't fit ever since we retrofitted the room with a puppy pen.

In our kitchen, we've installed another extra-large dog crate for Rollie, plus a decorative basket filled with dog toys, a cookie jar filled with dog treats on the counter, and the Frank bed.

As the fostering habit grew and more adjustments were made to accommodate it, I worried that Nick would one day say, "ENOUGH!" There were occasional grumbles, but for the most part he'd been a very good sport about this and I couldn't do it without him.

Recently we were enjoying a rare date when he said, "I know I give you a hard time about it, but I'm really glad you're doing this thing with the dogs. It's fun."

To my mind, sweeter words had rarely been uttered. He'd had a few glasses of wine at that point. Sometimes the honesty of alcohol is a good thing.

---

* Now that marching band had started up, instead of propping up the sagging wooden baby gate with the mellophone case, we'd installed a sturdy, metal four-foot gate.

NINE

Puppydom

Having three large puppies in the house sometimes felt more like I'd invited several hundred toddlers for a visit. It was loud. It was messy. They broke things. But gosh, they were cute. We were entering week three of life in puppydom. As veteran parents, we are familiar with the work that comes with caring for toddlers. We even understand that sometimes a toddler might bite you. They might pee on the floor occasionally. They don't take direction well. Even so, despite the cuteness and my understanding, sometimes it became too much.

Shut up, I thought when I heard Chism holding forth one afternoon. *Shut up, shut up, shut up!* I knew she was just a puppy; she couldn't help herself, but she was so darn loud. There was nothing quiet or soft or gentle about that pup. And I was trying to write. I had a deadline to meet.

I was trying to finish the first draft of my third novel. I loved this story, but the constant interruptions were making the final edits torture. I needed quiet to think. Addie can do homework while simultaneously watching *Parks and Recreation* and listening to music on her earbuds. Ian watches YouTube videos while he eats, texts, and studies for a test. I've begun to think this generation functions best with their attentions divided. Not me, though, every noise is a distraction to me. Even my laptop's internal fan shifting on interrupts my thoughts. It'd been doing that a lot lately and I briefly wondered if it was overloaded with too many words. Was that possible? Could you max out a laptop?

A familiar, gnawing sound attracted my attention and I ran from my office, slammed through the baby gate into the kitchen to scold Rollie for once again attempting to eat my kitchen cabinets. There was no way to put the cabinets out of reach, so I put Rollie in her crate. I tossed her three tennis balls and a treat and got back to work.

Soon enough, the pitiful cries of Charm pulled me from my work. She could only take so much of Chism and her endless need to play. I grabbed a leash and took Charm outside. I found a sunny spot on the hillside and sat down in the grass with her. She rolled over and leaned against my leg as I scratched her belly. Puppy bellies are calming. *Ten minutes*, I thought. And then I heard Chism's loud howl from the house. *How much longer until you go away?* Three weeks was too long to have three nearly-grown puppies.

Charm's potential adopters hadn't responded to my email, so I was beginning to think they weren't very serious. Puppy adopters were usually overeager for information and would practically bribe me to ignore OPH's two-week hold* so they could get their hands on their puppies. Chism's adopters, on the other hand, had many questions. They sounded concerned (as they absolutely should have). I wasn't

---

* OPH requires that a foster hold puppies for two weeks and dogs for one week to ensure that the animals are healthy and ready to go to a forever home.

sure it would be a good fit, but they were coming down the following weekend to meet her.

Rollie was going to be adopted by Mer's daughter, Shannon. It only took us a few days to realize that Rollie was a level-headed, super-sweet, smart dog—exactly what Mer and Shannon were looking for; although truth be told, Shannon just wanted a dog. *Now.*[*]

Hoping for the best, I left the three pups to play in the kitchen and went back to my laptop. Ten minutes later, I heard a familiar gnawing sound . . .

Years ago, when I was home with my three small kiddos, my days blurred together. The work (and joy) was endless. At the end of each day when Nick would come home and ask, "What did you do today?" I would shrug my shoulders, unable to remember anything I'd actually gotten done. My days lately had an eerie sense of déjà vu. But then, one by one, the puppies left.

First, Rollie, now Molly, went home with Shannon and Mer. She easily charmed their elderly beagle and Mer's hesitant husband.

Chism's adopters came to meet her and after she terrified her potential fursister (a sweet little dog, the kind who wear bows and require a groomer), they decided to adopt Charm instead. Since Charm's adopters had still not made plans to come meet her, OPH was fine with the switch.

I'd worried for weeks that Chism would never find someone who could handle her. She was smart and so, so much dog, but a few days later an adopter materialized. He was a sizeable guy who drove a truck and wore camo and probably knew his way around a power tool. His girlfriend, who'd come with him, said to me, "She's going to be his only daughter and you know how that goes . . ."

He had planned on naming her "Betty," but once he met her it didn't seem to work. She definitely wasn't a Betty. Whatever her name would be, she'd have space to roam on his family's farm and a fenced yard

---

[*] Shannon had been the approved adopter for Texas and so both OPH and I were happy to have found her a puppy.

where she could hunt bunnies. *The adoption magic happened again*, I wrote on my blog. Just when I thought it would never happen—*boom*! Perfect adopter.

All my puppies were set and we were finally dogless. Except Gracie. She lay next to me as I worked on my laptop, snoring and farting, happy to have me all to herself again. It was too quiet. I missed my puppies. Nick observed my sadness and said, "You're jonesing for a puppy, aren't you?"

I was.

Usually, when one dog left, we were already prepping for (or in some cases already had) a new foster dog. It kept me distracted from the sadness of letting the last one go. This time there was no dog waiting in the wings.

Nick and I were taking a short trip to Virginia to celebrate our twentieth anniversary. The leaves would be awesome, the weather looked good, we were taking the bikes, and I'd researched which wineries we'd visit. I love my husband. I love Virginia. I love wine. It would all be good.

But I still wished I had a dog.

I watched the list of dogs and puppies on the next transport. We can't take one, I reminded myself. Besides, we needed a break, didn't we? We'd just survived a month of three puppies. Absolutely silly. I would not volunteer to take a new foster.

But if I didn't, then I'd have to wait another week without a foster dog.

This was how bad the addiction had become . . . while on our wonderful vacation with my wonderful husband, I was quietly communicating with another foster about picking up a dog from her on our way home. I had a serious problem. I knew this, but I figured it was way better than cocaine or gambling or Internet porn.

The foster dog in question, John Coffey, was not getting along with one of his current foster's dogs,* so I was contemplating helping

---

* See what I mean about the confusion of calling the person fostering a *foster* and the dog they are fostering a *foster*? I'm still learning the logic of rescue dog language.

everybody out (the foster, the dog, me!) by stopping by and grabbing John Coffey on our way north.

We'd had a wonderful vacation—the wine, the weather, the oysters were all wonderful. If I hadn't done a face-plant during our first hike it would have all been perfect,* but I was ready to be home and to have a new foster dog. I thought Nick wasn't paying attention as I sent frantic emails and quizzed him repeatedly on what route we would take home from Virginia, but he knew me well and as we packed up the car that last morning, he left a dog-sized space between the suitcases in our backseat (the trunk was full of wine), and placed a comfy blanket in the space.

"It's on our way home," I told him.

"Sure, it is," he said and hugged me.

"See? That's why we're still married," I told him.

On the drive home, we met Livia in the parking lot of a Wendy's just off the highway in southern Maryland. John Coffey was one squirming bundle of happiness. It came out his pores. He couldn't wag fast enough to express his joy and emitted tiny little whimpers of ecstasy when you petted him. He resembled a Boston terrier with black-and-white patches on his head, but he had more white than black and there were traces of brindle in some of his black patches. He was very handsome with a sparkling personality to match.

"I owe you," said Livia, almost teary as she said goodbye to "Coffey," as she called him.

I promised to send updates, and we waved goodbye and placed John Coffey in his section of the backseat. It was immediately evident the backseat would just not do, not when there were TWO people less than an arm's length away who could be petting him. He rode the entire hour and a half posed like a hood ornament on the console between our seats, alternately licking a face or nuzzling a shoulder.

When we got him home, the energy did not dissipate. Luckily for us, John Coffey had smarts in equal measure to his energy and was eager

---

* I sported a lovely black eye and a sore wrist, and yes, Nick made the requisite jokes about our fight.

to please. I'd decided that his full name fit him, as in "John Coffey get down. John Coffey that's enough. John Coffey DOWN." He was like a small, excitable child whose mother needed to use his full name on a daily basis. And so he wouldn't be JC or Coffey, but John Coffey.

I looked up the name on the Internet. John Coffey was the character played by Michael Clarke Duncan in *The Green Mile* (based on the book by Stephen King). He was on death row in Aiken, South Carolina. Our John Coffey had originally come from a shelter in Aiken, where he was also on death row. In addition, Google revealed that there was another guy named John Coffey who had a PhD in Positive Developmental Psychology. All his papers on LinkedIn were about *happiness*. This was the most positive pup possible who had just escaped death row in Aiken, South Carolina. Finally, a foster dog with a perfect name!

Left alone for twenty minutes in the kitchen the next morning, John Coffey rearranged the furniture. He moved the Frank bed to the middle of the room, ostensibly so he could lie on it and still see around the corner to where I was in the living room. He pulled a dictionary (a big dictionary, think unabridged, hardback) down off the kitchen table and I found it, unmutilated, but open to the J's!* He dragged the toy basket to the center of the room, right next to the Frank bed, which made it easier for him to sort through the plethora and take out all the yellow plastic tool casings and make a separate pile of them by the door.†

Livia told me that John Coffey had gained nine pounds in his three weeks with them, but he was still so skinny I couldn't imagine what he looked like previously. She said he was a "skeletor," and I believed it. We tried to pile on the pounds, but he preferred to eat his food scattered across the floor so I wasn't entirely sure how much he was taking in. Each time I put a bowl of food down, he promptly dumped it. I didn't know if this made dinner more *interactive* for him, or if he was complaining about the service.

---

* I'm not making that up!

† Was he planning to take them with him when he left?

If my nephew/dog whisperer Brandon lived closer, I would have adopted John Coffey and found him an agent. He was a goofball-funny, ball-chasing, potential movie star trick dog. He was crazy athletic, intensely paying attention, and as eager to please as a used car salesman. Throw in a tiny little bit of manic, and you had the makings of dog headed for Hollywood, or at least dock-diving. At any rate, John Coffey needed a job.

I could run him four and a half miles in the morning, and he would still be dancing (for minutes at a time) on his hind legs as I prepared dinner.

He would chase a ball all day. I'm not exaggerating. *All* day. Our dog, Lucy, had faithfully retrieved every ball Nick shot with his lacrosse stick for about fifteen–twenty minutes, but after that she'd keep the ball to herself and find a comfy spot to lie down. *Not* John Coffey. We had to put the balls where he couldn't find them to end the game and he'd still spend a few minutes searching for them.

Tennis balls exist in multitudes around our house, thanks to Brady's efforts to make the high school varsity tennis team. He used to spend hours hitting balls against the garage, breaking a garage door window and forcing Nick to hammer boards over the rest to protect them. His grandparents encouraged this habit and regularly showed up with a half-dozen cans of tennis balls, barely worn but not good enough for the retirement community courts. John Coffey discovered that he could usually find a ball or two (or five) under the furniture in nearly every room and littered all over the yard. He generally had two or three going at a time. No person to toss one? No problem. *He could toss them for himself.*

Nick pulled out an old basketball one night and John Coffey went bonkers. The wiggle-spin-whine excitement was off the charts. It was hard to throw a basketball safely in the house, but we tried. When everyone else tired of it, he gnawed on the ball with a maniacal gleam in his eye, beyond happy.

The basketball was exciting, but then Ian got my exercise ball/desk chair—I thought John Coffey's head might explode! It was the first time I'd heard him bark. His mind simply could not contain the idea of a ball of that size. I worried for his heart.

Despite me bragging about his ball-catching ability on his OPH webpage and my blog, he garnered no adoption applications. The next weekend, I took John Coffey to an OPH adoption event. The activity and the other dogs sent him into sensory overload. He was an intense little guy who paid attention to everything, but it was pretty much impossible to pay attention to everything when everything included five or six other dogs, dozens of people, a busy parking lot, yummy food smells, and even an entire bag of tennis balls someone thoughtfully brought along for him.

He was frantic, pulling at his leash and barking. The only way to calm him was to pick him up, so I did, but at thirty-five pounds, that didn't last long. Luckily there were several teens volunteering that day and I gratefully handed him over. They had that teenage ability to see right through bad manners and noise. They happily cruised him around the parking lot, hunkered down with him on the far edge of the event, and sat with him in the kissing booth.*

I was frustrated that all anyone was seeing was the bad side of John Coffey. I'd hardly ever heard him bark before that day. He was actually a quiet dog. No one who was in Hanover for the event that day would have believed me. He rarely pulled on the leash, but at the event he was gagging and coughing from the effort. He growled and barked at the other dogs. Who wanted to take home the barking, gagging, bully dog? No one, apparently.

I couldn't even distract him with tennis balls. When I picked one up, his gaze would lock on it and he'd chase after it, only to drop it the moment another dog/person/food/noise/car came into his view. He was too distracted to show off his superior catching skills.

All anybody got to see was a nervous, frantic, barking bundle of snarly nerves. That was not John Coffey. I felt badly that I'd put him in a situation where his best self couldn't be seen.

Especially when he had such a great best self.

---

* Which he rocked, by the way. John Coffey was a first-rate kisser.

We'd settled into a routine with John Coffey and Gracie (who had become great buds) when I saw a plea for a foster home for a returned puppy. I was openly owning my puppy addiction at that point. Or maybe I just wanted to ease the heartbreak that surrounded any return. I knew the puppy would be confused. I knew the adopter would be in turmoil. Whenever I saw a notice on the OPH page about a dog or puppy being returned, I wanted to swoop in and take them all. Make it better. No dog should have to stay where she wasn't absolutely wanted and loved.

It made me think about why I kept Gracie. Was it just the guilt? There might be a sliver of it there, but it was mostly that I made a promise to Gracie (and the kids who loved her). Fostering had given me a new appreciation for her. She was consistent. She was trying. She was doing the best she could. There was a lot to appreciate in that.

So that Wednesday, Foo Foo* moved in. She came with a plethora of pink—two pink collars, two pink leashes, many pink toys, a pink harness, a pink sweater, and even a puffy pink jacket. There was a hot pink crate, but I declined it as we already had three crates cluttering up our house.

Foo Foo herself was not pink. She was gray. Steel gray. Even her eyes were gray. She was sleek with a long nose and skinny head that made her look very much like a seal. Pink looked nice with gray, but in honor of her new start, I slapped a gender-neutral neon yellow collar on her. It was padded and more comfortable than the stylish skinny pink one she'd been wearing when she arrived. I'd never been a girl who would suffer for fashion. I didn't imagine this puppy was either.

At thirteen pounds, Foo Foo was a total cuddle-muffin, and everyone wanted to hold her. She was fine with this. We set up the puppy pen in our kitchen where she could have front row seats to the

---

* Who had been named Daisy and seemed to answer to it despite only having been with her new adopter for two weeks.

action. John Coffey was decidedly jealous. He peed on her puppy pen the first night. Foo Foo's presence sent him into overdrive. He competed hard for everyone's attention.

John Coffey was much bigger and heavier than Foo Foo, and I worried he'd hurt her, but he quickly realized his role as the big brother. He let her attach her alligator-like mouth to his neck and walked around the kitchen dragging her like a fancy scarf. He'd wrestle and play with her, but it wasn't the hardball he played with Gracie. When she got too big for her britches, he'd sit on her or knock her down with a quick swing of his hips.

When an adopter turns up, I trust that OPH did their due diligence and the pup is the right match, but sometimes it's completely clear that there is magic at hand, as well. Once again, I was going to lose a dog I could have happily adopted. Loving these dogs and letting them go wasn't getting easier. They were only ours for a few weeks. And then their lives were upended once more, but hopefully they left us healthier, more confident, and with a heart all shined up and ready to love.

The family that arrived to meet John Coffey were quite obviously his people. He knew it immediately. Three boys—all for him! He circled them, his butt wagging in overdrive. They'd followed his progress on my blog and were well prepared for his enthusiastic personality. John Coffey was so anxious to get going that he leapt in their car as soon as a door was opened. We had to bring him back out to take a picture. When I snapped the shot, he had a huge smile on his face. That's still one of my favorite adoption pictures.

It was a super-duper awesome adoption. One that made me absolutely sure that what we were doing made a difference. Of course, now I had all my fingers and toes crossed that he would not overwhelm them with his happiness and enthusiasm, and that he would NOT break into the "Lego room" that their four-year-old told me about!

Just before John Coffey's family arrived, I got word that the puppies were being born!

What puppies? (You sound just like my husband!)

Cara with her first puppy litter.

Bambi.

ABOVE: Carla. BELOW: Carla watching for her adopter, Carol, to arrive.

ABOVE: Whoopi. BELOW: Berneen (Bernie).

Lafayette, the almost foster-fail.

ABOVE: Chuggy Alabaster and Pigweed. BELOW: Hamilton pups (seven weeks).

Cara with her injured knee and the culprits, Bambi and Lucy.

ABOVE: Gingersnap and her mile-long tongue. BELOW: Tennessee, Frank, and Texas.

John Coffey.

ABOVE: Oberyn. BELOW: Rooney and Lucy during the pee wars.

Wheat Penny, always on top of something.

Cara with Edith Wharton's puppies.

ABOVE: Hadley. BELOW: Itz Luv (Luvie).

ABOVE: Oak tries to cheer up Bernie. BELOW: Lucy, the quintessential hound.

Catalina, aka Cat.

Gorgeous Lily.

ABOVE: Symphony, aka Stitch. BELOW: Galina and Gracie.

Luvie and Lily wrestled endlessly.

Momma Bear outside.

Edith Wharton with one day old pups.

ABOVE: Fannie. BELOW: Schuyler has had enough of being the mom.

Gingersnap and Whoopi watching me outside.

Shiny clean Stitch after her bath.

Cara and Frank.

These would be the unborn puppies I'd committed to fostering when they were weaned. Chris, the mama dog's foster, works full-time and could only commit to foster if someone agreed to take the puppies once they were weaned in about five weeks. She didn't have to ask me twice. I tried to stay away, but as I might have mentioned, I have a puppy problem. "Hello, my name is Cara and I'm addicted to puppies . . . it's been three months and twelve days since I last smelled puppy breath."

While John Coffey was claiming his people and I was explaining the paperwork, my phone buzzed with texts that the puppies were arriving. *(Number three is here!)* As we took a picture, handed off the food and forms, and said our last goodbyes, my text went off again. (*Four!*)

As soon as their van cleared the driveway, I was racing across town to Chris's house. I arrived amid a crisis. Puppy number two had been born with a cleft palate and was fading fast. Chris, her friend Sam, and daughter Caitlyn were distressed and scrambling to try to help this tiny soul. OPH medical was advising by phone how to tube feed the pup.

Fostering pregnant dogs and litters takes a special heart.* This was Chris's second litter and the second time she would lose a newborn puppy. Tears ran down her face, as she took the tiny puppy from Caitlyn who had been holding it against her skin to keep her warm. Sadly, there was very little any of us could do. The puppy passed quietly and peacefully as Lily gave birth to puppy number five.

Despite her current circumstances, Lily was a beautiful black Lab with a wide expressive face, kind eyes, and a generous soul, allowing me, a complete stranger, to sit beside her for a front row seat to each birth. I tried to be a calm, helpful guest, but in my mind I was jumping around, shrieking, *Oh my God! Did you see that? She just had a puppy! Look at all*

---

* Many pregnant moms don't make it out of the shelters because no one wants to adopt a pregnant dog, and shelters aren't equipped to whelp puppies. And even if they did, young litters living in a shelter would be in grave danger of being exposed to parvo and other contagious diseases that their immature, unvaccinated immune systems couldn't survive. Many arrive in foster homes having had no prenatal care.

those puppies! In contrast, after the tears over the lost pup, Chris, Sam, and Caitlyn calmly watched the miracle unfold, quietly joking about the aggressive pup trying to nurse on his mother's leg. I had to wonder if I could be as composed and capable in their shoes.

I'd seen horses give birth, but this was my first canine birth. While Lily didn't need our assistance at all, I'd like to think our presence gave her a measure of comfort. We chose flower names for the pups in honor of their mama. The nine pups looked like skinny guinea pigs with their smashed noses and eyes squeezed shut. Chris told me their noses were squished to make it easier to nurse, but they probably wouldn't be like that forever and their eyes would only stay closed for two weeks. The whole scene, bloody towels and all, was amazing. I doubted anyone in that neat little neighborhood with the matching houses and solitary tree in the front yard had any idea a miracle was taking place right on their street.

I had promised Chris I would take the puppies in five weeks when they were weaned, but now I tried to picture nine puppies in my mudroom. It was a terrifying thought. Six had been overwhelming, but nine? There was probably a limit to Nick's willingness to indulge my addiction and this might just be it. I batted those thoughts away. I had five weeks to figure it out.

When the births were finally over, Chris and I opened the bottle of wine I'd brought to celebrate. We watched Lily resting with her puppies. I learned that Chris is a registered nurse which explained why she handled the grosser elements of the days' activities so well. I knew who I'd be calling if I ever took in a pregnant mom of my own.

By the time I came home to my lone foster puppy, Foo Foo, I was pretty high. Foo Foo looked enormous to me, even though she was only a bitty thirteen pounds (the newborn pups were all about one pound). I carried her to the couch and recounted the entire birth for Nick, whose only comment was, "Wow. Nine?"

"But we might not have to take all nine," I told him. "Chris said maybe she could keep a few of them."

Nick shook his head and went to bed. I took Foo Foo out for a last walk before putting her in her crate. We climbed the hill in the darkness.

I sat on the fence, while Foo Foo battled with a cornstalk that had fallen over. The air was crisp, and I could smell all the woodstoves warming homes up and down our hollow. The stars were especially bright and for once, the lights from the Walmart across the valley didn't seem to dull their shine. Foo Foo tired of the cornstalk and pulled me back toward the woods. I took one last look at the star-soaked night and thought, *I witnessed a miracle today.*

I also thought, *Someday I'm going to foster a pregnant dog.*

TEN

Hero Dog

oo Foo's adoption was imminent, so when I heard about a very special dog on the returns list, I jumped at the chance to invite her to our house.

Momma Bear was from Iraq. I'd followed some of her story via the OPH Facebook page, but had never met her. Upon introduction, she leaned against my leg, humbling me with her instantaneous affection. I was struck by her intelligent, trusting eyes.

The details of her story were third- and fourth-hand. I recovered most by combing through old emails and badgering other OPH people, but as all of it had taken place nearly a year ago, it was old news in the world of dog rescue where the present tragedy quickly supersedes the previous one. Here's the gist of Momma Bear's story:

The previous winter, Oscar and his wife* were working in Iraq, living near a university. They were attempting to help rescue dogs in a dangerous and unstable country.† The enormity of the problem made for heartbreaking work. Oscar and his wife had rescued seventeen dogs through their own efforts and money when they learned of three dogs living on the university's campus that would soon be exterminated per campus policy. Hearing that one of the dogs was injured, Oscar went to the campus to see what he could do. There he found Momma Bear, along with the injured dog.

When Oscar attempted to assess the injured dog, he was surrounded by a pack of male dogs. Momma Bear put herself between him and the pack, using her large size and the ferocity of a mama bear to defend Oscar and the injured dog. He was impressed by her bravery, and experienced it again when he returned to the campus to help another dog who had just given birth. Once again, this remarkable large white dog accompanied Oscar around the campus and protected him from other dogs.

Oscar named the dog "Bear" because of her large size, white fur, and clipped ears and tail, which made her look like a polar bear. Ultimately, he rescued all three of the dogs, along with the new puppies, and put them in boarding kennels while homes were sought. Three months passed and all of the puppies and one of the dogs found homes. Oscar and his wife were preparing to leave the country, so they contacted Nowzad‡ to see if they might be able to help. Was there any way to get

---

*   I've never been able to speak with these people and so I don't want to use their names. I couldn't even figure out if they were American or not, but guessed they might be British. Oscar is a name I've always wanted to use in my fiction, so indulge me here.

†   Stray and feral dogs are a huge problem in war-torn countries, as families are separated and homes are destroyed. Tens of thousands of pets are left behind to fend for themselves.

‡   Nowzad is a British nonprofit organization originally started with a mission to reunite servicemen/women with dogs they adopted while serving in Afghanistan. Nowzad now runs the only shelter in Afghanistan, just outside Kabul, and works with rescues to rehome dogs from war-torn areas.

Bear and the remaining dog, Sultan, to the United States where a rescue organization might sponsor them?

Nowzad agreed to help bring the dogs to the United States and reached out to OPH to see if they would foster the dogs when they arrived stateside. OPH agreed and found foster homes for Bear and Sultan. OPH doesn't reuse names and there was already a Bear in the system, so they added Momma to the name after hearing her story. Sultan became a foster fail, but Momma Bear was eventually adopted.

Now, nearly six months after she arrived in the U.S., she was being returned to OPH. I glanced at the return notes, but they contradicted themselves and didn't square up with the notes from Momma Bear's previous fosters. Many times we don't know the real reason a dog is returned, and for my part, I wasn't interested in the why, only the when. A few days later, Momma Bear arrived at our house.

I sat beside her on the floor her first morning, stroking the long white fur on her back. She glanced up at me and licked my hand. She was a young dog, but her life had not been easy. Her back was swayed, and her ears and tail had been cut off by kids in a local village. She had a bare patch on one elbow, and who knew what other scars hid beneath all that fur. She regarded me with large, brown eyes and licked my hand again.

She had won the hearts of plenty at OPH as she'd journeyed through the foster system regaining her health and confidence, being adopted, and now being returned. So many people were pulling for her, and I could see why. She was special. I would write about her for the newspaper, I decided.

The next day, I sat down at my computer and glanced behind me. Where was Momma Bear? She'd been my shadow up until that point. I found her standing at the entrance to the hall that led to my office.

"C'mon, girl," I coaxed.

She stood in the doorway wagging her stumpy tail. I tried luring her with treats, but she refused to step into the hallway. I put on a leash and pulled, but she panicked at my efforts. She would not set foot in the narrow hallway.

"All right, you win," I told her. "Let me get my laptop."

I worked in the kitchen that day to keep her company. Later in the week, I went back to my office to work, but she did not join me, always stopping at the hallway entrance. I wished she could tell me what had happened in a narrow hallway that made her refuse to chance it. What nightmares had this dog brought with her across the Atlantic?

I tried to sort out her story so I could explain it clearly in the article for our local paper, but as I got to know her it was hard to reconcile the pictures of the sad, skinny dog in a barren land or the complaints of the returning adopter with the sweet dog lying in my kitchen.*

When Gracie growled at her upon introduction, Momma Bear looked at her with patient, knowing eyes, waiting for Gracie to let go of her threat. Gracie backed away, and after that she watched Momma Bear warily, but she never again threatened her.

Momma Bear was an easy dog to love. Her big heart and gentle nature couldn't be missed. Ian was smitten upon first sight, and after the first day Nick said, "Tell them there's no rush in finding her a home." I even caught Addie lying on the hard, cold kitchen floor, arms wrapped around Momma Bear, quietly whispering her secrets.

Foo Foo fell in love hard, following Momma Bear everywhere. She would most likely pine more for Momma Bear than for me when she left that week. Momma Bear tolerated Foo Foo's affection, allowing her to climb all over her, hang from her collar, and chew on her legs.

She was a large dog, as big as a small bear, but never seemed to be in the way. Her watchful eyes missed nothing and it was rare to see her truly sleeping. Somehow she managed to stay out from under my feet even as she followed me everywhere, like my large protective shadow. And she was perfectly housebroken. And when I say perfectly, I mean

---

* She would not use the Frank bed, instead she slept on the floor beside it.

it. No accidents. At all.* Unlike pretty much every foster dog we'd had, Momma Bear was quiet and saved her barking for important things like the UPS guy on the porch waiting for a signature or Brady when he was locked out at 2:00 A.M.†

"She's the best foster dog we've ever had," said Ian, petting Momma Bear as he sat next to her on the kitchen floor.

"She is," I agreed. I was busy getting ready for Thanksgiving. My extended family would be arriving from Ohio, New Jersey, and New Mexico, plus friends from Maryland. I loved our crowded house at Thanksgiving—the competitive cooking, the excessive eating, and the cousins reconnecting. It was my favorite day of the year.

"So why don't we keep her?" Ian asked, not for the first time.

"We've been over this," I told him, leveling my eyes at him before moving on to the task at hand—one hundred homemade crescent rolls.

"Don't you love her?" he asked.

"I do," I told him. "But that has nothing to do with it."

He sighed and hugged Momma Bear, who licked his bare head. Ian has alopecia areata, which means he has no hair anywhere on his body. It's an autoimmune disorder he developed when he was four years old. There is no known cause or cure at this point. Those first years after his diagnosis were hard on me as a parent. I was grateful that alopecia wasn't life-threatening, but as I told so many people, alopecia was life-altering. I hated that my kid would have to explain his baldness time and again. It's hard to be different when you are young, and I worried that he would be teased.

---

* I'm gonna let you in on a little secret about foster dogs. They are *rarely* perfectly housebroken. The write-up might say *housetrained*, but that's almost always an optimistic take. Nearly every dog we've ever fostered has peed in our house at least once, usually more. I've accepted it as part of the deal, and no longer freak out when it happens. I figure, who wouldn't be wigged out after a twelve-plus hour van ride in a cramped dog crate, only to be dumped in an unfamiliar house with a snarly, socially awkward girl dog? I'd pee, too.

† His father forgot he was home on Thanksgiving break and accidently locked him out.

For the most part, that hasn't happened. But what has happened is that Ian has grown up to be more sensitive to other people. He's kind to everyone and looks beyond physical appearance. We're all different, Ian's difference is just more obvious.

Another way Ian is different, beyond the lack of hair on his head, is that he expects the best of people. When he was little, and even now occasionally, people mistake him for a cancer patient. They treat him generously and kindly. When he was five and the security guard at Hershey's Chocolate World gave him a huge chocolate bar, he told us how nice the policeman was, never realizing that it was a sympathetic gesture. That same scenario played out again and again, leaving Ian to believe that most people are friendly and nice. And so *he* is friendly and nice. He's also learned to have a sense of humor about his condition. That's not to say he doesn't ever wish he were like other kids. That pain is there too, but it's made him a stronger person. Maybe he loved this dog so fiercely because he knew what it was like to be different. Momma Bear looked like no other dog I'd ever met.

After only a few days with Momma Bear, Foo Foo left for her forever home with a young teacher from Virginia who laughed when Foo Foo bit his nose upon introduction. I was glad he had youth on his side and hopefully the patience of his profession. I would miss my puppy, but it would be good to have her out of the house as Thanksgiving was upon us and cousins were arriving that evening.

Momma Bear handled our crowded house and the chaos of dinner for thirty just fine. Our Ohio cousins stuck around a few extra days after the holiday and we enjoyed board games, hiking, and possibly more wine than truly necessary. Ian, teenage cousins Delia and Ben, and I took Momma Bear to the pet store for a fancy bath one day. She hesitated when we led her into the busy pet store, but walked obediently up the ramp at the bathing station, filling the entire tub and standing like a statue as Delia and I bathed her. She even tolerated the blow-dryer.

We also took Gracie for a bath because as usual, she stunk of the horse manure she'd rolled in the night before. Ian and Ben were tasked with bathing her, since they were teenage boys and not afraid of a little wrestling. Despite Momma Bear's example, Ian and Ben were as wet as Gracie when they finished. In retrospect, I suppose the busy pet store and our chaotic Thanksgiving household were nothing compared to the chaos Momma Bear had endured in her homeland.

Many, okay, pretty much *all*, of the dogs we have fostered have won our hearts quickly and given us as much love as we've given them, but Momma Bear's love was different. It was almost reverent. Maybe that sounds odd speaking about dogs, but her affection was embarrassingly honest. She adored us. But then, she seemed to adore everyone she met.

Considering her history, this was more than remarkable. Her cut ears and tail and the large pink scar on her elbow were the obvious signs that life had not been easy for this girl, but there were a few other clues, as well.

She continued to avoid the front hall, and walked a long detour around the island counter in our kitchen, circumventing the narrow passageway it created. She simply took the longer route around the other side of the island where there was more open space.

Something very terrible happened to this sweet dog in a passageway. Something worse than humans cutting her tail and ears. When I watched her walk the long way around to the kitchen door, I was angry that so many in this world do not value the life of an animal. Angry that someone could hurt a dog as gracious as Momma Bear. But then I looked at her sweet, trusting face and I realized that her heart was bigger than mine. So I tried to let my own expand a little. Forgiveness seems to come easier for dogs.

Momma Bear's paperwork said she was between two and five years old. As she began to relax at our house, she became more puppy-like, suggesting she was closer to two than five.

A few days after Thanksgiving, I was shocked to retrieve Addie's red-polka-dotted slipper shoe out of Momma Bear's mouth. For some reason, known only to the canine world, those shoes were the best tasting ones in the house. Pretty much every foster dog had savored them. Somehow they'd survived the onslaught, although several dogs ago, Addie had to use blue flowered duct tape to resecure the liner to the bottom of the shoe.

It wasn't just Addie's shoes. She'd gnawed on the directions for my new iPhone, multiple ballpoint pens, and then she found a box of packing peanuts. They were the kind made of cornstarch that disappear when wet. She poked her long snout into the box in the corner of the kitchen and fished out one peanut, and turned to take it to her favorite chewing spot only to discover it was gone! She returned to the box and grabbed more, repeating the process until I put the box up because I didn't know if cornstarch was poisonous to dogs.*

Momma Bear was such a pleasant, easy dog; I couldn't imagine why anyone had returned her. Her adoption coordinator was working hard to be sure the next adoption stuck. The more we got to know Momma Bear and the more she revealed her true personality, the better chance we all had at finding her the right adopter. I think plenty of returns happen because adopters are thrilled with the dog they adopt, but after the dog settles in their home, the dog relaxes and reveals new behaviors. Instead of adapting or seeking training help, adopters sometimes have second thoughts about this *new* dog, who is so different from the one they adopted. While my kids are reportedly excellent guests in other people's homes, here they feel free to leave their dirty socks on the kitchen floor and their wet towels in the hallway. I imagine if they stayed a few weeks in another home they would eventually reveal their dirty-sock-and-wet-towel-leaving habits. Maybe dogs act the same way.

Rescue dogs have experienced a lot of uncertainty and until they're certain they're really home, they might not be acting like their true selves. A dog might not be as quiet as it was at first. As it relaxes, it might be more playful, chewing things it had no interest in touching when it arrived. The dog might find its confidence and its voice, and

---

* It isn't.

begin barking more. These are all good things—they mean the dog feels safe. It feels at home.

Momma Bear was due to meet her new adopter in a few days and possibly go to her forever home. I hoped this time her adoption would stick. I hoped that she would be happy there and that within a few weeks she'd be chewing up the shoes, racing around the furniture, and leaving her wet towel wherever she wanted.

ELEVEN

The Healing Power of Safety

I t was still several weeks before Lily's puppies would move in, so I combed the latest transport list and picked a beautiful eight-month-old puppy named Hadley. She had brown and white patches, and one of her eyes was ringed in black—like a pirate patch! She wasn't a big dog—about thirty pounds or so, the perfect apartment-sized dog that OPH seemed to bring up by the dozens. All the week before transport, whenever I told anyone about the new puppy, I said, "She's a pirate puppy!"

"Wait? What about all those other puppies we're getting?" Nick asked.

"They're weeks away and this puppy is so cute—someone will want to adopt her straight away. She'll be gone long before Christmas!"

"Famous last words," was all he said.

We picked Hadley up Friday night from transport and she cowered silently in her crate the whole ride home. There was nothing pirate-y about her. When we got home, I coaxed her out of the cage, clipped on a leash, and set her on the ground. She froze. I tugged on the leash and she reluctantly followed me, creeping close to the ground, eyes darting every direction. *She's freaked out from the long ride*, I thought and picked her up.

She was filthy and smelly, so the first order of business was to bathe her. She sat still, trembling in the tub as I scrubbed her all over and the water ran brown. Finally clean, I carried her to her crate in our puppy room and spent a few minutes with her. She retreated to the back of the crate, burrowing under the blankets and towels, avoiding eye contact with me.

The next morning when I opened her crate, she pressed herself against the back wall. I knew she had to be hungry and thirsty (she'd refused food and water the night before), so I left the crate door open and the bowls nearby and went for my run.

When I came back she hadn't touched either. I reached to pet her and she allowed it, but tensed up and wouldn't look at me. We left her alone for the morning, figuring she was just shell-shocked after her journey from South Carolina. When she still hadn't emerged from the crate by afternoon, I pulled her out and took her outside. She followed me, crouched close to the ground again, as if under sniper fire.

Later that morning Momma Bear's new adopter arrived to take her home. She took to him right away, even whimpering softly in happiness as he petted her. I liked that when he met her, he knelt down to be on her level and talked to her, not me, as they got to know each other. I was happy for her, even as I endured the wrath of Ian who was furious that I let her go. He made me promise that if she was ever returned again, we would keep her.*

---

* He even forced me to shake on it.

I said goodbye to our sweet Momma Bear, and took my already lonely heart back inside to sit with my cowering puppy. I wished we knew what Hadley needed. Since she couldn't tell us, all we could do was love her even though, right then, it didn't seem like enough.

Hadley spent the rest of the day Saturday and all day Sunday lying on the back edge of the Frank bed, against the wall, watching all of us. We gave her toys, but she looked at us blankly, not touching them. She refused to eat and wouldn't even sniff at the treats we offered.

Exasperated and worried, I finally placed a few pieces of kibble in my hand and held it out to her. She sniffed at the food and then tentatively ate one tiny piece at a time. Twenty minutes later, she had finally finished her whole bowl, piece by piece. "Good girl," I told her. I leaned close and she turned her face up to me, touching her nose to mine, like an Eskimo kiss.

In the days that followed, we each took a turn, sitting with her; sometimes offering her food, sometimes just our presence. She allowed us to pet her, holding very still for each touch. Ian curled up with her often, always letting her sniff his hand first. He told me he'd read somewhere that it was important to let the dog smell you. Seeing my nearly six-foot-tall teenager curled up on the hard floor talking sweetly to Hadley reminded me what a good and kind child we were raising.

I spent hours petting her softly, talking to her, reassuring her. She endured my touches, tensely braced for some unknown danger. Every now and again, I would feel her soften against me, but that always seemed to be about the time my leg fell asleep and if I shifted my position at all, she became rigid again, the whites of her eyes flashing.

By Wednesday the only improvement evident was that she now lay in the center of the Frank bed, instead of at the back, pressed against the wall. But she remained there all day long, only getting up occasionally to creep to the edge of the bed where I'd placed a water bowl, before resuming her spot. She continued to eat only when I fed her by hand. Each time we finished, she looked up at me and waited for me to lean down so we could touch noses like Eskimos. I think it was with this little gesture that she stole my heart.

I'm a storyteller, and I wanted to know Hadley's story. We all did. And while we probably never would, it didn't stop us from guessing. Had she spent her entire life in a crate? Was that why she was terrified to move in open spaces? Was she raised on the streets? Maybe that would explain why she was so uncomfortable with human touch.

Just being near Hadley hurt my heart. I wanted to fix her—NOW. I'm not the most patient of people, but I did understand that this was only going to happen in her time and in her heart. I didn't know what had closed it up so tightly. If I did, I might have driven down there to South Carolina and done something that got me arrested. My foster coordinator, Mindy, told me, "I wish we knew their backgrounds, but sometimes I'm glad we don't." She was probably right.

When Gracie met Hadley, she snarled. Gracie, in human form, would be an insecure bully who is all bluster. She seemed to consider it her duty to threaten each new dog. It was probably a pack thing. Animals need to know where their place is in the pack. Each time Gracie did this, I scolded her. Most likely all this little interaction ever did was make it clear to our new guest that I was the alpha dog, not Gracie. Most likely, Gracie was a frustrated alpha-dog wannabe. Since that first introduction, Gracie had reined it in, though. I guess even she sensed that Hadley was a fragile soul.

After more than a week of Hadley spending her days/nights either frozen on the Frank bed or burrowed in her crate, Nick, who had always been the hardliner when it came to animals on the furniture, carried her to the couch to watch football with him. She seemed content tucked between him and the back cushions of the couch. She even closed her eyes and slept.

Eight days after she arrived I opened her crate as usual in the morning and she thumped her tail and crawled to me (as opposed to me crawling in the crate with the leash and dragging her out). That was a first. And then later when I touched noses with her after her breakfast, she actually licked my nose.

I was certain that Hadley wanted to be loved and was on the verge of returning it. Someday maybe she'd be like the cat I once rescued from a hoarding situation who'd never been touched. Once she discovered what a loving touch was, she followed me everywhere, even climbing in the bathtub for attention. It was as if she wanted to make up for lost time.

As the month wore on, Hadley scuttled between her "safe zones"—the Frank bed in the kitchen, her crate, the dog bed next to my desk, and the space behind the couch cushions on the sofa. She moved between them, head down, tail clamped to her side, in a crouched position as if she were ducking under the laser trip wires like the bank robbers did on TV. On the plus side, this meant she never stopped moving long enough to pee and consequently seemed to be more or less housebroken.

There were other signs that she was opening up. She'd begun chewing on a few select toys and toted some to her bed. She was especially fond of my shoes and Gracie's flat fox (what was left of it). To Gracie's credit, she never said a word about the interloper dog making off with her favorite stuffy.

Hadley also began to come alive outside—wagging her tail and prancing on the leash. Walking around the pasture, she raced ahead until a leaf fluttered to the ground or she heard a car on the road below, then she hurried back to my side. Most of the time on our walks around the pasture she seemed genuinely happy and I was treated to glimpses of a joyful little girl just waiting to join the world.

When I found the remote control dismantled and bearing obvious chew marks, I first looked at Gracie. She didn't usually chew up anything except stuffed animals. I waved the ruined remote at her and she yawned. Either she didn't take my threat seriously (as usual), or she wasn't the one who chewed it. And then I found Ian's favorite set of earbuds stripped of their buds and lying next to a whole host of shredded nerf darts. Apparently, Hadley was getting around. We rarely saw her moving about the house, but the evidence was clear. She was most attracted to things that smelled like us—shoes, devices, playing cards, etc.

Hadley's confidence was growing. One night, after finishing her dinner, she trotted off to her favorite spot on the couch, only to discover Ian already occupying her space. He was lying on his stomach reading a book, filling the entire couch. She glanced around anxiously and then hopped up and sat on his back. In the picture I snapped she looks awkward and uncomfortable, but determined.

Hadley's progress screeched to a halt with the holidays. In addition to my mother-in-law visiting, Brady was home from college, so the household dynamics shifted. Hadley, being such a sensitive soul, picked up on that and regressed to some of her earlier insecurities.

She was back to staying in her crate for hours on end—running for it at every frightening new sight or sound or visitor. Brady had noisy reunions with friends who were also home from college and they took over the kitchen laughing and talking and eating pizza.

"Do they always have to hang out here?" asked Nick, as we ate our dinner on the living room couch with Hadley. There was no room for us in the kitchen. "Can't they go to someone else's house sometimes?"

"I like them here," I told him.

We listened to them for a moment. "Yeah, I guess it's only for now," he said.

And he was right. Every time I saw Brady I realized we were on a countdown. Soon he would have his own life and we would be his parents back in Pennsylvania. Noisy, messy, constantly-eating young people in my kitchen? The more the merrier.

Hadley watched them nervously from her crate and I watched Hadley. It was frustrating to see her hiding in her crate again, but I knew it was her safe place. We all need a safe place, so I let her be. I looked up fearful dogs on the Internet and read that you couldn't force them to interact or they could become aggressive. I couldn't imagine Hadley ever being aggressive about anything, still I didn't think we were pushing her hard enough. Her regressive behavior was frustrating me.

My (and I believe Hadley's) favorite time of the day was in the evening when we snuggled on the couch. Even if she was cowering in her crate, the moment I sat down on the couch, I'd have company. That's what made me so sure what she really wanted was to love and be loved. Like all of us.

The coming week would be a big one for Hadley. We planned to cut down a Christmas tree, install it right next to her crate and pile presents under it. And there would be puppies! *(What?! Did I say puppies?)* Hadley's little world was about to explode.

It was time to pick up the puppies from Lily's litter at Chris's house. In the end, Chris had decided that she could handle caring for four of them and would only send five with us. They were arriving just a few days before Christmas. I couldn't imagine a better Christmas present! Most already had approved adopters, so we'd only have them for a few weeks until they were old enough to go home.

They now looked like little chunky Lab puppies. If you've ever seen Lab puppies, you know that it doesn't get much cuter or busier. At five weeks, they had no qualms about walking through, playing with, or even sleeping in each other's poop. I tried to stay on top of it,* but with the Christmas chaos, visitors, my own work, Hadley, and the fact that I had to bake six dozen cookies and package them beautifully for a neighbor's cookie exchange, it was pretty much impossible to keep the puppies poop-free those first few days.

Fearing Hadley would be overwhelmed by the puppies, we kept her in the kitchen. This didn't last long as we had plenty of untrained guests who didn't remember to shut the gate. A few hours after they arrived, Hadley crept into the mudroom, wide-eyed at the puppies. She lay down and pressed her side against the pen fence and let the puppies sniff her all over. After that, whenever they whined she would get up from wherever she was hiding and trot to their pen. Then she'd lie down beside the pen and let the puppies poke at her and lick her through the wire. She seemed genuinely concerned for them. I immediately started filling in the blanks of Hadley's story—maybe she was taken from her litter too early, maybe she was so scared and sad because she had never been socialized by her siblings. I'd never know, but if those little

---

* So to speak.

cherubs could help Hadley come out of her shell—it would be my best Christmas present.

Everything I'd read said we should wait for Hadley to come out of her crate on her own. And that made total sense. She was insecure and needed to know she had a safe place she could always go to, but here's the thing—some of us need to be pushed from the nest.

I'm not a huge fan of change. I like to have my little routine in my little world. Things like software updates, new technology, attending public events, even parties make me anxious. There's no avoiding most of them, so I plunge ahead, stuffing my worries and nerves aside. And you know what? It almost always goes well. And then I'm happily chatting with new people or marveling at how much easier my work is with this new whiz-bang system. I wasn't going to venture out of my crate on my own, but once you force me—hey, this is pretty great!

I thought maybe Hadley and I were kindred spirits in this, so one day I let her out of her crate in the morning and then I closed it behind her. At first, she seemed worried. She clamored up in her couch cushion cave and hunkered down. But after a day or two she was boldly trotting through the kitchen, snagging a bag of cookies abandoned by some kid, and slinking back to the couch, hoping we didn't notice. Nick followed her out and retrieved the cookies, and a moment later she was back, sniffing around the backpacks.

I had to shut Gracie's crate also because otherwise Hadley would take up residence there, so Gracie claimed the Frank bed. The first time Hadley attempted to join her, Gracie snarled and Hadley scooted away, but an hour later, I found them sharing the bed like the matched set they were.

When I took Hadley out for her walk, she fearlessly approached one of the cats and was game to chase it if it wasn't for that silly leash. Next, she grabbed a stick and carried it around with her as we toured the yard. *Who was this dog?*

I knew it wasn't just the closed crate; the puppies were key to Hadley's blossoming. She loved the puppies. Her giddy joy when I carried a puppy toward her reminded me of the Looney Tunes Abominable

Snowman when he picked up Daffy Duck. *I will hug him and squeeze him and name him George*, her excited wiggles seemed to say.

To keep the puppies safe from Hadley's overly enthusiastic affection, we took the same approach we did when an older sibling wanted to hold the newest baby we brought home years ago. We got her comfortable on the couch and then we handed her the swaddled infant, or in this case the wiggling bundle of happy puppy. Then we supervised the interaction.

For their part, the puppies loved Hadley right back, climbing over and under her, lounging on top of her, chewing her tail, and giving her all manner of kisses. We kept all the action up on the couch and supervised, because Hadley could get overly excited and forget her size, plus Gracie was acting like the neighborhood bully who trotted by and snarled threats at them.

The puppies all had adopters, so there was no pressure to advertise their cuteness; still, I couldn't resist and regularly posted pictures on my blog and Facebook. In no time at all, they had fans all over the world.

We celebrated the New Year in much the same way we had every year—dear friends, board games, leftover Christmas cookies, and plenty of beverages. I left Hadley's crate open so that if she was overwhelmed by the presence of so many new faces, including a three-year-old, she would have a place to hide. She surprised us all by joining the party. As we gathered around the game set up on the coffee table, Hadley hopped up on the couch. She hung out the entire evening, despite the three-year-old instructing her to get in her "room," so she could latch the door (she'd already tucked Gracie into her crate for the night). Hadley sat gamely* beside me through a loud game of Telestrations and plenty of rounds of Apples to Apples.

It had become clear that for all her fear and trembling, Hadley loved people. She was ready to find her family. My New Year's hope was that she would find her forever home quickly so she could start falling in love with the right person.

---

* So to speak.

Hadley and I were both distracted by and in love with the puppies. Not much was getting checked off my to-do list. Just like my other litter, I spent hours standing in the puppy room doorway watching the entertainment. The battles were epic. Hadley watched them from the other side of the fence, racing back and forth and whining to join them. When the puppies tired, they slept in a pile against the fence where Hadley lay on the other side.

Having a birthday at Christmas time is tricky. Instead of more presents, it's become our tradition to go away for Nick's birthday. This year was a monumental birthday, so I decided to surprise him with a visit to nearby Gettysburg.* This meant leaving my teenagers in charge of the puppies.

I left detailed instructions and paid the kids per poop. In one twenty-four-hour period, Ian cleaned up sixteen poops and Addie put the rubber gloves on and held her nose long enough to deal with seven. If you're doing your math, that means five puppies produced twenty-three poops in twenty-four hours. That's nearly one poop per hour! Consider that the next time you think, *hey, it'd be fun to foster puppies*!

---

* Plenty of monuments there to celebrate the monumental birthday. I even found an obscure blog with an obscure walking tour I could download that would make my nerdy husband happy.

TWELVE

There's an Adopter
for Everyone

'd never heard Hadley make a sound in all the time she was here, but somehow the house was quieter once she left. I missed her. Nick missed her. Ian was once again not happy with me for letting one of our dogs go.

Everyone else went to see the new *Star Wars* movie on Sunday, but I stayed home to dig out my desk. New year, new start and all that. I thought clearing my desk might clear my mind, and yet my mind kept finding its way to Hadley. I'd forgotten to ask the adopters what they would call her. I couldn't stop picturing her sweet, terrified eyes the night we brought her home six weeks ago. I kept trying to replace that image with the playful gleam she had when she was wrestling a puppy or the way she often glanced up at me when we walked outside—checking that I was still there. Maybe it hurt so much because she was the most broken dog we'd ever fostered. We'd watched her come out of her shell, going from a terrified, shut-down dog to the happy, playful puppy she was meant to be. I should have felt proud of what we'd done, not sad. Happy for Hadley, not worried that she missed us or would regress without our support.

I sifted through a stack of papers to file and shook off my worry. Clearly, adoption magic had happened once again. Evelyn* adopted Hadley, but her adult son Dave would spend his days with her. Dave and his teenage daughter lived with Evelyn. Dave was on disability for a condition that had already required numerous surgeries. He was home full-time. When he introduced himself to Hadley, she licked his hand. I think she sensed his gentle spirit. She was as relaxed as Hadley could be in the company of three new people.

There's a lot of pressure on a dog and a family at a Meet and Greet. One of the biggest benefits of the foster system is that by the time dog and adopter meet, there's been plenty of information passed back and forth between adopter and foster. Anyone who picked out Hadley in a shelter and adopted her for her adorable looks would have been completely unprepared to deal with a puppy so shut down. Dave had followed Hadley's story on my blog and commented several times. He was drawn to Hadley and understood, perhaps identified with, her fearfulness. He knew a challenge lay ahead. She was doing well here, but her progress might have come faster if there hadn't been the constant teen traffic and puppies and grumpy hostess dog and busy, busy foster mama always doing ten things at once. Her soul would do well with a quieter home. Evelyn and Dave knew it would take time. They seemed like patient people.

These were the things I kept reminding myself of, but still, I checked my email incessantly, hoping for word. I busied myself working on a new journal. Crafting homemade journals, using discarded scrapbook papers

---

* Not the actual names of these adopters, as I want to respect their privacy.

and old books, always helped me find my happy. This one would be dog-themed and I'd use it to document the dogs we fostered. We'd fostered twenty-five dogs in our first year. If we'd had one more, Pennsylvania would have required us to have a kennel license. I'd decided we needed a license—just in case. The journal would help me keep the details straight for the dog warden who would come for twice yearly surprise inspections.

Although I tried not to be a "helicopter foster mom" after my dogs were adopted, I couldn't help but reach out to Dave the next day. I needed some morsel of good news to beat back my worries. I sent him a quick note, "Just checking in," and then waited for a response.

While I waited and worried, I took care of the puppies. Thank goodness for the puppies—they were a joyful, constant distraction.

Finally, I got a call from Dave. Hadley was doing great. She was going for walks with him in the neighborhood and a young relative of theirs had come for a visit and Hadley lit up at the sight of a child. She'd also made friends with another dog already. She was fine. I could stop worrying.

On Monday, Chris, Melissa,* and I took the puppies for their first-ever vet check. Because the puppies were born "in rescue" they hadn't had a wellness check. Most OPH dogs have a vet check before traveling northward. These pups came north in their mama's belly. Before we sent them home with their new families the next weekend, we were headed to a local vet to get them checked out.

The logistics of getting nine puppies to the vet required two cars, three crates, and five people. Melissa rode along with me. We chatted happily until we smelled the unmistakable scent of a car-sick puppy. The road to the vet who treats OPH dogs at a discount is long, winding, and narrow. There was nowhere to pull over and nothing we could do, but get there as quickly as we could. When we arrived, we discovered that the puppies had cleaned up the mess themselves.†

---

* Remember her? My foster mentee? She was taking a break from fostering to adopt Begonia for her teenage daughter.

† Yes, puppies are disgusting.

Chris was already there, and it was fun to see how much the rest of the litter had grown. Edelweiss was over thirteen pounds! And I thought my Foxglove was big at twelve. Although to be fair, we weren't totally certain that was his weight because he couldn't stop wiggling and wagging on the scale long enough to get a clear read. He was the only puppy to wag his tail enthusiastically while having his rectal temp taken!

The vet said they all looked healthy, and she also said some of them were pretty large. "Might be some Great Dane in there," she remarked. I looked at Chris and we both shook our heads, a silent agreement not to mention this idea to the adopters.

Everyone was weighed, had their temperatures taken, and was examined. They were all perfect—except Pigweed. Something was amiss with the joints in her legs.

As the vet spoke, I spun back through my time with the puppies. Had I done something wrong? Was this my fault? After Texas's unexplained death, I'd harbored a secret doubt as to whether or not I was qualified to be fostering. I didn't know enough about dogs, sometimes neglected to pay attention to details, and was disinclined to read directions or ask for help. Between my shoddy housetraining skills, multiple mix-ups with worming schedules, Hitch's escapes, and not realizing Homeboy was a girl, I'd certainly lowered the bar for OPH fosters. And now I'd screwed up a puppy.

I watched the vet write notes on her chart and wondered if I should mention the phone call we'd gotten from Brady while on Nick's birthday getaway in Gettysburg the previous week. When my phone rang, we were at an Irish pub. We'd both already had a beer or two, so there would be no rushing home. Hopefully, this had nothing to do with the puppies.

Brady's voice was panicked. "I think I broke one of the puppies," he told us.

"What?" I said. "You can't break a puppy."

"She jumped out of my arms and went splat on the floor. I think something's wrong with her front leg. She's holding it funny."

I quizzed him. Yes, the puppy could walk on it. No, she wasn't crying anymore. Yes, she's back to wrestling with her litter.

"She's fine," I told him. "Puppies are pretty bendable."

But now I wondered—*should I tell the vet about that fall?*

As it turned out, Pigweed wasn't permanently damaged from her inadvertent leap from Brady's arms; what she had was a hereditary condition. It was called luxating patellas, which sounded like a delicious Italian dish, but wasn't. It meant that the kneecaps in her hind legs* could float out of position. It didn't bother her now—which was clear if you'd ever seen her racing around my puppy pen. The problem with luxating patellas was that later on it could grow worse, or . . . she could grow out of it. So, it was random and treatable and might be nothing.

Of course, I read all the blather on the Internet about the condition, and still obsessed that we had caused it in some way. I told Nick, "If we broke her, we have to buy her." I watched Pigweed, and carried her around obsessively. I wanted to keep her safe and not let anyone think she was less than a perfect puppy.

Because that was the thing—she *might* be a perfect puppy. She might never have any pain from her crazy wandering patellas. The vet had said that if she was fed well, watched her weight, and got plenty of exercise she might be fine all her life.†

And besides, there was no such thing as a perfect puppy. The vet pronounced the other eight as just right, but who knew what was lurking inside their DNA?

I wasn't naïve enough to think this puppy would have a hoard of takers. She'd need a little extra care and she might need vet treatment at some point. But luxating patellas were not a death sentence. They were just a more intentional life sentence. I hoped that all the adopters planned to feed their pups well, keep them at a healthy weight, and be sure they got plenty of exercise.

---

* I had no idea that dogs had kneecaps in their hind legs. See how much I don't know?

† True for all of us, no?

Not long after Pigweed's diagnosis, I watched a video of another writer talking about battling breast cancer at the age of thirty-three. Near the end of the video, she said something to the effect that having cancer upset her at first because she thought, "I'm going to die!" but then she realized that had always been true.

We are all going to die.

So we should probably take full advantage of the day before us, because tomorrow was no guarantee—for any of us or for our puppies.

Four out of five puppies took off for their forever homes the next weekend. All adopters are happy, but puppy adopters bubble over with excitement. Who isn't over-the-moon happy to be taking home an adorable puppy? Some of that happy might wear off after a few days of cleaning up poop, but for that thirty minutes or so when they are meeting their puppy and signing the papers and taking pictures, they are THE happiest. And that's fun to see.

Sneezewort (now Cooper) jumped all over his new boys and Snap Dragon (now Rocky) gave his new mom a facebath. The grins on the faces of Foxglove's (now Teddy's) new mommy and daddy practically split their faces, and seeing the dreams come true for one teenager when she snuggled Begonia (now Calypso) made my day.

And that left Pigweed alone. It was a long, tough night for that little girl. We learned she could bay like a hound when she was VERY sad. It would take a week for an adopter who was not worried about luxating patellas to come forward and until then she would be alone in the puppy pen.

After her first long night of crying, Ian asked, "Next time we do puppies, can you make sure they ALL go home on the same day?"

Yup. That would be ideal.

I tried to head off this predicament by claiming a very small foster dog—a sort of puppy impersonator who could keep Pigweed company. Chuggy Alabaster (who could resist a name like that?) arrived on Saturday afternoon. He was a pug/Chihuahua cross and weighed a little less than Pigweed. He had a smashed-in, turned-up nose, plus a mini-Superman build—svelte waist and broad chest. He was about a year old and had lots of small dog energy. The perfect playmate.

The only problem was that while Chuggy may have been puppy-sized, he was not a puppy. After two thousand laps around the kitchen island and several hundred tackles, he was done. He sat down in protest. Pigweed, being a mere eight weeks old and having only ever experienced the nonstop roughhousing of her siblings, didn't know how to take a hint. She had yet to be schooled in dog-to-unrelated-dog etiquette.

Between the puppy that just wouldn't quit and the snarly, socially awkward girl dog who wouldn't give him the time of day, Chuggy must have wondered whether this was a step up from the shelter. I'd heard small dogs could get testy, but he had yet to snap at anyone. He dodged the mean girl dog and humored the HAPPY puppy, but what he most wanted was to snuggle in my lap. I really needed more than one lap. Three laps that week would have been perfect.

Chuggy's story was one of the ones that made me angry and grateful. He'd had a home until a few months ago. Then his owner surrendered him to a shelter when Chuggy developed a stress-induced skin condition that had caused him to lose most of his hair. And here I must remind everyone: DOGS ARE NOT DISPOSABLE.

Maybe I was more than a little sensitive to this one because written on his owner surrender form was the word "alopecia." Ian has alopecia. And while that diagnosis turned our world around eight years ago, in the end we were all better because of it—healthier, more grateful, and much more aware that everyone has their own hurdles in life. Ian has no hair, but he has a loving family, a supportive community, and a great sense of humor. Maybe the owner had other reasons besides the puppy losing his hair, but it just hit me in the heart to see that diagnosis written on the form of a dog being thrown away.

I was grateful for the shelter that took him in, treated him, and three months later sent him northward with OPH. The only evidence of his history was some scarring on the edges of his ears and a baby-soft new coat.

I didn't have a lot of experience with small dogs. I could see the appeal—they made much smaller messes, they didn't eat much, and if they didn't listen, you could just pick them up and move them where you needed them to be. They fit so nicely on, and were so happy in, your lap. But I needed more DOG in my dog. There was something about a big dog—just the substance of them—that I appreciated. I promised Addie when we began this odyssey that we'd foster some small dogs, preferably purse-sized, but I didn't know how well I could keep that promise. Chuggy was great, and he was awesome with Pigweed, whereas a large dog might have accidentally hurt her, but I was probably going to stick with big dogs, or at least *bigger* dogs after this. I was the one picking up the poop around here so I figured that made it my call. And besides, I didn't have enough laps to go around.

Life got easier the following weekend. Fiona, the puppy formerly known as Pigweed, took off for her forever home with a previous OPH adopter who was more than thrilled to get her. Chuggy (and the rest of us) were missing Pigweed, but cute as they were, Pigweed and the rest of the puppies were a LOT of work. Chuggy was not. He was a delightful and gracious houseguest.

Chuggy Alabaster was a very expressive dog. He wasn't pushy like so many fosters before him, but he was SO READY. I'd call his name, which he seemed to know a little, and he'd cock his head, as if to say, "Might you be talking to me?"*

He bustled around with his toenails going *clip, clip, clip*, like an efficient little supervisor. He was so quick to follow me that I'd turn around to look for him and not see him standing beneath me. More than once, I'd almost stepped on him, but he seemed to be used to this possibility and had lightning reflexes.

That whole week, he had been a perfect babysitter. He'd kept Pigweed entertained, happy, and even a tad bit disciplined. I could

---

* In my mind, he had an English accent.

imagine him saying, "Okay now doll, it's nap time. No more of those shenanigans."*

I googled Chuggy Alabaster thinking it must be a name from a book or movie, but I came up empty. The only Chuggy I found was THE Chuggy, residing right here in my home.† I suppose he got his name because it fit. Someone, somewhere, looked at him and thought, *Chuggy Alabaster*. Clever soul. Whoever it was should be put in charge of naming all the rescue dogs.

I decided I still wasn't a small dog person, but I was a Chuggy Alabaster person.

---

* Now, somehow, he had a gangster accent.

† I'd written about him on my blog.

THIRTEEN

What Lies Beneath

With Chuggy launched, I told Nick we'd be foster dog-less until after we got back from our big vacation. We were headed to Grand Cayman Island in two weeks to celebrate our fiftieth birthdays with my brother and his wife. I'd promised Nick I wouldn't spend the week worrying about some foster dog at home, but he'd been married to me long enough to know how serious that promise was.

Because, you know, twist my rubber arm. Plus, the dog in need of a foster home that I wasn't supposed to be offering wasn't just any foster dog. This was a Lily, the puppy mama. How could I possibly say no? I'd been smitten by this gorgeous girl since the first time I laid eyes on her, back in November when she was giving birth to all those beautiful puppies.

Now that the puppies had been weaned and adopted, Lily had perked up and her energy was taxing Chris's home. She needed more space and a lot more running around, so Lily would be my running partner for a few weeks until it was time to be spayed and go to her forever home. She couldn't be spayed until a month after the last puppy left, so she had time to kill before some lucky family could adopt her. While we were in the Caymans, Lily would again stay with Chris, but for two weeks we enjoyed her happy energy.

When you considered what she'd been through—she was pregnant, abandoned in a shelter, and shipped a day's drive north where she gave birth to ten puppies with four birth attendants that she'd only just met. Considering all that, you'd think Lily might be a little shy. Maybe suspicious. You'd think she might have trust issues.

Well, you'd be wrong on all those counts. Within hours of being here, Lily loved us like her own. When Ian came home from school, she bounded up to him, wagging her body in side-to-side U-shapes. She whined for me when I hiked up the hill to the barn to feed the horses. She leaned into Nick as he crouched down to put wood in the woodstove. This dog was oozing love and trust and happy energy. If only we could all be like Lily. Imagine *that* world!

Kind of like any young mom who had just been freed from her mothering responsibilities, Lily could get a little wild. Maybe it was the stored-up energy, but when I watched her race through our house, tossing stuffed animals in the air, and making Gracie run for her crate, I imagined she was yelling, "Wahoo! Free at last! Let's do shots!"

It was unreasonably cold that first morning with Lily, hovering just under ten degrees with a nice slicing wind. On a normal day, I'd return from the barn work and say, "Time to hit the treadmill. I'm not going out *there* again." But watching Lily careen around the kitchen on her slippy toenails, I realized that was not an option, so out we went.

We'd only run two miles. I figured she'd been cooped up with the kids for quite some time; she was probably out of shape. We should start slow. Ha. We made it to our split in record time and I assumed she'd slow down on the return journey. Silly me. Lily dragged my sorry, cold butt all the way home like an out-of-control towrope. And then she spent the better part of the day in my office chasing tennis balls and ignoring my pleas for her to "Lay down right here next to the heater on this super soft doggy bed . . ."

This dog was not an old person's dog. It would probably be optimal if her adopter had a serious running habit, a large fenced yard, and/or a pitching machine to toss balls. I hoped to take her over to the fenced-in tennis courts for a good run and fetch session on Thursday. After that, we'd stop in to see Chuggy!

Chuggy Alabaster had won the lottery in terms of adopters. Jim and Rosie owned a local pet store and he'd be helping them run it. Having a family that owns a pet store was probably like being a kid with parents who own a candy store. Think of the free samples! I was really happy for Chuggy. The trip there may have been a little turbulent, but he sure landed in a great place.

After Chuggy, Lily was a BIG dog. She was SOLID and had a tail more like a beaver's than a dog's. That appendage was strong, and could level anything in its path. Plus it was set on nonstop wag due to her happy heart. Lily had adult-sized teeth with a puppy-sized urge to chew. So far, besides my slippers and my gloves, she'd destroyed pretty much every dog toy we'd given her.

What Lily wanted more than anything was for Gracie to play with her. *C'mon, just one game of tear around the house? Ya wanna?, Ya wanna?, Ya wanna?* I had to supervise their interactions. Gracie didn't have a nice indoor voice, it always sounded like she was threatening to kill Lily, even though I knew she was all bluster. And Lily had no idea that she could squash Gracie in a flash. Still, I couldn't take a chance on that changing.

The week before we were to leave for our trip, the snow fell relentlessly, piling up to nearly four feet. Nick had to use the snowblower to create pathways for the dogs. Lily loved the snow—barreling through it like a dolphin to chase tennis balls and then disappearing under the snow in search of them.

I watched the snow and fretted that we would not be able to take our long-awaited trip. I needed sunshine. I needed blue water. I needed rum drinks.

And still the snow did not relent. It was historical. Everyone seemed so pleased with it. School was canceled. Work was canceled. Lugging water to the barn through the drifts, I truly didn't see what everyone thought was so great about so much snow. It was like that crazy relative who came for a visit and was so darn much fun, but the next day you were hungover and tired and really in no mood to deal with his needs. *Go away,* you thought. But he didn't go away.

Thankfully, the roads were cleared and the weather warmed just in time for us to make our break for the islands. Lily knew something was up. She'd seen the bag packing, my ramped-up stress-level, and the cleaning (perhaps the most obvious giveaway of all). She was underfoot. That last morning as I picked up her toys so I could run the vacuum, she followed me around, retrieving each toy I put in the basket, only to drop it wherever she was to get the next toy I put away. Ian watched from the breakfast table and said, "Is having Lily around what it's like to have a toddler in the house?"

When I finally put the basket out of reach and got the vacuum, she offered her assistance with that task too, and I learned that I *could* play fetch and vacuum at the same time. Later, I dropped Lily at Chris's house and made up the guest room.*

The week went just as planned. The kids and grandparents had some nice solid time together with no dogs, except Gracie, underfoot. The snow did not fall, so I didn't have to worry about my parents and ice and snowblowers and our hilly property. The weather was beautiful on Grand Cayman, the snorkeling amazing, the rum drinks flowing. The only time I thought of dogs was when we visited Stingray City on a sandbar where the bay meets the ocean. The gorgeous blue water is only a few feet deep. It looks just like a picture postcard.

When our boat anchored there, the captain explained how to interact with the stingrays circling our craft. I thought of *The Crocodile Hunter* and wondered if it might be a little crazy, jumping out of a boat into a herd of stingrays. The captain told us to shuffle our feet so we

---

* Lily ate the corner of the quilt on the guest bed in honor of the g-parents' arrival.

wouldn't step on a stingray. If we shuffled, he said, we would have zero chance of being killed by their poisonous barbs. *Uh, huh.*

The gentle, giant creatures circled our legs in search of treats. It reminded me of Chuggy following me around the kitchen hoping for a treat, and the many times I'd nearly squished him. I'd shuffled then too. Other than trying (unsuccessfully) to make friends with an island dog, that was my only dog-thought all week.

Mostly, the week was a total break from my life—just what I needed.

When we returned, Lily came back too. Ian said she was a snow-caller because her reappearance coincided with another big snow. The cats were none too happy to see the return of Lily. Because of the snow, they were sheltering in the warm kitchen. They didn't hesitate to reassert their dominion, smacking Lily from where they perched on the counter stools every time she wandered by. I loved having Lily around. She was great company, despite the fact that on her first day back she ate my new lipstick.

Everyone settled back in and I checked email and saw one from Foxglove's (now Teddy) adopters. They'd had a DNA analysis done on their pup and sent me the results. It turned out that Lily was no black Lab after all. The family tree indicated that Lily was a boxer-rottweiler mix.

I have to confess that had I known Lily was a rottweiler mix, I would have never agreed to foster her. Is that horrible? Yes, you're right; it is. I liked to think of myself as a nonjudgmental person, but when it comes to dog breeds, most of us have plenty of judgment to pass around. My aversion to rottweilers came from an incident that happened over ten years ago when my young nephew, Parker, was attacked by two rottweilers. He was walking down a sidewalk on the air force base where my brother lived when he was attacked and narrowly escaped with his life thanks to quick-thinking soldiers who fought off the dogs with a shovel and a car. Parker required hundreds of stitches and a hospital stay. I'd been afraid of the breed ever since.

Lily taught me that it wasn't the breed. It was the owners. I should be afraid of people who do not care for their dogs properly, raising them with an unkind hand. I should be afraid of irresponsible people who don't secure their aggressive dogs. I should not be afraid of rottweilers.

Lily was gentle and sweet and one of the most obedient foster dogs we'd ever had. I trusted her completely. I could still picture her the day I met her giving birth in Chris's basement after a long journey northward. I remember being stunned at how brave and loving she was. I drove home thinking, *How could anyone give up a dog like that?*

Now, when I looked into her wide face, I could picture her rottweiler daddy. He gave her those strong limbs and broad shoulders. He gave her those powerful jaws. But he also gave her a sweet temperament, a sharp mind, and happy manner. Shame on me for judging him sight unseen based simply on his breed.

Another life lesson for this foster mama. We had no right to judge the heart of another based on their heritage—dog *or person*. Maybe that was one of the best things about adopting a mutt. You couldn't hold their pedigree against them. You could only love the dog before you right here, right now.

Speaking of mutts, Itz Luv joined our dog party after arriving on the Valentine's Day transport from South Carolina. Luvie was listed as a beagle/shepherd, but you could probably make a case for nearly any dog breed being part of her family tree. She was medium-sized; her fur was not short, not long. She was mostly brown with black edges. Her nose was long, but not too long; her ears were pointy, but flopped over. Her tail curled around in a "C," and was usually wagging. I searched in vain for the little plastic dog that came with Addie's dollhouse years ago. I swear it was a spitting image of Luvie. She simply looked like a classic dog.

She was a happy, easygoing girl who took everything in stride. She sat nicely for her bath, was appropriately grovelly in her introductions to Gracie, and then eagerly took on Lily with some full-contact, hard-core play. Both dogs grinned ear-to-ear as they slammed around the kitchen, wrestled over toys, and had never-ending tug-of-war matches.

That sigh you heard? That was me relaxing because now I'd get some uninterrupted work done.

It was refreshing to have such a simple dog. No issues, no barking, no whining, no pining, not even very much peeing-in-the-house. She was happy in her crate; she was happy out of it. She slept through the night, walked nicely on the leash, and ate her meals with no hesitation. If they were all this easy, everyone would foster. I picked up my phone and called my friend Allison who had been searching for a dog for months. She'd come to meet plenty of my fosters whom I claimed would be "perfect for your family," but this time, I told her, I meant it. *This is a good dog.*

Luvie's only issue was cats. She was a bit obsessed. She raced from window to window, tracking their activities outside. So far, she'd done nothing other than be certain we knew where the cats were at any given moment. She didn't get close enough, or they didn't allow her close enough, to discover her true feelings about cats.

Allison was approved to adopt Luvie, but it would be a trial adoption. All adoptions to houses that had cats were by default trial adoptions. I was pretty sure this adoption would stick. If she had to choose a side, I was certain Allison would go with Luvie. Who wouldn't? Besides, cats and dogs work these things out. They've been doing it for centuries. Her trial period would come and go and she was indeed a good dog and is still in her happy home as I write this.*

That week Lily went to be spayed. This was the last step before she could go home with her very excited adopters—a wonderful family that included an ultramarathon-running dad. Finally, Lily would have someone who could keep up with her!

When Lily came home from the vet's office, we pulled the Frank bed in front of the woodstove and she remained there the whole night. It was eerily odd to see Lily so still. I sat with her reading my book and stroking her soft ears. I loved the heart of this dog. Here was another dog I could have adopted. She loved us and we loved her. So, why was I, once again, letting a good dog go? *She had perfect adopters*, I reasoned. *There were so many more dogs to come*, I told myself. And yet, the tears came.

---

* And Allison's cats are still not happy about it.

FOURTEEN

Trust

Our newest foster, Meredith, was due to arrive on a transport van at 7:00 A.M. on Saturday. Another foster mom, Deb, graciously offered to grab Meredith when she picked up her new foster. Thanks to Deb, instead of trooping down to the bowling alley at the crack of dawn, I was able to roll over and hit the snooze button. As I was having my morning tea, Deb texted that they'd had some difficulty with Meredith. She didn't want to come out of her crate when they'd unloaded her from the transport van. She was terrified and snapped at them. They'd had to dump her out, slip a leash around her collar-less neck and deposit her in their backseat where she was now cowering, fur raised, as they drove toward my house.

The idea of a snapping, terrified dog terrified me. I paced the kitchen and watched Lily as I waited for them to arrive. Lily was still resting from her surgery. What if this new dog was mean to Lily? Or bit me? Or one of the kids? Then what? This was bound to happen eventually, right? I mean, every dog can't be a good dog, can it? I hadn't considered that one might bite me.

When Deb and her husband, Scott, arrived with Meredith, I went out to meet them. We all peered in the window at Meredith. None of us wanted to touch her (and clearly she didn't want to be touched). We debated a few approaches, and finally Scott used treats to distract her and slipped a collar on. He pulled on the leash and she hopped out of the car, glancing around, hair raised, tail tucked between her legs, terrified. He handed me the leash and I thanked them. Meredith stood next to me, growling quietly as we watched them head out the driveway. I looked down at her. *Now what?*

My only other experience with a traumatized dog like this was Hadley, and she'd taken hours that turned into weeks of patience. But she'd never growled at anyone. I suppose it was surprising that more dogs didn't arrive like Meredith. Considering they'd just spent the last month or two in a noisy shelter all alone after wandering lost or being abandoned, then they'd been spayed or neutered, vaccinated, and a few days later loaded into crates stacked three or more high in a van and trucked north for ten hours or more. On Saturday, it was barely dawn when strangers reached in to drag Meredith out of the crate to take her to what she could only assume would be another scary place. So sure, I'd be reluctant to come out too. I might snap at a few hands myself.

I led Meredith to the Frank bed. She stood next to it like a statue. I sat down on the bed and patted the spot next to me. She took a tentative step forward, but retreated as soon as I reached for her, the hair on the back of her neck standing in a ridge.

OPH says the best plan for handling dogs like this is to do a "shutdown." Bathe her, feed her, water her, potty her, and leave her alone in a comfy, quiet, safe crate. No stimulation, no forced contact, just consistent calm, kind touches, and good food. This can take days, even weeks. I followed protocol, giving her a careful bath, taking her for an unproductive walk, and feeding her a watered-down mix of food (she refused water). Lily was lying in front of the woodstove watching all of this, so I put Meredith in a crate in the living room to let her decompress. Then, I went outside to prune the fruit trees in the day's unseasonably warm weather.

I clipped branches and hauled them to the woods and tried not to think about Meredith. Instead I thought about my next novel, *Girls' Weekend*, which was to come out in May. I wasn't happy with it, but I couldn't really say why. I'd edited it to death, perhaps cutting too much of the heart out of it. My editor, copy editor, beta readers, and proofreaders all loved it. "Stop moving furniture around," one of them said to me. I'd have to trust them on this, but I still felt like the book wasn't saying what I wanted it to say. Mostly I didn't want people to think the book was a lot of whining about first-world problems from overprivileged women. But maybe it was. And maybe a lot of readers were dealing with first-world problems. That didn't change the fact that they were still problems, *right*?

I waved to Addie as she pulled out of the driveway. She was headed to her first meeting for the York County Distinguished Young Women program. She'd recently been selected to participate in the program, formerly known as the Junior Miss Pageant. Addie was decidedly not the typical Junior Miss participant, what with her head nearly shaved on one side with a long swatch of red-dyed hair on the other side. Add to that her eclectic wardrobe, liberal attitudes, and passion for fringe issues, and one doesn't picture the typical Junior Miss participant. Still, I was proud of her for stepping out of her comfort zone. There was a lot of scholarship money on the line, and I knew that's what was behind her decision to apply. I hated that everything *did* seem to be about money lately. And I hoped it wasn't the only reason she'd applied.

When I returned to the house a few hours later there was an all-out nerf war being waged between middle-school boys in the living room—over, around, and occasionally, inside Meredith's crate. *Great*, I thought. *We're so good at this shut-down thing.* I shooed the boys away and carefully coaxed Meredith out of the crate. To my surprise, she'd perked up. It seemed the *entertainment* worked some kind of magic.

By dinnertime she was wagging her tail, and by the next morning, she was happily sauntering along next to me on a walk. Her happiness level and energy quotient grew with every passing hour. The next morning when I opened her crate, she tumbled out. And when I reach out to pet her, she fainted to the ground in ecstasy and whined out her happiness as I scratched her belly. *Who was this dog?*

Her attachment and affection became comical. When I would return to the room after any kind of absence (like when I went upstairs to change the laundry or out the door to grab a log for the fire) she leapt in the air with joy and threw herself on me. Never had a dog been so happy to see me. We made a short film of it for my blog. All week, I watched it when I needed a laugh.

Lily was restricted to leash-walking and supervised play sessions with Meredith, many of which involved Meredith stealing Lily's toys and then Lily sitting on her until she dropped them. Meredith was a mini-me of Lily. She had the same shiny black coat and white markings on her chest. She had the same wide head and floppy ears. If you glanced in the kitchen quickly, it was easy to mistake one for the other. They shared the Frank bed, sleeping in a large black lump.

The snow finally began to melt and it was almost time for Lily to go home. Lily had been AP for the past month with us. In a wine-induced moment of weakness, I had agreed with Nick if for some crazy reason the adoption fell through, we would adopt Lily. It was easy to make this promise because I was confident her adopters would love her, and they did. Upon introduction, they fell instantly in love. We stood in the driveway and watched as they threw tennis ball after tennis ball for her. She raced up over the mounds of plowed snow and leapt back down to return the balls. The kids' big smiles and the parents' smart questions made it very clear Lily was headed for a good life.

The next weekend, after four months in OPH care, in which she gave birth to ten puppies, overcame health issues, weaned her puppies, discovered her love for tennis balls, showered her devoted and vocal love on everyone in her path, was spayed, and regained her svelte figure,

Lily left with her forever family. Gulp. The Frank bed seemed much bigger without Lily.*

My heart felt a little bruised. This one was tough. Her adopter sent an email soon after they'd arrived at their home in Virginia telling me how well Lily was doing and how much they already felt she was part of the family. I was sure that in the coming week Lily would chew up something important and her energy level might be over the top, even for this ultramarathon-running dad. But I was equally certain that Lily had already stolen their hearts. An email from them earlier in the week confirming the details of picking up Lily said it all, "We feel a little guilty getting such a special dog in our family!"

---

* Not long after she was adopted, her adopter set up a Facebook page, Trail Running Dad and Lils (her adoptive dad called her "Lils," the same nick name I'd used on her). It was great to follow their adventures and inspiring to read how they were encouraging other runners to adopt rescue dogs and run with them.

FIFTEEN

In the Groove

When a purse-sized Chi-weinie* popped up on the foster list, I couldn't resist. We named him Okieriete.† He was a tiny ball of unending happy who resembled a very small Doberman, with big round eyes and one crooked ear that folded sideways. I picked him up on a chilly Friday night and carried him to our car; he was only three months old and per the quarantine rules his little baby feet couldn't touch the ground. He felt like he weighed nothing.

---

*   Chihuahua-dachshund mix.

†   We rarely got to name our foster dogs, so when we had the option of naming this puppy I gave Addie the honors since he was a purse-sized foster, in her honor. Addie was currently obsessed with the musical *Hamilton* and chose this name in honor of one of her favorite actors in the Broadway production. It was a mouthful and we generally called him "Oak."

The next morning when I opened the door to the puppy pen, Okieriete began to bounce at the sight of me. He jumped up and down in place nonstop, sometimes bouncing so high his head cleared the side of the pen, not unlike a Mexican jumping bean. I closed the door quickly and yelled for Ian, who was the only other person awake. "Come see this!"

Once he stood beside me, I opened the door, Okieriete immediately began his Mexican jumping bean impersonation. We laughed as we started him up again and again—closing the door and then opening it. Okieriete bounced so long, I grabbed my phone and made a YouTube video of it for the blog.

When I tried our smallest collar on him it was like a reenactment of the scene in *How the Grinch Stole Christmas* when the Grinch ties the antlers on his dog and the dog tips over from the weight. The collar weighed as much as he did. As it turned out, Okieriete didn't need a collar anyway; we carried him everywhere. At four pounds, he wasn't a heavy load.

Later that same week, I took a quick trip to Florida to meet with a book club near Tampa to discuss my debut novel, *I'm Not Her*. I was happy to forget about *Girls' Weekend* and dive back into the characters I loved from *I'm Not Her*. It was like visiting old friends; I trusted those characters and the message of that story. The women I met were smart and had excellent questions, but somehow we still ended up talking about my foster dogs. They asked what everyone asked, "How can you give them up?"

"Sometimes it is terribly hard," I told them, and then tried to change the subject. When we started fostering, I never thought about the giving-up part. I was in it to find an animal to keep. But now I had loved and lost over two dozen dogs, what did that say about me? Maybe there is more of my suck-it-up-and-do-what-you-have-to-do mother in me than I realized. My mom grew up poor, the oldest of ten children, in coal-mining country. Even at eighty, she still worked tirelessly to fix, mend, help, and lift up others; always finding a way to make a difference.

"It's terribly hard," didn't begin to explain the giving-up part of fostering, but it was simpler than telling them about the sick feeling I always got in my stomach and how much I wished I could keep each one. And yet, in reality, my pain seemed like such a small price to pay to save another dog. If my mother taught me anything it's that making any kind of difference in this world always requires a sacrifice.

Mahatma Gandhi said, "The greatness of a nation and its moral progress can be judged by the way its animals are treated."

When I read of animals saved by our rescue and others like it, who have been starved, neglected, beaten, abandoned in unsafe places like dumpsters or highways, or worse, I simply don't understand. What kind of person could treat an animal like that? I understand being financially or physically unable to care for an animal, but to intentionally cause it to suffer? Who does that? Why do we stand for it? And what does it say about us as a society?

On several occasions, I've been asked why I don't foster children instead. I know this is a loaded question. It wreaks of judgment. Usually I say, "I couldn't handle it," and leave it at that, but I do know the point the questioner is trying to make. Don't people matter more than these animals? Sure they do, but that doesn't mean these animals don't matter. They absolutely matter. And this is something I can do. I can't foster children for a multitude of reasons that we'd have to discuss over a few hours and a few bottles of wine. But dogs? I can do this.

So, yeah, it does hurt to say goodbye. *A lot.* But that's nothing compared to the pain of doing nothing. I can't do nothing.

I don't think that there was ever a dog happier to see me come home than Meredith when I returned from Florida. She nearly lost her mind—leaping through the air, yelping with joy, only to throw herself on the ground and wriggle around before tearing around the house and repeating the process ad infinitum.

Even when Okieriete's quarantine was over, I hesitated to put the two of them together because I worried Meredith would squish four-pound Okieriete. The energy level alone with the two in one room could power a football stadium. They were the perfect antidote to the winter that wouldn't end.

When he arrived, Oak was frighteningly skinny and had a croupy sounding cough. We kept him sequestered in the puppy room with the baby plants and the humidifier to breathe in healthy air and gain weight. The cough cleared up and he gained enough weight to cover his ribs, but was in desperate need of more stimulation and rearranged his blanket, pee pads, toys, and food/water bowls pretty much hourly. Nick pointed out that the steady micro-activity coming from that room sounded like there was a mouse in the wall. A week into his confinement he began a sad wail that was painful to hear. He wanted out of his prison. There was a whole big world to explore.

When the sun finally peeked out, I fitted Oak with a tiny kitten harness.* Outside, he took his jumping enthusiasm horizontal! It was a very good thing he only weighed four pounds—I couldn't imagine holding on to the leash of a full-sized dog with his enthusiasm!

Oak's history was another mystery to be solved. Thanks to some kind of glitch in his records, I'd been exchanging comical emails with Gina, who was in charge of records, trying to sort out whether Oak had been neutered. I explained that he had no tattoo,† no scars, and no visible "peanuts." It remained to be seen how we would determine if a vet appointment should be made, but Oak quickly grew tired of my investigations.

Not long after Oak arrived, I had a call from Chuggy Alabaster's mom. "He's a little hero," she told me. Chuggy had a fursister named Sail, a rescued greyhound who was elderly and prone to seizures. Apparently, late in the night Chuggy sensed one of Sail's seizures coming on and rushed to Rosie and Jim, jumping on their bed and barking to wake

---

* The same harness Addie had used to show one of our chickens in the Pet Parade at a local festival. The festival in which she won first place (a basket of dog toys).

† Rescue dogs are usually given a green or blue tattoo after they've been altered. It's nothing fancy, just a little slash. I've always thought it should be something more fun, like a smiley face.

them so they could help Sail. In a teary voice, Rosie told me, "We were meant to have Chuggy."

Chuggy's story was not the first story I'd heard of dogs who had some kind of super power, for lack of a better word (or maybe that's the right word). My best friend Linda's teenage daughter was diagnosed with Type 1 diabetes the year before and I'd been hounding her* to look into the diabetes-detecting dogs I'd read about. Samantha would leave for college in a year and having a dog with her who could detect drops in her blood sugar could save her life. Plus, how cool would college be if you got to bring a dog along?

We were nearing our one-year anniversary of this fostering adventure, and fostering had so become our way of life that visitors didn't bat an eye at the keys hanging out of the front door lock (on the outside) because they knew that some of our fosters (Meredith, Tennessee, John Coffey, and Frank) knew how to work a lever handle door. Even if we were only going out for a piece of wood for the fire or to throw some scraps to the chickens, we locked the door behind us.

The stacks of towels, bags of food, and random collars that littered the landscape of our house didn't look so out of place to me anymore. I just dusted around them (if I were to dust).

Best of all, there was no need to explain the random crates, assorted dogs, or that funny smell to anyone who stopped by because they knew all about my dog habit. Fostering began to feel second nature as multiple dogs came and went that spring.

Meredith took off for her forever home and with the help of Chris, an RN, we determined that Oak was indeed intact. In preparation for him to go to his forever home, I took him to the vet for his neuter operation. It was a much simpler process than with the girls and he was back to his bean-dancing in only a few hours. Oak went home later that week to a local family who surprised their excited little boy by meeting him when he got off the school bus with his very own puppy!

---

* So to speak.

Berneen was next to arrive. She was billed as a border collie, but other than her black-and-white coloring she didn't resemble one. She had obviously given birth recently and was still carrying swollen teats and a few extra pounds. She was medium-sized, round, and your basic dog: semi-pointy nose, curving tail, soft brown eyes. There was something about mama dogs. It was as if they knew something other dogs didn't.

I remember a similar feeling after giving birth to my own first born—like I'd entered some kind of secret club. The world seemed a little more complicated, while at the same time what really mattered was much clearer to me. I'd gained perspective. Berneen* had clearly been a mama. Her body would testify to that, but so would her heart.

She spent the first two days with us on the Frank bed unmoving. She lay with her legs tucked under her so that she resembled a furry black-and-white seal. She seemed exhausted, not even raising her head when we moved about the kitchen. I wondered if she was mourning something or someone, or if the last months of being a stray and giving birth and then living in a shelter were very hard, and finally she was in a safe place where she could sleep.

Bernie perked up a little more every day. When I took her outside I caught glimpses of the playful dog buried beneath her solemn demeanor. She'd dash about on the leash, but her excitement never lasted long, ending as suddenly as it started, as if she were embarrassed for her outburst. Bernie landed in a stellar forever home that very next Sunday. Her new family sent me pictures later in the day that showed Bernie (now Zora) making herself right at home.

"This is how rescue is supposed to work," I told Nick as I showed him pictures of Bernie relaxing on the couch in her new home.

With Bernie happily ensconced in her new home, I decided to stop by a local OPH adoption event and pick up another dog from the handful who were pulled from boarding to attend the event.

"You don't want to take a break this week?" asked Nick.

---

* Or Bernie, as we'd taken to calling her, as she was also a bit of a rumpled underdog—like one of the candidates running for president at the time.

"Why?" I asked.

"No reason," he said with a shrug.

It was as if he knew he should protest, but he also knew there was no point. As I drove to York, I wondered if fostering was an addiction. I thought it was puppies, but maybe it was the whole rescuing gig. It felt so good to help a dog and to help a family. A happy drug. I needed another hit.

If OPH had a trademark dog it was "black Lab mix" or BLMs, as I referred to them. The very first dog OPH rescued was a black Lab and rumor had it that OPH's founder was partial to them. BLMs were prevalent in the site's listings most days. Nothing wrong with a BLM, mind you, but I was a hound girl myself.

Catalina was a skinny (seriously skinny), leggy, long-nosed BLM who resembled a German shepherd in her size/shape/nose length, but had the short black coat of a Lab. When I met her at PetSmart, she was nervously guarding her own personal space—happy to meet people, but snarling at dogs that crowded her. Perhaps a week in boarding after a month or two in a shelter had made her a little defensive and suspicious. Who could blame her? Not me, so I hooked a leash on her and carted her home. She shook the whole way.

It didn't take long for her to settle in. She was nothing like the dog I witnessed at the event. She was warm and affectionate, sweet and eager to please. It took less than twenty-four hours for her to go from running from Nick (*maybe she doesn't like men*) to jumping all over him with kisses (*maybe she likes men best*).

Ian thought she looked like Sirius Black when he was in dog form in *Harry Potter and the Prisoner of Azkaban*. I thought she was gorgeous— long legs, shiny coat, sweet face, big smiles.

Catalina was a major fan of the cats, so we nicknamed her Cat.* She kept tabs on the cats' whereabouts and announced any sudden

---

* Also because *Catalina* made me think of the sickly sweet, red-colored salad dressing I used as a kid to cover the taste of vegetables. I could eat anything green covered in that dressing.

moves they made on or off the porch. While Cat was large and leggy and full-sized, if underweight, she was still a puppy, so the chewing damage was major league. The first night she ate a baseball. Like a cat, she was very quiet and stealthy and no one noticed her with the ball during dinner when she was being so well-behaved, lying on the Frank bed. The only reason I knew she'd eaten a baseball was because she barfed it up overnight.

Have you seen the inside of a baseball? Endless white string. The next morning, when I found the mess in her crate, I thought, *Crap, she's got SERIOUS worms.* But upon closer inspection, I realized that there were bits of red leather mixed in and there couldn't possibly be worms *that* long. Hunting around for the one red baseball we possessed confirmed my suspicions. She'd eaten it.

While I was cleaning up the crate and sorting out the barf mystery, Cat removed the butter plate, Ian's cereal bowl, and Nick's coffee thermos from the counter. She licked them all clean and left them on the Frank bed. In the afternoon, she decapitated my car phone charger and ate a portion of the cord. I waited for days and eventually, like the penny one of my kids swallowed as a toddler, the cord worked its way out. Fostering is nothing if not humbling. Certainly, examining excrement for any sign of valuable objects will take you down a peg or two.

"I'm a little afraid to tell you this," said my friend Amy.

"What?" I asked, suddenly worried. I consider Amy one of my closest friends, despite the fact that she lives four hours away. We were having one of our long-distance wine chats—drinking wine while catching up at the end of the day via cell phone. We usually did this when one or both of our husbands were traveling for work and we needed adult conversation.

"We're talking to breeders about buying a puppy," she said.

Amy and two of her kids have severe allergies to dogs. They have to take medication in order to visit my house. They'd tried adopting a rescue dog about six months before but it had been a disaster, despite how much they loved the dog. It was physically impossible for them to keep it and they'd tearfully taken it back to the shelter.

I hated that she thought I might judge her for her decision. I understand why people buy purebred dogs, and I would never presume to judge them, but I thought about my tweets of late. I often ended with #adoptdontshop. Was that a bad thing? Was I unintentionally offending people? I certainly didn't mean to, and I told Amy this now.

"Your kids want a dog. You want a dog. Get a dog."

Sure, I wished they'd been able to adopt a rescue dog; they did too. But it would have been very difficult and because of the unknown factor in any rescue dog's pedigree, it could have ended disastrously once again. Hypoallergenic dogs in OPH get adopted in seconds. Adoption coordinators keep lists of people waiting for one.

When they brought their golden-doodle puppy, Chewie, home, I fell in love with him too. He's a great dog. But now I wondered about my friends who bought purebred dogs simply because they liked purebred dogs. Was there something wrong with that? *Did I think there was?*

No, I decided, I didn't. Responsible breeders were not the cause of dog overpopulation. It wasn't purebred dogs we were pulling from the shelters, not that we didn't get a few. The dogs who were being thrown away in this country were the result of irresponsible people. You want a purebred dog? Get one, and don't apologize for it. Just take care of it. And if you would, have it spayed or neutered. Leave the dog breeding to the professionals.

SIXTEEN

Pup Overload

The email said, "A momma and 3 pups just posted on Facebook."
Mindy knew I was jonesing for some puppies. I checked the
OPH family page. The pups were adorable—barely two weeks
old, their eyes not even open. The mom even looked a little like Lily.

"I'll take 'em," I emailed back.

Yay, puppies for Easter, I thought before remembering that I'm not
the only one who lived here. I went for a bike ride with Nick and broke
the news.

"Puppies? This weekend?"

"Yeah, but only three and they're little guys."

"Well, hopefully Cat will take off this weekend."

"Yup, that's the plan." Cat had approved adopters who were friends
of ours, so I had no doubt that her adoption was a sure thing.

As soon as we got back from our ride, I sorted out the puppy room. I stacked the clean towels and mopped the floor. Then I removed all the accumulated kid flotsam, as the room had been vacant ever since Oak left. I even tidied the "garden." The puppy room was also where I raised geraniums and begonias under lights, and in the spring started vegetables and petunias from seeds. I trimmed up the bigger flowers and pulled all the dead leaves off the geraniums. I made a mental note to look up whether geranium leaves were poisonous to puppies.*

Everything was set. Then I checked my email. There was a message from OPH medical that said my nine puppies would be arriving on the Friday transport accompanied by their vaccines.

Uh . . . NINE?

I knew one thing—the next conversation with my husband would need to take place over a beer. Or several.

It was a beautiful night, so we took Cat and a six-pack and hiked up the hill to our favorite spot to survey the manor. We talked about the garage we were planning to build that summer, the three college boys who were due at our house in a few hours for Easter break, how funny it was that our cat Crash loved to torment our foster dog Cat. We talked about the first-run copies of *Girls' Weekend* I'd received that week that had the pages all mixed up. I suggested maybe the print screwup was a good omen. Kind of like how bad weather on a wedding day was supposed to mean a good marriage. On our wedding day, everything that could possibly fall from the sky fell from the sky, and it had been a pretty stellar marriage for twenty years. It was a nice conversation. Finally, I confessed the news of our multiplying puppies.

Amazingly, Nick laughed when I told him there were going to be a few more than three puppies coming. Six more, exactly.

"Really?" he asked.

"Really."

---

* Yes! They are! The ASPCA says geraniums are fully and totally toxic to all dogs, not to mention cats too. I moved the geraniums to the back of the shelves so there would be no danger of falling leaves.

"How'd that happen? I thought there were three."

I shrugged and waited for him to say something to the effect of, *well, you're on your own with this one. Six puppies was too many last summer. No way am I helping with nine.*

"Well, that should be fun," he said, chuckling. "How is it puppies seem to multiply with you?"

I looked at him—checking for sobriety—and he smiled at me. I squeezed his hand.

"You're pretty great," I told him.

"Why's that?"

"You just are," I told him. See? You really can teach an old dog a new trick.

"So, now instead of twelve dogs, we only have eleven," I explained to my parents when they arrived for Easter dinner. I'm sure I never imagined I'd say that in my lifetime.

Cat had left the day before. Her adoption would make it harder for Nick to get his favorite contractor out here ever again. She was being adopted by Heather, whose other half was Barry, our go-to guy for all matters involving digging, block laying, paving, or moving anything large. He'd built a rock wall, regraded our hillside, yanked out a few trees, addressed our barn flooding issue, and paved our driveway in the past, and now we'd hired him to lay the block and pour the floor for our garage-building project.

Heather met Cat the day she and Barry were here to quote the job. When Heather told Barry she wanted Cat, he said, "But we've almost gotten rid of the kids . . ."

He was a softie, though, so he called a few hours later and said, "What do we have to do to get this dog?" I doubted he'd be in a hurry to come out the next time Nick called him with a job.

Meanwhile, we were getting to know our newest guests. Addie had taken charge of naming them, and came up with a list of cast names from her beloved *Hamilton*. Alexander Hamilton, Eliza Hamilton, Lafayette, Hercules Mulligan, Angelica Church, Maria Reynolds, John Laurens, Peggy Van Rensselaer, and Theodosia were little furballs who swaggered and swayed like tiny, fuzzy drunk sailors as they wrestled with each other and jostled for position at the milk bar named Schuyler. Schuyler was a great mom, even though she seemed to still be a pup herself. Another BLM, she had a sweet face and a white bib and white paws. She was always happy to see me, climbing to her feet to greet me with several puppies still attached. I remember that feeling, that desperate need for adult company. Being the mom to little ones was never easy—whether you had one or nine.

Many times, Gracie was a tough dog to love. For seven years she had rolled in horse manure every chance she got, spent entire days barking at imaginary dangers in our neighbor's yard, and chased the cats. She had never (ever) come when she was called and threatened to take out the poor UPS guy every week.* She had regular barking fits aimed at nothing visible to the rest of us—running up and down the steps, circling the living room, racing from door to door and back to us as if she was clearly trying to tell us something. Nick would tease her, "What is it Lassie? Did Johnny fall down the well?" Whenever I complained about her, the kids came to her defense. They loved her.†

One stormy Saturday night not long after the puppies arrived, Gracie began one of her barking episodes. It was nearly 3:00 A.M. and I was exhausted. I'd stayed up well past midnight waiting for Addie to get home from a cast party thirty minutes away. Worried about the storm, and knowing that she would be high on the excitement of a good show, I tracked her progress on my iPhone and imagined the worst. Even after she made it home, I slept fitfully and it seemed like I had just fallen

---

* She bit the FedEx guy, and now he will only lean out of his truck and drop our packages on our retaining wall.

† They claimed to love her, but were never willing to go track her down in the pouring rain when she'd run through her invisible fence and spent hours wallowing in horse poop.

asleep when I woke to Gracie barking intensely, racing up and down the stairs between our door and the living room. I nudged Nick and got no response. I waited a few minutes hoping Gracie might settle down on her own. Nothing doing, so I dragged myself out of bed and went to see what was up.

Gracie ran down the stairs still barking frantically. I followed her, intending to put her in her crate, but when I reached the bottom of the stairs, I heard it—a puppy wailing.

When I opened the door to the puppy room and turned on the light, all the puppies were up and Schuyler was whining, pacing frantically around the pen. It took me a minute to spot the source of the screaming. Peggy V had her head stuck between the puppy fence and the board we used to extend the puppy pen. The fence is connected to the board by small carabiner clips. I never imagined there was room for a puppy in the small gap between the fence and the board, but apparently there was. Much like a monkey who put his hand in a jar, Peggy had somehow gotten her head squeezed through and when she straightened up and pulled back, it didn't fit back out. She was trapped.

I quickly lifted up the entire fence and board, and slipped her out. Schuyler gave her a complete once-over and then licked her until she calmed and started nursing. I snuggled a few puppies to settle myself down, then barricaded the corner so that no puppies could get trapped before we had a chance to solve the problem in daylight.

I gave Gracie a treat and long talking to, telling her that she was my hero. Had Schuyler gotten too frantic and pushed at the walls of the pen, she could have inadvertently strangled her own puppy. I thanked my lucky stars, the powers that be, and my sweet Gracie who saved the day (night). Then I lay awake for a long time thinking how crazy it was that OPH trusted me to foster these fragile pups, and once again I'd screwed up. I knew I'd never rig up a puppy pen without thinking carefully about how all the panels were connected, but how many lessons did I need to learn? And how many lucky breaks would I get?

I remember having similar feelings when I fumbled with my own babies years ago. Leaving the hospital with firstborn, I thought, *They're going to let me just take him? Shouldn't someone make sure I know what I'm doing?*

But I had help—parents, friends, and books, and while there were a few close calls, my kids all survived toddlerhood more or less intact. I suppose that's the way it's always been. No one can do more than the best they can do. It has to be enough, and thankfully, most times, it is enough. Maya Angelou, one of my greatest writing inspirations died that year, and her words said it perfectly: "Do the best you can until you know better. Then when you know better, do better."

We had five more weeks with these precious babes . . . how would we keep them safe? Now everything looked like a potential choking hazard or a threat to their safety. *Is it too hot? Too cold? Can that one breathe on the bottom of the pile? Is the water bowl too full—could one fall in it and drown? Was that a sneeze?* After the Peggy-stuck-in-the-fence episode, my worrying was ratcheted up a few dozen notches.

Sometimes when the puppies slept, they slept so hard I thought they were dead. SPDS—Sudden Puppy Death Syndrome—is there such a thing?* I didn't know, so I lay a quiet hand on a belly to check for breathing. Lafayette and Peggy slept so deeply they didn't move, even when other puppies trampled them or I lifted their heads trying to get a reaction.

And the laundry! Just like when I had babies and toddlers at home, the laundry was endless. Towel after towel after rag after blanket. Truly unending.

The sounds were also reminiscent of living with babies—there was crying and whining, but there was also that wonderful snuffly sound they made when nursing. They were just learning to work their vocal chords, and the volume and repertoire grew daily.

Probably the greatest similarity was that my days again revolved around poop. Changing the towels, cleaning up the poop, taping down

---

* No, there isn't, but puppies have fragile systems and organs and need proper care and vaccinations. Puppies born in shelters or dumped at shelters sometimes have neither, so they are much more likely to succumb to a preventable ailment than a puppy born to a healthy mother who has received prenatal care.

new puppy pads, only to do it all again twenty minutes later. And just like babies, I'd get the pen all clean, fresh towels set out, clean water bowl filled, and then someone would poop and everyone would run through it.*

Schuyler reminded me of every new, exhausted, overspent mother. She loved her babies, but she was *always* ready to get out of that pen when I appeared with the leash. And then predictably five minutes after we'd been away from the pen, something would trigger her worries—the neighbor's coonhounds baying on a scent, a squabble in the chicken pen, my bad-boy horse knocking over the water trough. Any commotion would have her pulling on the leash back toward the house. She wanted to be certain her babies were okay. Of course, five minutes after she was back, she'd be standing at the gate to the pen hoping I'd happen by with the leash.

As I assisted Schuyler in weaning her own pups, I sometimes wished Nick and I had someone directing the weaning of our own kids. It would be nice to have someone say, "Okay, at exactly 16.75 years of age, your child is ready to drive the car on the interstate in the rain with another passenger whom she might or might not have a crush on. Then at 16.83 years of age, she will be able to . . ."

Teaching them to take care of themselves without me is the ultimate weaning. I want them to become adults who are capable and independent, yet also compassionate and kind. Weaning was a little bit easier for Schuyler as her darlings were penned up in our mudroom. She knew exactly where they were and what they were doing. And she had me—directing her days.

As the pups embraced puppy food, Schuyler seemed less enamored of them and preferred to hang with me when given the option. They were nearly five weeks old and now when she went in the puppy pen, she didn't even lie down to nurse them. She stood there looking mostly miserable until they'd had their fill. She never made herself comfortable.

---

* Okay, my own children never did that—but I do remember that it was usually when they were all clean and dressed in the fancy outfit saved for special occasions when they would have one of those horrifying poop-all-the-way-up-the-back episodes.

She had no plans to stay. Schuyler was ready to move on. It was clear in the way she'd begun straining at the leash to chase after squirrels or deer. She was more puppy than mom when she rolled on the rug, shook the stuffed animals, and attempted to engage Gracie in play.

The puppies began bonding with me the same way my teens preferred their friends over us. Schuyler seemed WAY less upset about her pups moving on than I was. I wished my kiddos clamored for my attention the way Schuyler's pups still whined for her. At the same time, I was proud that my kids needed me so little. That month, Addie went to visit American University without me. This was partly because I was once again writing to another deadline for my third book and partly because she was enamored with the idea of a solo adventure in the city.

Sixteen-year-old Addie drove herself to the metro station in Silver Spring, rode the train into D.C., visited American University, and met up with friends. They rode the metro to a museum and then dinner and then back to Silver Spring, before she drove home. Aside from three or four phone calls (*The parking lot is full! The copier at the D.C. library is out of service! I can't find the admissions building!*), she managed just fine and had a great day. She learned that she could drive on the D.C. Beltway, utilize public transportation, didn't want to attend American University, city food was expensive, and you take Route 83 *north*, not *south*, to get home.

I tracked her with my phone all day long, keeping her activities on the back burner of my mind, but I also trusted that she was capable and smart and independent, so she would be just fine. And she was. She didn't need me and that was a good thing, I reminded myself.

Schuyler seemed to be coming to that same conclusion. Now, when she heard the pups scuffling or whining in the other room, she didn't stand at the gate and whine as she did for the first few weeks of weaning. Instead, she canvased the kitchen for food scraps and begged to go outside. (Or let herself out if we forgot to lock the lever-handle door!)

At six weeks, her pups went from "on hold" to "available for adoption" on the OPH website. They couldn't be adopted for two more weeks, but this was the beginning of the end for me. The hardest part was writing a little "blurb" on each pup for the website. They were *all* cute. They were *all* wonderful. They were *all* the best one. I would keep every single one of them. But we weren't running a dog farm, here, despite what the cats told the neighbors. How could I write nine different descriptions of these sweet little, poopy butterballs?

Not easily. Take Peggy. When the other pups rushed me each time I entered their pen, she hung back. She knew that after I had greeted all the others who simply wouldn't wait as she could, I'd reach for her and snuggle her under my chin, away from the flailing mob beneath. Was she *shy*? That made her sound less attractive. She's *careful*, I wrote.

I wrote nine different descriptions, trying to be honest without throwing anybody under the bus. These were my assessments, but in the end, the kind of dog these pups grew up to be was 90% on the adopter. The pups would need love, that was the easy part, because who *doesn't* love a puppy? But they also needed intentional, consistent training. And boundaries. And good food, not the cheap stuff. And plenty of exercise, socialization, and snuggles. Every one of them could be *the best dog ever*.

Nick petitioned hard to keep Lafayette—the white pup with the solitary black patch over his eye. He tossed out names like Target, Targette (French pronunciation), Spot, and Spanky. Lafayette was a great pup. He had a wonderful sense of humor and could easily be voted most popular in the puppy yearbook. I entertained the idea through one bottle of wine on a gorgeous evening, but later decided, that, no, I didn't have time for a puppy. And if I'd learned anything from my sweet dog, Gracie, it was that I am not a good puppy trainer. No puppies would be staying; that way there would be room for more puppies to come. (Don't tell Nick.)

SEVENTEEN

The Best-Laid Plans

Every day that passed revealed another layer of Schuyler. She was no longer *Mama Dog*, as we'd called her when she arrived with her brood of nine pups. Now she was Schuyler or Sky. Her mothering duties were over and she was ready to be a *dog* instead of a mama. This meant she was tearing up toys/stuffed animals/pens/pencils/egg cartons (plus the eggs inside them—*who left that on the counter?*). She was not just a chewer; she was a destroyer. So far, the saving grace had been Kong toys—she couldn't make a dent in them and was happy to gnaw away for hours in her efforts. As I worked in my office, I could hear the *squeak, squeak, squeak* of her chewing, like sneakers on a tile floor.

When I was asked her breed, I always said "dog," because other than her kind-of-Lab-like appearance there hadn't been anything to suggest a particular breed. Lab mix was the default breed for rescue dogs with short hair, ears that didn't stick up, a curving tail, and a medium-large size. I wasn't suggesting she wasn't Lab, but I could easily have agreed she was nearly any breed you wanted to suggest. If anything, she was a classic mutt. I saw that as just one more of her many attributes.

Like all good mutts, she was devoted. Schuyler *loved* me. Never mind that Nick spent more time with her than any of the other dogs we'd fostered, and suggested almost daily that we should keep her. Schuyler liked him very much, even giving a little squeal when she saw him pull in the driveway. She liked Ian too, greeting him with happy wags when he appeared. She even liked Addie, who took loud offense at Schuyler's friendly, snuffly nose.

But she had chosen *me*.

When I worked in the kitchen, I could feel her eyes following my every move. When I went outside, I had to lock the door because she quickly figured out how to work the lever handle door so she could let herself out to follow me. While I did barn work or garden work, she waited at the kitchen door, watching, vigilant. If she caught sight of me, her excitement spilled over and she would leap at the door. Nick told me that she would jump so high her head reached the top panes of the French door.

She was athletic and getting stronger every day. We'd been running together regularly and she was up to about 3.5 miles. She loved our runs and bounded out the door in the morning, spinning excited circles.

Six puppies left one by one that second week of May, and as they did I felt my energy draining. Were they taking my happy with them? The last few weeks had been a whirlwind of activity and stress in my life—both good and bad.

My second novel was released, and like when *I'm Not Her* was released, I held my breath. I like to tell my creative writing classes that you have to be brave as a writer—you're working without a net. Once a book is out there you can't take it back. And *Girls' Weekend*, more than my first book, laid my heart wide open. I would be judged by the quality of the writing, the story itself, the cover, and the sales figures, but more than that, people would have a view into what went on in my head. If one of my characters cheated on her husband, would people think I had? Or if they had embarrassing personal hang-ups or didn't like their mother, would everyone assume I had these same thoughts and habits? After all, I wrote them. Again and again, at book clubs and at signings, I was asked, "Which character are you?" as if this was an autobiography. I would say, "I'm none of them, but I'm all of them," and I meant it. A writer's stories can't help but be shaped by the experiences she's had and the person she is. As Brady's favorite T-shirt says: *Careful or you might end up in my novel.*

It was hard not to be distracted by the reviews and the comments online. I needed to focus on finishing the latest draft of my next book, but stilling my mind to enter that story wasn't easy.

The weekend after the book came out, Addie competed in the York County Distinguished Young Women program. She'd been preparing for it for months, groaning about the dress requirements—not too much sparkle, a hem that hit exactly below the knee, no excess skin or cleavage. She'd spent weeks working on a speech focused on one issue, only to be informed on the day before the contest that the requirements dictated she talk specifically about a different issue. She'd missed several meetings because she was rehearsing for the school musical, and somehow she'd missed that directive. She had to pull a new speech together in hours.

The physical-fitness portion required that she wear a gaudy, embarrassing outfit with capris and a glittery top, plus black tennis shoes with *NO* label.* It was the sort of outfit she might have swooned over when she was four, but at sixteen she looked and felt ridiculous. The talent portion was the only part she wasn't stressing over. It was the one piece of the competition she would enjoy. She'd wear a gaudy gown she'd found at a consignment shop for a dollar and sing a tongue-in-cheek operatic piece she'd always wanted to perform but never had the opportunity.

---

* This led to Nick shopping for black, ladies tennis shoes at Walmart and then making a mad dash to the rehearsal site to deliver them.

On the morning of the competition, she asked if I would drive her to the venue. I was a little surprised as she had driven herself to every meeting and rehearsal for months. As we drove to York, we talked about the interview portion of the competition. She was the rare teen who paid attention to politics and international news, but still she worried she wouldn't have the answers. I asked her if she'd made any friends during the program and she told me the other girls were nice, but no, she hadn't really made any new friends.

When she got out of the car, I helped her hand off her dresses and the rest of her gear to the volunteers who would take them backstage. And then I hugged her. She held on to me a long time and I could feel the nerves she so rarely showed. "I love you and no matter what happens up there today—I'm proud of you," I told her. I forced a smile. I didn't want her to see that I was terrified for her. She nodded, holding back tears. "And remember," I told her as she started to walk away, "You're just playing a part."

I smiled and drove out of the parking lot, but then had to pull over to cry. I hated leaving her there to be judged. She was so much more than a rehearsed dance number and exercise routine. More than makeup and hair and a just-right dress. I felt jangly all day, imagining what was happening backstage in that huge auditorium. She would compete in the interview portion and then have rehearsals, hair, and makeup before the public portion of the competition that evening. I'd recruited lots of her friends to send well-wishes and gifts that would be delivered backstage an hour or so before the evening's competition. I sent sparkly blue slippers to put on her feet after she took off the painful, proper pumps she was required to wear. I'd done all I could to support her, now I could only hope. I didn't care anymore about scholarships or winning, I just wanted her to feel good about herself when it was over.

Watching her on stage that night, I was incredibly proud, but also terrified and a little bit sad. Just like with my new book, Addie was putting herself out there in the limelight to be judged. My heart broke with her bravery. The contest required her to conform her dress and behavior, and to me it went against so much of who she was and who I hoped I'd taught her to be. My daughter is nothing if not an individual. She had always marched to the beat of a different drum and she'd always been the one to beat that drum herself. I was beyond proud to see her step up to this challenge, but I felt her terror at the same time.

Addie didn't win, at least not on that stage, but to my mind she did. She won over her own doubts and fears. She did something crazy-scary and pushed herself outside her comfort zone. And she inspired me—I needed to stop being such a chicken in my own writing and explore the parts of my heart I held too close, afraid to share, afraid I'd look stupid or silly. Being a true artist requires a level of bravery very few possess. I wanted to be an artist like my daughter.

That week Brady finished his finals and returned from his first year of college, which should have lessened the stress. No more wondering about what he was doing and whether he was taking care of himself. Now he was under our roof again. The first night he was home, I couldn't sleep as I listened to him laughing with friends until late and then pacing the kitchen after they left. Brady's year at college had solidified his nocturnal nature, and the next night Nick put a box fan set on high in our room to muffle the sounds.

The following weekend at a soccer game, Ian sustained a concussion, taking a ball point-blank to the face from an equally large opponent. The referee rightly insisted he go "get checked out," so Nick drove him to a local clinic where it was confirmed, that yes, he did have a concussion. No sports for one week and then a reevaluation.

I'd always worried about Ian's head, now I worried more. Besides having alopecia areata, Ian was prone to migraines. He'd been getting them ever since he'd fallen off a truck (while it was parked) when he was three and suffered a skull fracture. Reading the concussion protocol from the soccer league, school, and doctor caused me to revisit the cause of those migraines. We'd kept a journal of what he'd eaten and done before the onset of each migraine, but we'd not yet been able to find consistent triggers. We'd lessened their frequency by eliminating food dyes, MSG, and artificial ingredients as much as possible, but he still had about four migraines a year. Each one took him down for several days—lying in the dark, vomiting with any movement, miserable. He was starting high school in the fall. Maybe it was time to revisit the neurologist. I wrote myself a reminder note and taped it to the corner of my desk so that I wouldn't forget to follow up amid our suddenly chaotic life.

As the puppies left with their very excited adopters. I made careful notes in my kennel record as to where they went and when they left. There had been a rumor that the dog warden would be coming by for an inspection that week. I kept the puppy pen as spotless as I could, considering there were still three large, busy puppies left, and I quizzed all the kids on where the fire extinguishers were on each floor of our house, as I'd be told that was the most common reason people failed an inspection.

It didn't help that the weather seemed to be stuck in a succession of gray, rainy, cold days. Gray days got to me. That made it very hard to slap on a smile and put up with the daily messes and stresses. I don't know how people manage who live in the Pacific Northwest. Maybe you get used to it. It was May, though, so the gray weather was inappropriate and draining.

As summer bore down on us and regular routines flew out the window, I became absolutely certain of one thing—the presence of animals was critical for my survival. I could not have survived those stressful, gray, rainy weeks without those puppies. Research says that people who own dogs live longer. No less than Harvard Medical School proclaimed that, *Having a pet—a dog in particular—likely lowers the risk of heart disease.*[*] I'm pretty sure it's not just the increased exercise that's so good for your heart.

Six of the puppies were safely set in their forever homes where reports abounded that they were love and adored, and susceptible to car sickness (just like their mom). One of the adopters started a Facebook group for the puppies so they could stay in touch and share their news. The one thing that makes giving up a dog you've spent weeks, sometimes months

---

* Harvard Health Blog, October 29, 2015.

nurturing is knowing that they are safe and happy. Some adopters are good about sending me updates, but many don't take me seriously when I say, "Stay in touch," as they pull out of my driveway. The puppy page on Facebook was a bright spot in my day. Seeing a notification that someone had posted a picture always put a smile on my face, and I took time to look at it, even if I was in the middle of something.

Schuyler was soon to have her spay operation and then she would go home with her forever family who had been following her progress on the blog. Her remaining puppies, Maria, Peggy, and Eliza were all due to go home that week also. The puppy room was emptying out.

Maria's adopter arrived early on Wednesday morning to pick her up. We'd had very sporadic email communication. He was the only adopter who hadn't inundated me with questions and excitement over his impending puppy adoption. I contacted his adoption coordinator and expressed my concern that he wasn't as excited about his puppy as he should be, especially since he was adopting one of my favorite pups. She assured me that it seemed like a good home. There had been some complication and delay in the adoption only because the adopter wanted Maria to be a surprise for his girlfriend, and the adoption coordinator had to say, "No, we don't do surprises at OPH. This is a dog we're talking about. A lifetime commitment." Eventually, the adopter assured her that the girlfriend was in the loop and would be coming to pick up Maria with him.

Knowing this history, I was concerned when he turned up on my porch with no crate, no toys, and no girlfriend. I offered him a towel to cover the seats of his very clean car into which he was about to place Maria for their two-hour ride home. I warned him that several of the puppies had gotten carsick. He chuckled at this. I handed him Maria whom he held awkwardly, as if she might spring a leak at any moment. I asked, "Have you ever had a puppy before?"

"Oh yes, my family had puppies."

I assumed this translated to his mother/father fed-watered-walked-housetrained and cleaned up after the puppy, and he and his siblings played with the puppy. At least that's how it went at our house. Someday my kids would be adopting a puppy and someone would ask, "Have you ever had a puppy?" and they'd say, "Oh yes, my family had LOTS of puppies—hundreds." But would my kids actually know how to care for a puppy? *Maybe.*

After the adopter left with Maria, I emailed the adoption coordinator, "I have a bad feeling about this—can you please check on this puppy?" She assured me she would. I crossed my fingers and hoped I was wrong—dreams and good intentions can only take you so far.

Eliza's adopters arrived that evening and couldn't be more excited or prepared. Such a difference from earlier. They'd smartly come with towels, which was a good thing because Eliza barfed all over her new mommy on the car ride home.

The last puppy, Peggy, left on Friday. Her family brought us a donated bag of dog food as a parting gift. They adored their new girl and we stood in the driveway and fawned over her at length before they loaded her up with the kids in the backseat and took off. We were all especially happy to see Peggy leave as she had cried for nearly two days since Eliza left. I spent the two days typing with Peggy on my lap and learning to do many things one-handed. It brought back memories of when I had a baby in the house.

The puppies were gone and Schuyler was due to leave the next week. I told Nick, "We'll be dog-free by Thursday." Which was perfect because we were due to leave that Friday for Carapalooza.*

But then I saw Debbie's post.

Could somebody take Gingersnap?

I scrolled right past. I couldn't take Gingersnap. I had a big weekend planned. No room at the inn.

But it nagged at me. Gingersnap had been in rescue for ten weeks and had already been in two different foster homes. I knew how hard

---

* And before you think that there is a festival all about me—let me explain. Each May we travel to our beloved Shenandoah Valley, Virginia, to attend a fabulous Wine and Craft Festival in Front Royal. Sometimes other couples join us, sometimes it is just us. My little brother named it Carapalooza because it almost always falls on my birthday weekend.

it was on dogs to readjust to a new environment and everything I read about Gingersnap said she was a sensitive girl who would take those adjustments to heart. If no one stepped up, she would land in a boarding kennel for who knew how long. Debbie was having surgery and could no longer foster her. I looked at Gingersnap's picture again and read the description. I scanned her OPH page. She had no adoption applications. I looked at her big grin and read Debbie's notes. She was excitable and sweet. She was housebroken. She was great with kids. She needed plenty of exercise. A boarding kennel was no place for her long-term.

I mentioned to Nick I wanted to take in another foster. "But she's housebroken and crate-trained. She'll be no work for the kids to look after while we're gone."

He sighed and rolled his eyes, but he didn't say no. It was almost my birthday, after all.

Debbie dropped Gingersnap off on Sunday. She filled the house with her crazy energy and Schuyler was happy for the company. They romped around the kitchen, eventually ending up side by side on the Frank bed chewing tennis balls.

Gingersnap was the same color as my horse, Cocoa—liver chestnut, which is a sort of burnt red, penny color. She was thirty-nine pounds, smaller than Schuyler, but those thirty-nine pounds were all muscle. She was not a quiet dog. In any way. But wow—such a huge heart. Gingersnap LOVED every dog and person she met. She loved them so much she couldn't hold back and launched herself at them, licking faces and wiggling her whole body as if this new person was the BEST PERSON SHE'D EVER MET!

Gingersnap had the same reaction to other dogs. Because of this, she couldn't attend adoption events—apparently, she considered the whole scene one big giant playdate. Not all dogs* wanted a new friend RIGHT NOW. Especially a friend who was extremely physical in her affections and perhaps a little manic. Schuyler, on the other hand, was ripe for a playmate and the two of them spent the week wrestling and

---

* Gracie would be one of those dogs.

chasing and fighting over who got to sleep in the laundry basket (which was too small for either of them).

Despite the manic enthusiasm, or maybe because of it, Gingersnap was my kind of dog. She was misunderstood, but had an enormous heart and brimmed with unbounded personality. She just needed the right adopter—someone who had a serious running habit, a large fenced yard, and/or an enthusiastic canine playmate. I was sure that person was out there and eventually would find Gingersnap. Until then, she'd found a home here.

On Tuesday, I got word that Maria was being returned. I was not surprised by this. The adopters said she was crying and barking too much. *Hello? You just brought home a puppy who left her siblings for the first time—this is what they do.* I was frustrated, but at the same time Wednesday evening couldn't come soon enough. I wanted my puppy safe back in my arms. She'd likely had a confusing and frightening week going from our puppy pen and all her siblings to a solitary life in an apartment with two people who didn't know how to care for her. Upon her return, I lavished Maria with attention. Schulyer did too; they snuggled and played together on the Frank bed. It made my heart happy, but it also complicated things. So much for a dog-free house by the weekend.

Schuyler, Maria, Gingersnap, and Gracie made a colorful, happy bunch. The next morning a Facebook memory popped up in my feed from the year before when we were still relatively new to fostering. It was a picture of me with four dogs the weekend we'd babysat for Kylie and Hitch, and still had Carla. I'm laughing in the picture, amazed that we have four dogs in our care. Now four doesn't seem so crazy. In fact, as we watched our merry band of four, I said, "I like our little herd," and Nick said, "Me too."

When Schuyler was spayed, she'd been tested her for heartworm and had returned questionable numbers. The vet's office sent her blood out for another test and it had come back negative. Heartworm is always a scary thing, but for now, it appeared she was negative. It could stay that way, or the numbers that appeared could indicate she was developing heartworm. Either way, we all breathed a sigh of relief when her adopters assured us that they understood heartworm and were prepared to adopt her no matter what.

On Thursday Schuyler went home to her forever family and soon after, her adopters* posted pictures on the Hamilton Puppy Facebook page. Seeing her happy and settled was the best birthday present I could have gotten.

We were all set to leave for our weekend in Virginia, but first I had to draw up a puppy-care schedule for the kids. I listed "walk puppy" every two hours all day along with "clean puppy pen" and "play with puppy." The schedule was two pages long. It reminded me of when we went away and left the grandparents in charge when our kids were young. I'd drawn up menus and directions and lists upon lists of activities. Looking back, I'm pretty certain they ignored my lists, but I needed to write the lists for me, not them. I hoped the kids wouldn't ignore my lists, but figured they would learn how to take care of a puppy.

On the way out of town, we dropped off Gingersnap at boarding. It would only be for the weekend, I promised her. They wouldn't mind her barking as much as my teenagers would. Plus, I wouldn't lie awake thinking that she'd slipped a leash or gotten out a door or frustrated her caretakers with her endless energy and barking.

---

* Who would keep her name and were now *Hamilton* fans!

EIGHTEEN

Breed Racism

Despite three days of rain, we had a fabulous weekend of fun, wine, and family in my favorite place on earth. As we walked around Front Royal on our last morning in search of somewhere to eat lunch, I tried to picture us living there. My grand plan is to move to the Shenandoah Valley after all the kids are finished college—when we are broke, but still young enough to hike and play. Now I tried to picture our life there with dogs in tow. I briefly wondered if adopters would drive all the way to Front Royal to adopt a dog from me. Maybe we could create custom winery tours as a bonus for adopters. I didn't share any of these thoughts with Nick for fear he would think that the dogs were taking over our lives.

As we were driving home, my cell phone rang with an unfamiliar number. I answered tentatively.

"Is this Cara Achterberg? This is the dog warden."

My heart began racing. When I was growing up, the dog catcher was pretty much the worst bad guy out there—driving around looking for loose dogs to catch. I wrote stories in elementary school about escaping the dog catcher. Once, my brother and I found a stray hound dog. We dug an underground kennel for it near a stream to keep him safe from the dog catcher (and so our parents wouldn't know). The dog hung around a few days and then disappeared. I was certain that the dog catcher got him.

The woman on the phone didn't sound like the kind of person who locked up innocent dogs. She sounded perfectly nice. She informed me that she was sitting in my driveway. I could hear Gracie barking at her in the background, verifying that fact. I hoped the kids had followed the directions on the puppy chart. If they had, Maria should be having naptime in the puppy pen right at that moment.

"Will you be home soon?" the dog warden asked.

I looked at the clock on the dash. "I probably won't be home for a while," I told her. Nick gave me a questioning look. We'd be home in less than thirty minutes, but I didn't know how long she would hang around and I definitely wasn't ready for my first kennel inspection.

The warden said she would try to come back later in the week.

"What are you so afraid of?" asked Nick after I hung up.

"I don't know. She just scares me." We pulled into the boarding kennel to pick up Gingersnap, who went ballistic in the tiny kennel office when she spotted me. Wow, it felt good to be loved at that level (and she'd only known me a week!). Gingersnap was MUCH more enthusiastic about our return than the kids.

When we pulled in the driveway, I looked at my phone. "Chris will be here in ten minutes," I told Nick.

"Who?" asked Nick as he hauled a case of wine into the house.

My answer was drowned out by the squealing of Maria, not at the sight of me, but at the sight of Gingersnap. They rolled and tumbled while I filled Nick in on our newest foster who was about to arrive.

"But we still have Gingersnap and Maria," he protested.

I pretended I hadn't heard him as I carried my suitcase up the stairs. I've found that in situations like this, it's always better to ask for forgiveness rather than permission. And besides, Maria was leaving soon, and Gingersnap would need a playmate.

Sure enough, ten minutes after we arrived home, Chris pulled up the driveway with Fannie. Fannie was a beautiful white-and-tan hound dog who came in on transport Friday while we were at Carapalooza. She was picked up by a volunteer, cleaned up, and taken to an OPH adoption event that weekend before being dropped off with Chris on Sunday to hold for me until Monday when we got home. My network of enablers is very dependable.

Fannie was sweet and cautious, and not quite sure how to handle the exuberance of Maria and Gingersnap or the snarling welcome from Gracie. But she adjusted within the first hour and assumed her role in the pack—watcher. She watched Gingersnap and Maria wrestle and quietly took the toy they forgot about.

Maria was scheduled to go home in a few days to become Lafayette's neighbor. I loved that she would be near her brother, and they would grow up together. Fannie was such a doll baby that I knew she'd be adopted quickly, and she was.* Which left Ginger; we'd all taken to calling her Ginger, except Nick who often called her, Snapper. She still had no applications, but she was an excellent running buddy. I decided we'd stick with just Ginger for a while. She was more than enough dog for me.

Two weeks later, we had friends over for dinner and drinks. Food was fabulous, wine was flowing, kids were enjoying themselves.† Ginger greeted them in her you-are-the-most-exciting-guests-we've-ever-had way. She eventually settled down and observed us from her perch on my favorite lounge chair. Ginger knew getting on the furniture was by invitation only. I raised my eyebrows at her, but let it slide because she rarely left evidence thanks to her low-shedding coat.‡

---

* She was adopted by a local family seven days from her arrival on transport.

† Always iffy when we're talking about teenagers thrown together for the sake of their parents' social life.

‡ A VERY nice change after the run of hairy black Labs we'd had that spring.

It was all going swimmingly until someone commented that Ginger was a pit bull. I don't think it was meant as a slight, but I took it as one. I said, "She's listed as Lab mix on the website."

"I'd bet that dog is 90% pit bull," my guest replied.

I didn't think too much of it, but then I did. *So what if she's a pit bull? Is that really a bad thing?*

All the next day while I gardened, I thought about my own feelings about pit bulls. Not Gingersnap, but *pit bulls*. I didn't know anything about pit bulls. Not really. I knew they were bred for fighting and being a Philadelphia Eagles fan, I'd followed the Michael Vick story like everyone else. When we toured a few shelters before we decided to foster, I was astounded at the number of pit bulls. I didn't want one, but it wasn't because of some personal experience, it was simply their bad rap and the fact that they didn't have long, floppy ears.[*]

Ginger was the first pit bull I'd come to know and love. She reminded me of my beloved Lucy, who was a foxhound and not the least bit pit. Ginger adored me as Lucy had. She was intense and smart, like Lucy was. And she always had a big smile for me, just like Lucy did.

I decided I should learn more about pit bulls, so I looked them up. What I learned saddened me. Of the many, many dogs euthanized each year, the breed most often euthanized is pit bull.[†] Some put the figure at 40% of the dogs euthanized.[‡] This broke my heart. It seemed like a canine form of racism. Dogs unwanted, feared, misunderstood, and euthanized simply because of the way they looked.

---

[*] I have a thing for long floppy ears.

[†] Per ASPCA Professional blog.

[‡] This was cited again and again but I couldn't find an official report giving hard numbers. After reading the data though, it's not hard to imagine that it's accurate, maybe even conservative. One article said that the Humane Society claims 50% of all dogs euthanized at shelters are pit bull breeds, and that 75% of shelters euthanize all pit bulls, regardless of temperament, age, history, etc.

I learned there is Breed Specific Legislation (BSL), laws that make it a crime to own a pit bull. *What? This was a real thing?* As I read, I realized I'd lived up here in la-la land much too long imagining a rainbow world of dog-loving people. I was relieved to know that Ginger and I weren't breaking any laws in York County, still, forty-two of the fifty states have BSLs. Even without a BSL in place, though, some landlords refuse to rent to families who own pit bulls, and some insurance companies deny or cancel home owners' coverage for pit bull owners. No wonder pit bulls so often end up in shelters.

As I was doing all this research, Ginger sat beside me adoring me with her eyes and occasionally licking my leg when she couldn't resist any longer. I couldn't imagine a dog as smart and sweet as Ginger being euthanized.

Just the day before, Addie was explaining to me how Ginger was the best foster dog we'd had and that we should adopt her. She was laying out for me all the reasons, and I was hard-pressed to refute them. At the time, I was sitting at my desk and Ginger was lying nearby, stretched out on her stomach. Addie was sitting in the other chair in my office about ten feet from me. Ginger lifted her head, cocking it to the side as she listened to Addie's plea. Then she began slithering toward her like a snake, pulling herself with her front paws and dragging her body. When she reached Addie, she lay her head on Addie's foot. Her groveling gratefulness was apparent.

At a neighbor's party, I overheard a man talking about an incident in the news recently in which a pit bull had mauled its owner. He categorically blamed the breed for the incident and said no one should ever trust a pit bull. I didn't know the guy, and normally I hold my tongue in these situations, having learned the hard way it's a waste of breath to try to change the mind of person blindly committed to a belief. Particularly a person who has already had several beers. But I thought of Ginger and I couldn't be quiet. Before I'd unknowingly fostered Lily, the rottweiler, no one would have changed my mind about that breed either. So much of our own prejudices about dogs, and probably people, are rooted in a single experience (or a story repeated by a drunk guy at a party). And sometimes, those experiences color future experiences—we see and hear what we expect. It takes a personal experience to change a mind. I was certain anyone who encountered the enormous heart of little Gingersnap would walk away changed.

I was sorely tempted to drive back down the street and grab Ginger, but didn't. Instead, I inserted myself in the discussion by asking the guy for more details about the incident he'd been referencing.

"Did they give you any background on the dog? Or the owner? Had it been trained to fight? Was the owner abusive? Were there any other dogs involved?"

He didn't have any answers, he just shrugged and said, "It was on the news," as if that made it so.

We talked more and I shared my belief that dogs become what their owners make them. They aren't born mean. Just like people aren't. We teach them to hate and fear and not trust. That's our doing. I told them the only dog that had ever bitten me was my own dog and she was a hound. Does that mean hounds are dangerous? No, but dogs and people can be dangerous given the right circumstances. Maybe it was the red wine, but I was on a roll, so I told him about the book I'd just read by Jim Gorant about Michael Vick's dogs. Fifty-one pit bulls were rescued from that operation, but only one was destroyed because it was too aggressive. The rest went on to find forever families and have the lives they were meant to live. And none of them mauled their owners, despite being bred and trained to fight. As I learned with Lily, it's not the dog that has the problem, it's the people.

To the guy's credit, he did say, "You've given me something to think about, but I just couldn't ever own one." And then he excused himself and avoided me the rest of the party. Can't say that I blame him. Like Ginger, when I'm excited about something, I can get a bit over the top with my enthusiasm.

When I got home, I took Ginger for a walk in the dark and wondered how many people were like that guy at the party. Would anyone ever take a chance on her, or would they recognize her pit bull ears and build and face, and click to the next dog?

We all loved Gingersnap. Whenever I made any positive comments about her, the nearest family member would say, "See, we should keep her!" I'd shake my head. I did love Ginger, but her intensity and devotion raised the energy in the house threefold. Choosing to keep her would mean choosing to stop fostering. Nick and I argued this fact again and again, but he knew I was right. We loved dogs and we loved Gingersnap, but she took up all the available dog-space in our home.

"She's the most like Lucy we've had," said Nick in one final plea.

"She is," I told him. "But I'm not ready."

NINETEEN

Vacation

We settled into the knowledge that Gingersnap might be here all summer. It was time to get a new foster dog. I scanned the list of dogs arriving on transport and dogs being returned. Among the returns was Whoopi, an eighty-pound bloodhound. Here was the big dog that Ian was always begging for.

Whoopi was even bigger in person. As her adopter talked to me about the difficult decision to return Whoopi, and details about her likes and dislikes, I simply marveled at the enormity that was Whoopi. All that skin. Hanging everywhere. I wanted to get her a headband for the extra flesh on her face so she could see better. She had a white scar ringing her hips where at some point in her life she must have been caught in a fence or wire, the result now branded her for life. Her long ears had hard, tiny lumps near the edges where shotgun pellets were embedded. I learned that when she came to OPH originally, she was heartworm positive and had been treated successfully. The rescue road had been long for Whoopi and it was far from over.

After the returning adopters left, Whoopi ambled into the house, drool hanging from her enormous snout. I watched as Whoopi shook her head back and forth, batting herself with her mile-long ears, her face literally smacking her face, flinging dog drool on me, the wall, the cabinets, and Ginger who was standing there in awe.

I showed Whoopi to the deck, she glanced around, spotted one of the cats and let out a beautiful hound-dog bay. It was seriously loud. Louder than Carla or any of the other hounds we'd fostered. Ian said later that when Whoopi was barking he could feel it in his chest. Ian and Whoopi spent a lot of time together. This was because he was the only person in the house large enough and strong enough to walk Whoopi without great personal risk.*

As I might have mentioned, we live on a hill. Six acres of lovely countryside, but not a level spot of ground anywhere. Walking up the hill with Whoopi, she made a sturdy towrope and it was fairly easy going. Walking back down was another story. Once she had momentum on her side, I stumbled/ran/skied along behind her like some kind of Looney Tunes character, yelling, WHOA and pulling with both arms.

Once in a momentary loss of sanity, I decided to take both dogs with me on my run. It was a beautiful day and it didn't seem fair to take Ginger and leave Whoopi to howl her disappointment. Whoopi's tail wagged and her snout was high as we set off. I'd barely gone a half mile before I realized I'd made a horrible mistake. It reminded me of a boot camp class I took years ago at the Y in which we had to tow truck tires across a parking lot. This was just like that, only imagine that the truck tires were gunning it in the opposite direction. Each time Whoopi

---

* Ian sprouted up that summer and while he'd just had his fourteenth birthday, he was already six foot, 180 pounds. He'd taken up shot put that spring and had been lifting weights to improve his throw.

bounded off on a scent, I braced myself and yelled, "NO, Whoopi!" Despite my protest, I was dragged forward scrambling to retain control, and poor Ginger was towed along behind me like a toddler with no options.

Miraculously, we made it home, but I felt like I'd run a marathon. Whoopi plopped down on the deck for a nap. Ginger watched me faithfully as I stretched. I stroked her sleek head and wondered if Ginger and Whoopi would still be with us at Christmas. Not because they were bad dogs—quite the contrary—but there were complications involved with either of them finding a forever family.

Whoopi was a hit at events. Bloodhounds are notorious. We smile at the sight of them—picturing a big droopy dog lounging on the porch of a falling-down house while a hillbilly sits beside them guzzling moonshine and cleaning his shotgun. I took Whoopi to a large pet festival at a nearby college and everywhere we went people smiled and pointed—"Look at the bloodhound!" Whoopi drew loud cheers in the Pet Parade dressed as a butterfly.

Everyone loved her, yet no one filled out an application for her.

But that was the thing—Whoopi was not an impulse buy. She needed a hound person. If you've ever met a hound person, you know what I mean. These are people impervious to drool, who instinctively keep their counters cleared of any food items and store their open bag of chips on top of the refrigerator. They take no issue with sliding glass doors snotted up at eye level. And when they hear a hound let out a long, loud bay, they say, "Isn't that gorgeous?" instead of, "Will somebody shut that bleepin' dog up?" They are in awe of a dog with the ability to sense a dropped cheese curl at fifty paces or the trail of a chipmunk who sauntered through the yard several days ago. Whoopi needed one of these people who would offer her the room to run and the freedom to sing when inspired.

Gingersnap was lingering at our house for entirely different reasons. I hadn't witnessed her at an adoption event, but I had taken her to enough of Ian's baseball games to know that would be a disaster. She loved the excitement of the crowd *too* much. So much she couldn't help but shout about it—nonstop. And she loved meeting new people. In fact, she felt the only appropriate response to new friends was to jump on them and lick their faces. Not everyone welcomed a facebath upon introduction.

She also loved meeting other dogs, but she was that party guest who was still dancing on the tables when everyone else was looking for their coats. She couldn't tone down her enthusiasm and was never deterred by a growly new friend. So, I could only imagine how an adoption event would go. There would be people and dogs everywhere. It would be simply too much for the sweet girl. She was a lot like John Coffey, the maniacally happy, people-loving foster dog we had back in the fall who also couldn't attend adoption events due to his enthusiastic nature. John Coffey ended up in the perfect forever family, so I had to trust that Ginger would too. Still, because she couldn't attend adoption events and meet potential adopters, the only way her forever family would find her was through the OPH website.

The problem with that, though, was most people who paged through the website made their decisions based on pictures. And getting a good picture of Ginger was not an easy thing. She was in near constant motion, and when she wasn't moving it was because she was sleeping. She wouldn't hold still and sit pretty for the camera. What would be the fun in that when she could be licking the legs of the camera person or chasing down the butterfly that just passed by?

And more than that, her funny, sweet personality was difficult to capture on film. For instance, the night before she was chasing fireflies. Totally adorable. But was there really any point in taking a picture of a brown dog at night?

The next Saturday we were headed to the beach for a much-anticipated vacation. I could hardly wait for an entire week with two of our favorite families and most, possibly all, of my kids. Yay. No stalls to muck or weeds to pull.

But there was a problem: I still had Ginger and Whoopi. At first I considered leaving them with our house/horse sitter; after all, we were paying her, right? But while I was fairly certain she liked animals, it seemed unrealistic to expect her to deal with an eighty-pound blood-hound with an impulsive nose, a maniacally enthusiastic face-slurping pitbull, and a snarly, grumpy, poop-rolling Gracie *at the same time*. No, I couldn't ask this of my nice college-age house sitter who thought she'd been hired to care for the horses and water the plants.

I was all set to send them to the boarding kennel, when an adopter for Whoopi appeared out of thin air! Now, sure, several others had backed out once the idea of an eighty-pound pet with an overactive nose and a drool setting had sunk in, but maybe this was karma finally paying me back. Maybe Whoopi's forever family had finally found her. And then I checked Ginger's OPH page and *what*? Applications! Somebody/somebodies wanted Ginger?!?!! Yay Gingersnap! She'd been almost adopted too many times for me to count those chickens, but I did it anyway.

The reality of one or both being adopted before we left in four days was beyond even my optimistic nature. Applications were not processed overnight. References had to be checked, questions asked, interviews given. This takes time.

I packed and planned and worried. Another foster, Juanita, who lived just north of us, volunteered to take Whoopi while we were on vacation. Ginger, though, would have to go to boarding. The idea that they might be adopted while we were gone was hard to bear. I acted all tough and I'm-not-keeping-them most of the time, but Ginger was another story. Not being able to say goodbye would be awful. She'd wormed her way into our hearts, mine especially. Even Addie, who generally tried to ignore the foster dogs and actively campaigned for switching to fostering cats, was still pleading for us to adopt Ginger.

"I think this is the best one we've had," Brady said, after once again arriving home from working in the deli at Giant, smelling like fried chicken, only to be tackled by Ginger who proceeded to lick him head to toe—and not just because he smelled of cold cuts. She LOVED him.

And he loved her. Ian liked Ginger too. He enjoyed picking her up and cuddling her as if she were a lapdog.*

As we talked about our predicament, Nick looked at Ginger, smiled, and said, "If only you didn't bark." She had interrupted more than one conference call. And me? I loved that dog. The idea of Ginger going to boarding and then being adopted without me just about killed me.

By Thursday it was apparent that no adoptions would be taking place anytime soon. I made arrangements to send Whoopi to Juanita's. Juanita had a fenced yard and several personal dogs of her own. More than that, she had an enormous heart. When she heard that Ginger was going to have to go to boarding, she emailed and said, "I think I could try taking both of your dogs."

"You are the very best," I told her.

She picked up Ginger for a "test run" to see if she could handle her high energy and to see how she was with her three personal dogs (two of which were pit mixes and the third was a blind and deaf mastiff). Ginger hadn't been gone more than an hour when Juanita texted, "She is NOT going to boarding. She's 150% love. She fits right in."

We took off for vacation comforted by the knowledge that both Ginger and Whoopi would be safe and happy at Juanita's Puppy Palace. Meanwhile, the applications that looked so good earlier in the week faded away like all the others.

When we returned from *our* vacation, I picked up Whoopi and Ginger from *their* vacation. They were tired, fat, and happy—the way everyone should be when returning from vacation. While we were gone they'd been spoiled rotten by Juanita. They'd had free run with her pack in her big, shady, fenced yard; they were allowed on the bed for naps, and even had a doggie swimming pool to cool off in.

---

* I guess to a person of his size, she was a lapdog.

Ginger's chocolate coat was shiny and sleek, and with the extra pound or two she'd picked up on vacation, she looked even more like a seal. Whoopi was sporting an extra roll around her shoulders. Ian lifted a few of her layers and said, "You could fit another dog in this dog."

Whoopi and Ginger seemed happy to be back with us, despite the downgraded accommodations. Back to wearing leashes. Back to being stuck in the kitchen. Back to snarly Gracie-dog ignoring them. Back to being hissed at by unappreciative cats. Back to being shrieked at for licking passing legs and hollered at for barking at the squirrels they were not free to chase.

While we were on vacation, I had watched online as Whoopi's status went from *Adoption Pending* back to *Adoptable* and then *Adoption Pending* again. The new adopters had emailed me with questions and were planning their trip to come meet her—driving all the way from Rhode Island! Everyone was now holding their breath, hoping this was the one.

If there's one thing I'd learned about the whole fostering and adoption process, it's that the right family *would* eventually find these dogs. I'd seen it happen again and again. I remember thinking no one would ever adopt Carla and she landed in the perfect setup—in Indiana! And John Coffey? Same. Latest reports were that he was happy and healthy and very much appreciated in his forever home and still catching balls like a champ. Probably the one dog I worried the most would never be adopted was Hadley. And even Hadley found her person.

When friends asked, "You *still* have those dogs?" I'd say we were just babysitting while Whoopi and Ginger's future forever families were on vacation. They'd come for them soon, I wrote on my blog; I was certain. But what IF Ginger and Whoopi's families never materialized? What then?

TWENTY

Making a Difference

Whoop! Whoop! Whoopi found her forever family! She left early on a Sunday morning for the six-hour drive to her new home in Rhode Island! By Monday we were already hearing how happy she was in her big fenced yard near the seashore with her two new fursiblings.* It was a great story that made my heart very happy. I did have to admit, though, it was also nice to finally wash our slobbered windows and not have to jump out of the shower and run downstairs in my towel because I remembered I'd left the butter plate on the counter.

Ginger was still with us, with no adopters in sight. Ian said, "Maybe no one will adopt her and they'll forget about her and we can just keep her."

---

* Wiener dogs—I mean dachshunds! Can you imagine the trio they make?

"Probably not," I told him.

When Brady filled up our kitchen with college-age boys,* Ginger lay among them, licking their toes and waiting for the occasional treat. She was one of the gang.

I didn't bother with a leash when we went out anymore. I knew she wouldn't leave me. She loved me too much. Sure, she'd get that cat up in the tree for me, but then she'd be right back. She did indulge in occasional staring contests with the chickens, and I was guessing if given access to them she might have taken it a step further, but she respected the fence that separated them.

One morning I overslept, a rarity as I was normally up with the sun and hadn't used an alarm clock in years. Nick was the first one downstairs, and as soon as he let Ginger out of her crate, she bounded up to our room, leapt on our bed, and woke me with kisses. What a happy way to join the world. The more I thought about it, maybe Ian was right. Maybe it would be best if no one adopted Ginger and she just stayed here indefinitely.

I found it kind of telling that Ginger had lived in four foster homes in her nearly five months in rescue and every single foster family wished they could keep her. Her first foster mom stopped by to visit her the week Whoopi left. Ginger hadn't seen her in almost three months, but recognized her immediately—leaping and squealing with delight and covering Christine with nonstop kisses.

Her second foster mom had to pass her along to me because of impending surgery, but while she recovered she was acting as the adoption coordinator for Gingersnap, and every time I saw her she said, "We miss Ginger so much. Our house is just not the same."

And then there was Juanita, Ginger's temporary foster mom, who confessed, "I would totally foster fail with her if I didn't already have three dogs."

She was *that* special—and yet she still had no adopter, and of late, no applications. I really didn't understand it. The only explanation was

---

* *Boys* who were technically *men* except I'd known them since they dressed up in Harry Potter costumes and cast spells, so they would always be *boys* to me.

her pit bull appearance. How was it our world had still not gotten past appearances? Would we always judge a book by its cover?

That same week, ironically, I was wrangling with my publisher over the cover for my next book. It was hard to pick one image to sum up the complicated story I'd written. The cover was critical, though, it could compel readers to pick up my book or put it down. We had to consider every angle. Is a door just a door? What does it matter if the tree has fresh spring leaves or a splash of fall color? My ideas and his didn't mesh so we went back and forth again and again with images. I was waiting for him to say, "Okay, never mind, it's not up to you anyway." In some ways that might have made it easier. The picture was important, though, so I wanted my say.

This made me wonder what people thought when they saw Ginger's picture. Could they get past the appearance of pit bull to see the crazy-cool pup we loved so much? I tweaked her description again and again. Did *high energy* make her sound dangerous? Sure, she was excitable— prone to slurping on faces and jumping on clean clothes. But this was only because she was—as Juanita had put it—150% love.

Early on a warm July morning, I joined several other OPH fosters from PA and headed to a gathering for OPH volunteers at a brewery in Maryland. We weren't going for the beer, but to learn more about OPH and what we could do to save more dogs. I was excited to meet some of the people I knew only via Facebook.

I discovered that most people look nothing like their Facebook profile pictures, but then again, don't we all put our best faces forward on Facebook? Blond, charming, and passionate, OPH's founder Jen explained the history of OPH—starting with driving south in the family minivan to bring a handful of dogs north until now, six years and six thousand dogs later. As she told of the conditions in the shelters, I blinked back tears. She introduced other members of the board and guest speakers including a couple whose local organization provided dogs for veterans with PTSD. They specifically sought out rescue dogs and had brought two former OPH puppies with them. I learned what signs to look for in the puppies I fostered that might indicate they would make a good service dog—people-oriented, treat-motivated, and smart.*

Two women from Scott County, Virginia, one of the OPH partner shelters, were introduced. I went to school in southside Virginia a million years ago, so I remembered that part of the country as rural, blue-collar with field after field of tobacco. As a college student, I worked at a pub in Danville and waited on mill workers who called me "Yankee Girl" and never missed an opportunity to remind me that Danville was the last Confederate capital of the South. I can only imagine how the economy of that area has declined with the shuttering of textile mills in favor of foreign production and the decreasing demand for tobacco.

Rachel and Ashley didn't look like the image I'd had in my mind of the employees in the desperate shelters that euthanized so many dogs. They were young, articulate, and Ivory-girl beautiful. The heartbreak they faced on a daily basis was clear as they stood before us and shared their story.

The tears I'd been holding back all morning flowed down my face. I glanced around at the room full of mostly women with big, dog-filled hearts and tear-streaked faces. OPH began partnering with the Scott County Humane Society shelter in mid-2015. The impact that we'd had on Scott County was astounding:

Euthanasia Reports and SCHS Rescues Since 2013
2013—*355 dogs euthanized (68%), 42 dogs rescued*
2014—*245 dogs euthanized (65%), 38 dogs rescued*
2015—*66 dogs euthanized (18%), 197 dogs rescued*
2016 (6 months)—*euthanasia less than 3%, 95 dogs rescued*

---

* I did think to myself as I heard this, all my puppies had been people-oriented and treat-motivated, the smart part, however, wasn't always clear.

I'd had the privilege of fostering quite a few dogs from Scott County—the Pooh litter (Chick Pea, Jillie Bean, Boz, Homeboy/girl, Lug Nut, Marzle), Texas and Tennessee, Chism and Charm, Okieriete, and most recently, Fannie.

Clearly, rescuing dogs was not for the faint of heart. On my blog, I sometimes droned on about how hard it was on my own heart, but as I listened to these remarkable young women, I realized that they were far stronger than I'd ever be, and the little bit of bruising my heart took when I said goodbye to my foster dogs was nothing like what they'd endured as they witnessed who left through the front door of the shelter and who left through the back.

All the next week, I thought about the words I heard from Rachel and Ashley, and it made me less apologetic about my crazy house with the dog crates and the stained carpet and the baskets of dog toys and the baby gates. What we were doing was important. It was having an impact. It was making a difference.

"We're never going to adopt a dog, now, are we?" asked Nick, as I told him about Scott County.

I didn't know the answer to that question, so I said, "We have lots of dogs."

"True," he said, and left it at that.

Our next foster was a puppy named Little Lady. We renamed her Bambi because of her stick-like legs and fawn coloring. She even had white spots on her back near her tail. She was a greyhound mix and only six months old. Nick went with me to transport that night. When we pulled into the bowling alley parking lot, I jumped out of the car.

"You gonna go talk to your crazy dog people?" he asked.

"Yup," I told him, "They're my people."

When Bambi was unloaded, Nick clipped on her leash and tried to walk her, but she froze like a statue and refused to move. At home, I pulled her out of her crate and set her on the grass. She flattened herself against the ground, shaking. I peeled her off the ground and put her in a crate in the puppy room, deciding it was probably best to avoid Gracie's regular less-than-warm greeting and Ginger's overbearing enthusiasm.

The next day, I sat down outside Bambi's crate, and she cautiously crept out. She leaned into me, pressing her long nose against my side, wagging her backside. She had only a stump for a tail. Was it docked or was she born like that? No one knew. When I picked up a leash, she scrambled back into her crate, so I sat back down and waited.

This time, after she again climbed into my lap, I picked her up, snapped the leash on, and carried her outside. When I set her down in the grass, she repeated the behavior of the night before, pressing herself against the grass as if trying to disappear. When she did move, it was to sprint for "cover" (a bush, the tree line, etc.). She was a speedier version of Hadley.

Realizing that peeing was out of the question, I carried her back inside and set her up in the puppy room with puppy pads and toys. She took each toy I handed her and piled it in the back of her crate. We hadn't had a hoarder like that since Stitch.

Ginger and Gracie were curious about the new guest, but I kept them away. As the weekend wound down, Bambi improved only a little. Her big eyes wanted to trust and she eagerly climbed into our laps when we visited her in the puppy room. When I picked her up to take her in or out, she scrambled over my shoulders so that sometimes I was wearing her like a greyhound boa as we headed in or out.

"She's pretty freaked out," observed Ian.

Bambi wasn't nearly as shut down as Hadley had been, at least Bambi welcomed our attentions—on her terms. All she needed was a little patience. We could be patient.

And then . . . I got an email about a dog dumped on the side of the highway in southern Virginia who looked like she could be pregnant. Could I take her? Silly question.

But what to do about the puppy in my puppy room? If this stray dog was pregnant, I'd need that space. Bambi seemed to be relaxing in the puppy room, bounding out of her crate when we entered, but still terrified to walk out of the room on a leash. I decided to move the crate to the kitchen. She could watch the action from her safe place and the puppy room would be free, just in case.

Nick didn't argue when I told him about our new foster. He knew there were too many signs. I'd been wanting to foster a pregnant dog. I'd always wanted a Treeing Walker Coonhound. And if that wasn't enough. Her name was Lucy.

"But what about Bambi?" was his only question.

"I can deal with it," I said, as if I believed that.

The Lucy Train was coming in two days. She would be transported northward through a series of volunteer drivers from Wise County, VA, to Staunton, VA, and then from Staunton to Strasburg, VA, and then from Strasburg to Hagerstown, MD, where I would pick her up. She wasn't coming from one of our regular shelters or regular transports, so this was all new to me. Everything was coordinated via Facebook. It seemed to me modern dog rescue couldn't happen without Facebook.

Once installed in the kitchen, Bambi refused to leave her crate. Not wanting to push her and knowing she would eventually have to leave the small space to eat and drink and pee, I left her alone. I placed a bowl of water and some food just outside the crate, far enough away that she'd have to physically step out of the crate to reach them. I put a puppy pad nearby too. We kept Ginger out of the kitchen. She wanted so badly to play with the new puppy, but she made do with Gracie.

Bambi watched us from her crate. She accepted our touch when we crouched down and reached into her crate, but refused to follow us out.

"What if she pees in there?" asked Ian.

"I don't think she will," I told him. "She'll come out soon."

Thirty-six hours later, she had yet to leave the crate. I was amazed a dog could go that long without drinking or peeing. Finally, early on the morning that the Lucy Train was due to arrive, I saw her standing at the open entrance of the crate, looking longingly at the water dish. She leaned out of the crate toward the bowl, almost falling forward out of the crate before retreating back inside.

Next, she placed one paw gingerly outside the crate and touched the floor briefly before snatching her paw back inside again. She did this over and over as if testing the surface to be sure it would hold, and then she found her bravery and took the few steps to the water bowl. Her hind legs remained in the crate and she stretched her body to reach the bowl and drink. I wanted to rush to the crate and give her treats and congratulate her. Instead, I stayed on my side of the kitchen. This was her battle; she had to conquer this fear on her own if her confidence was to grow.

Just before we left to meet the Lucy Train, Brady said, "Hey, look!" and there was Bambi, standing outside her crate. She was smiling; her stumpy tail wagged ferociously.

"Good for you!" I told her and she scooted back inside the crate. I refilled her water bowl and gave her a treat before heading out the door to drive to Hagerstown.

My trusty copilot* and I were early when we arrived in Hagerstown to meet the Lucy Train, which was a good thing because it was running well ahead of schedule and Lucy and her chauffeur for the last leg of her trip were waiting in the parking lot of an Olive Garden restaurant. When I opened the back of our Pilot, she hopped right in, settled in the crate we'd brought and went to sleep. Obviously, she wouldn't be a high-maintenance guest.

This poor pup had clearly had a rough life, to date. She was riddled with scars, the worst one being a permanent pink necklace from where a collar had embedded in her neck. Her skin was inflamed and hot and covered in bumps and oozy patches. The vet in Virginia had diagnosed a flea allergy dermatitis, but because of the possible pregnancy, hadn't given her any drugs. The poor girl looked miserable.

When we arrived home, Bambi was a new dog, careening around the kitchen in her excitement at seeing us. Lucy greeted her and they did a few laps around the island before settling in to wrestle over the small stuffed pumpkin toy that was in Bambi's transport bag. The party was much too big to keep Ginger away and she snuck through the gate at the next opportunity. It was quite the dog party. Obviously, Lucy would fit in just fine.

---

* The only kid without a driver's license or a job that summer.

ANOTHER GOOD DOG

Thankfully, she didn't appear to be pregnant. As exciting as that would have been, the last thing Lucy needed was puppies. Lucy was a happy, friendly, easygoing girl despite her rough past and her present misery. The resilience of dogs was, once again, something to behold.

Lucy's dermatitis required us to keep a cone of shame on her head 24/7 so she wouldn't chew herself bloody. I gave her an oatmeal bath and my sympathy, but there wasn't much else I could do for her. We made an appointment with the vet a few days later to confirm that she wasn't pregnant and hopefully get a prescription for some serious drugs to help her out.

Lucy, it turned out, was unflappable, taking the inconvenience of her cone in stride. When the cone got caught on a chair or the doorway, she simply backed up and tried again. As I worked in the kitchen, she stayed close in hopes that I might drop whatever I was cooking. The cone poked at my legs, incessantly. I wanted to grumble at her to stay out of the way, but that seemed cruel since she couldn't help it.

She was a sweetheart with a hound smile and a playful nature, racing around the kitchen, banging into cabinets with her cone. Just like Gracie, she loved to shake the stuffed animals to *kill* them and then rolled on them once they were *dead*. Bambi and Ginger adored her and the kitchen was nonstop playtime. Occasionally Bambi grabbed the edges of Lucy's cone and yanked. Lucy waited patiently for her to let go and if she didn't, she just dragged her along for the ride. Ginger dodged the cone whenever possible, but otherwise was unfazed by Lucy's enlarged head.

Bambi zipped around with greyhound speed and Lab curiosity. After five days of refusing to leave her crate, Bambi was never again happy to be relegated to it. When I put her in her crate for morning naps and at night for bed, she had to be lured in with a treat. She barked at anyone who passed by, wagging her whole body and banging the crate sides, inviting them for a playdate. Outside she leapt and jumped like the fawn we'd named her after—bucking her leash and tearing in circles.

Nick watched her sprint by with a potholder in her mouth and asked wistfully, "What happened to the quiet dog cowering in her crate?"

213

TWENTY-ONE

Falling Down on the Job

'd fallen off plenty of horses in my time and rarely incurred an injury, but now falling hurt more. In fact, I was actively looking for someone to take my horse, True, on a long-term lease, as he was much too eager to land me on my butt. Seeing him in the pasture, doing nothing except irritating my two older mares and dumping the water trough out of boredom, plagued me with guilt. It was time to find him a job, and so that week I signed a contract to lease him to a young woman who was excited at the prospect of my big, gorgeous, playful boy moving into her field. To my mind, he was going to a foster home. He'd be back someday and hopefully by then; he'd have gotten out all his bucks. No more falling off horses—if only I could say the same about dog-induced falls.

In the eighteen months we'd been fostering dogs, I'd fallen down a lot. I'm not talking in terms of the direction-following screwups or the emotional breakdowns, there were plenty of those. I'm talking about actually hitting the dirt, physically.

Carla was the first foster dog to knock me over. She darted in front of me while we were running, taking me out like a football player making a clean block. Luckily (for me) she broke my fall. I only suffered a few scratches.

Then Frank pulled me over twice. When he slipped into the chicken pen as I was closing the gate, I chased after him and stupidly grabbed his collar while he was in full flight. You can imagine the rest. A skinned elbow and bruised knee were penance for my bad decision.

The second time Frank got me, I was walking down our steep hill in smooth-soled shoes and my feet slid out from under me. I'm not sure he had anything to do with that fall other than happening to be on the other end of the leash when I clumsily lost my footing. The result of that fall was only a few grass stains.

Tennessee took me out while running. Something behind us startled him and he panicked, slamming into me from behind and sending me sprawling. I ended up with two skinned knees and one skinned palm on that one.

After that I had a long run of not falling over, nearly a year, and then Whoopi yanked me over time and again when her bloodhound nose picked up a scent and I couldn't keep up. I did a lovely belly flop on the grass, skidded across the driveway landing on my elbow, and more than once went waterless-skiing down our hill, before turning over Whoopi-walking duties to Ian.

But on a clear and uncharacteristically cool Monday night in July, I hit the ground again, only this time I didn't get up. I was walking Bambi and Lucy at the same time in wet grass, in the dark, in sandals, down the hill. So, you can already see all the mistakes I made going into this. The two of them both lunged forward at the same time. I think Bambi was only excited, as she was a puppy, and I believe Lucy, who was not a puppy but had a puppy-spirit, simply joined in the fun.

They bounded forward suddenly and I slipped on the wet grass. I landed sprawled with my leg bent underneath me in a painful position. I didn't let go of the leashes and my screaming brought both dogs back to kiss an apology all over my teary face. Nick came and grabbed the dogs.

As I lay there waiting for him to return to help me, I was overcome with multiple thoughts. The first thought was probably not one that would be appropriate to share here, but suffice it to say, I was just SO MAD. Not at the dogs, but me. How could I have survived so long on this planet and not have learned a little common sense? What made me think I was invincible? Basically, how stupid could I be? And then I thought—*this just* cannot *be happening. I* cannot *be hurt. I have no time for this.*

Sadly, I couldn't will away my pain, though I tried. Instead of going for medical help, I insisted on waiting it out a bit. I popped a handful of ibuprofen and then took the pain meds left from Brady's recent wisdom teeth removal, and finally slept with my knee wrapped in ice and elevated on a pillow.

In the morning my knee seemed doubled jointed. I was pretty sure if I tried I could bend it both ways. So off to the local ortho clinic we went. I came home with a stack of prescriptions, sporting a stylish brace, and praying that when I went for my MRI later in the week the doc would say, "Why no, your meniscus is not torn. In fact, here, let me give you this pill that will make you all better by tomorrow."*

With the brace on, I was semi-stable, but it was the perfect excuse to get someone else to walk a dog for a change. The other positive of the knee debacle was that upon seeing my X-rays, the doc said, "You have beautiful knees." He wasn't hitting on me, but he was impressed that my knees had no arthritic changes or obvious wear and tear on the bone structure. This was AWESOME news. Both of my parents had recently had knee replacements. People, mostly nonrunners, were always telling me that running would ruin my knees, but see? Despite

---

* Remember, I write fiction for a living.

genetics and a long-term running habit, I was bucking the odds. I had *beautiful knees.*

Bambi went home that week with a family who had experience with greyhounds and a little girl who was in love. I smiled as she raced in circles around them, jumping on her new family. *Who was that dog?*

A few days later, Ian went with me to take Lucy to the vet. I needed his assistance lifting her in and out of the car as my knee couldn't be trusted. The vet confirmed that Lucy was not pregnant, and prescribed an antibiotic to help with the itching, along with a medicated shampoo. She told me the oatmeal baths I had given her were not helping; in fact, they were probably making it worse. Yay me. I scheduled Lucy for the first available spay appointment so that we could get that girl ready to be adopted.

As I've said, I have a fondness for hounds, but Lucy's houndness was wearing me out. Her energy and her need to sniff was making walking her a chore. She had a very hard time leaving scents lie so that she could take care of her potty business, and consequently walking her consumed hours of my day. Add to that the insatiable appetite, hardcore counter-surfing, and one serious cupboard raid, and my fondness for hounds was diminishing daily. Her beautiful bay wasn't so beautiful at five in the morning or all afternoon while I was trying to write.

And then the day finally came for Ginger to leave. I felt unprepared. Every other time when a dog was leaving, I had a plan in place. A new foster on its way or already in our house, or I had somewhere to go or be that would distract me. Not this time. I was still waiting to see a doctor who would have the answers about my knee, so I couldn't commit to a new dog. I wasn't a good patient or a patient person, so my hurting knee was dragging me down. Lucy was still here, but to my mind, it was well past her time to leave.

Without my usual props in place, I felt the tears gathering as I waited for Ginger's adopters to arrive. This was the hardest part of fostering. The heart-cratering pain that was so completely avoidable—*if* I just didn't foster dogs. If I could just commit to adopting one, I could stop fostering and avoid this self-inflicted, preventable pain, and yet I kept setting myself up for it. I limped around the yard, watching Ginger and wondered if maybe I'd had enough.

My bum knee had forced me to slow down and I'd finally gotten around to reading the book so many people had recommended to me, *Rescue Road* by Peter Zheutlin. It's the story of a man named Greg Mahle who drives a tractor-trailer full of rescue dogs twice a month from the Deep South to foster homes and adopters in the North. He'd helped rescue over thirty thousand dogs and had driven a million miles. I was trying to read it as fast as I possibly could because it was unbearable. Peter shared Greg's stories of the dogs he drove and the people he met. Every time I closed the book and moved back into my world I felt sad, unmoored, frustrated. How could there be people in this world, in this time, who would dump a litter of newborn puppies in a trashcan, or worse yet, set that trash can on fire?

How could there be state-run "shelters" that were no more than concrete holding pens completely exposed to the elements, where dogs were dumped all together (young, old, sick, neutered or not) to wait for no one (or maybe a rescue) to claim them before they died of preventable diseases or state-mandated euthanasia? The book broke my heart. Gone was my feeling of euphoria a month ago. Gone was my hope that we could make a difference.

Nick didn't say anything, just listened when I shared the stories I was reading. He said nothing when I lamented how impossible the situation was and how hopeless I felt. There were too many dogs dying every day because of ignorance, cruelty, apathy, and lack of resources. The maddening part was that this was a fixable problem. The Scott County shelter had proven that. Maybe that's what made me most crazy. Parvo, mange, heartworms, overpopulation—these were all preventable or treatable.

"Everything will seem better when your knee is back in order," Nick wisely said, but I didn't believe him.

All my mixed feelings and sadness was complicated by the fact that my knee was not healing. It limited me. Just that morning I fell, once again. Even though I had on my brace and my new super-grippy-but-incredibly-ugly shoes that Nick insisted I buy, my unstable leg still slid out from under me on a stick that fell in the storm the night before. Ouch.

And then there was Lucy.

As I read about these dogs that were used and thrown away, I pictured Lucy. I didn't know her whole story, but there was no doubt that she somehow escaped a life of neglect or possible abuse. She had given birth to countless puppies; this was obvious from the shape of her body, her elongated nipples, the scars. Her hair was thin, but growing back after being treated for the flea infestation. Living in a house was all new to her. House-training was slow, but progress was finally happening. When she first arrived, she peed in her crate and then simply lay down in it because most likely she'd lived a life where that was her only option. The nasty, thick scar that encircled her neck told of a life lived on a chain with a collar embedded in her neck. Who did that? What kind of person? Did she only serve a purpose for someone else?

In *Rescue Road*, Peter Zheutlin tells of dogs who were used solely to breed a new hunting dog—a male, before the other puppies and the mother dog were disposed of or dumped. Or dogs of no pedigree that were bred in the hopes that the owners could make a few bucks selling the puppies. When it didn't work out or there were too many expenses that canceled the profit, the dogs and puppies were abandoned. One vet office discovered fourteen puppies from two litters stuffed in a plastic tub with the lid on and left on their front step. If an employee hadn't come in early that day, they would have suffocated. Miraculously, they all survived and made it to forever homes thanks to rescue efforts of unsung heroes in Louisiana.

The true miracle here was that despite her early years, Lucy was a happy, loving dog. She shouted out a joyful hound greeting from her crate in the morning when she heard me on the stairs. When I let her out, she jumped on me, wagging and licking and so hopeful for my attention. How could anyone tie up and neglect a dog with a heart like this?

This is where my mind was as I tried to say goodbye to Ginger. The night before she left, for the first time in twenty years of marriage, Nick let a dog sleep in our bed. Ginger snuggled between us all night and in the morning after Nick left for work, she and I had a serious talk. I tried to explain to her that I had to let her go so that I could help more dogs. I cried and she watched me. I looked into her sweet face and I promised her, "I'm gonna save as many as I can. That's the only reason I can't keep you. I have to save more." When I'd finished, she rubbed a paw along her ear and eye, as if to say, "Aw, don't worry about me."

But it wasn't her I was worried about. I knew her adopters were ready and excited. They'd come to visit her twice and asked all the right questions. It was a wonderful home with a fenced yard, two runners in the family, and three little girls who were getting their very first dog! Ginger deserved a home like that and she'd certainly waited long enough (over five months).

No, I wasn't worried about Gingersnap. I just hoped I could hold it together so the adopters didn't feel bad. I didn't want my pain to lessen their excitement. When the adopters arrived, I talked about the details, the contract, the future. I tried not to think about Ginger. I took a picture of them with her and posted it to Facebook so that all of Ginger's foster mommies could see how happy she was. And she was. In that picture, she is smiling almost as much as the little girls surrounding her.

After Ginger left, I headed to the doctor's office to get the results of my MRI and find out what happened next in terms of fixing my leg. Until I knew the answer to that question, I couldn't commit to another foster. I hoped the news would be good because I felt a sense of urgency. I needed to do more to help solve this fixable problem. We needed more foster homes, more resources, more awareness, more education. I wanted to do more. Now, if only my stupid leg would stop tripping me up.

TWENTY-TWO

Second Chances

My MRI revealed that there was a lot of damage—deep bone bruising, strained Achilles tendon, and a small tear in my meniscus. The doctor told me all this, but in the days between when I had the MRI and when I'd come in for the appointment, my knee had been feeling much better. I still couldn't bend it tightly—no crouching down or crawling on my knees—but other than that it felt nearly normal; weak, but not about to collapse as it had felt the week before.

"The tear might be old. We won't know until the bone bruising and the tendons heal," the doctor told me, sitting on a stool and gazing up at the image of my knee on the screen.

"So that means . . . ?"

"You can go back to normal activities."*

"Running too?" I asked.

"If it doesn't hurt, you're okay to do anything you want."

Great advice. And not just about running.

I was back! Lucy and I quickly upped our walk times and I even began adding in some slow jogging. "Don't overdo," said pretty much everyone. But I wasn't inclined to listen to everyone.

As Lucy and I wandered the back roads, I was still mulling over my new commitment to dog rescue. The challenge was enormous and complicated and, heck, where did I begin? I felt the same way I did when my elementary school science teacher explained how long it would take to get to Pluto—an impossible journey to even fathom. My teeny, tiny part in rescuing dogs couldn't possibly put even the idea of a dent in the problem. But now that my leg was healing, I was ready to get back in the game. I was ready to save more dogs. I was all-in. I would use the only tool I had besides my willingness to sacrifice my carpet, my home, and the patience of family and friends—I'd write about it. I began working on a proposal for a book about our foster experience. I'd tell our story in the hopes that others would read it and they'd see that they could foster too. My blog had lots of readers. People loved dog stories. And I had a good one to tell.

Meanwhile, Lucy still didn't have a single application for adoption. No one wanted her. And in reality, she was a hard sell. She wasn't a puppy, she was high energy, she was VERY hound-like, and at that point, she wasn't even particularly housebroken, much to my frustration. That morning she had peed on the Frank bed. I was furious! Why would she do this? *Why? Why? Why?* I took her outside, waited for her to not-pee (since she'd already done that) and then I brought her back in and closed her in her crate.

"You shouldn't write about that," said Nick.

"What?" I asked. "Me yelling at her or her peeing on the Frank bed?"

"Her peeing. No one will ever adopt her."

---

* I didn't tell him that normal activities mean fostering a herd of rescue dogs.

"Apparently, no one will ever adopt her already. I might as well be honest."

"Maybe put a positive spin on it."

"Right."

For the sixty-gazillionth time I wished dogs could talk.

Lucy wasn't a puppy and she lived a long time under harsh conditions; it would take time to teach her differently. But we would get there. The fact that she was in my kitchen was really a small miracle. She'd already beaten some pretty long odds. Neglect, early (and repeated) motherhood, desperation, then a skin infection, and another possible pregnancy—by every count, Lucy shouldn't have been here. Any shelter, even a good one, would have put her on the euthanasia list. It was too much effort and expense for one dog who wasn't very adoptable. Those resources could be used to save five or ten highly adoptable dogs instead.

And yet, here she was. Because someone, somewhere decided she deserved another chance. But why her and not another?

I didn't know, but what I did know was that after the past few weeks with my injury, I needed a puppy. Bad. So that night I picked up Oberyn, a three-month-old shepherd puppy from North Carolina, and another Scott County dog named Rooney, a blue heeler mix whose picture reminded me of Gingersnap.

The house was full and I was busy. No time to think about missing Ginger or all the dogs we couldn't save.

Our new foster, Rooney, was striking looking with a grey/blue-flecked coat and a tail ringed like a raccoon. I looked up blue heelers and she seemed to be textbook heeler. Wicked-smart, quiet but observant, and already very loyal and protective. She arrived with a urinary tract infection, most likely from holding her pee for the entire ride north. We were giving her cranberry pills and taking her out frequently, but she definitely seemed uncomfortable. Rooney's UTI, in fact, was most likely how the whole war started. It was the first grenade launched.

What war, you ask? The one that began raging in my kitchen the day after Rooney arrived. I didn't know who started it. I didn't know how it could possibly be "won," but I'd had entirely enough of it.

Both Lucy and Rooney had large crates in the kitchen. Although there had been no growling, snarling, barking, or even any mean faces, it seemed they didn't like each other. For the first twenty-four hours or so, they took turns being loose in the kitchen or shut in a crate. When Lucy was out, she spent the time cruising for crumbs or lying in her open crate—unless someone was in the kitchen handling food and then she gave them her unwavering attention.

When Rooney was out, she would sit or lay next to Lucy's crate. She didn't interact with Lucy or even glance at her. She just sat there looking very uncomfortable, but not making a sound. At some point on Saturday morning, Rooney peed next to Lucy's crate. I cleaned it up, took Rooney outside for a bit, and then put her in her crate and let Lucy have time in the kitchen.

Lucy checked the kitchen for crumbs and then helped me pack my lunch (we were getting ready to go to an adoption event). I ran out of the room to get something, and when I came back, Lucy had peed in the exact spot that Rooney had peed. Game on, apparently.

I said a few things that shouldn't be repeated, cleaned up the mess, and left for the event. Just to be safe, I left Rooney in her crate while we were gone. I won't bore you with the details, but some version of this battle continued for the next two days. Lucy upped the ante after they were both loose at the same time by peeing in Rooney's crate. After that, Rooney attempted to get in Lucy's crate at every opportunity.

All of this was making me NUTS (that's the PG version of my feelings). Both of these dogs were really sweet and got along fine with each other, if never acknowledging the other or interacting in any way (even when standing side by side) constituted getting along fine. Basically, they ignored each other, but it was obvious they weren't *really* ignoring each other. This was some serious passive-aggressive maneuvering.

When the pee wars started, I thought, *if only they were male dogs, I could cover up those bad boys.* But then it occurred to me that there is a dog product for every need and every dog. So of course there must be doggie diapers out there. And sure enough, I found them at my local pet store. I wasn't sure yet which dog should be wearing it, but I'd decided to place blame on the dog who should know better, so Lucy was now sporting a lovely, turquoise-colored doggie diaper complete with a hole for her tail.

Meanwhile, our other new foster, Oberyn, was an adorable puppydoll residing out of the war zone in the puppy room per puppy quarantine rules. He was a crazy-cute, solidly built little guy with a face that begged to be cuddled. I couldn't get enough of his puppyness and retreated to his space many, many times a day, where I held him in my lap or played puppy games like chase-the-toilet-paper-roll or one-sided-tug-of-war (I didn't want to pull out a puppy tooth). I told him he was gorgeous and perfect and I lamented the pee wars going on in the next room and then I promised him that after the war ended, I was ONLY going to foster puppies like him. He understood. (And he never peed anywhere but on his pee pads!)

One morning, in an attempt to help Rooney and Lucy "bond," I took them both for a walk up our road. I had intended to do my regular four-plus mile loop, but we barely made it two. Lucy barged ahead, straining at her harness, as if she had someplace to be. Rooney scuttled along behind me like the heeler she is. Each time Rooney stopped to pee (a lot), I had to haul Lucy back. Pretty much the entire walk, my right arm was stretched out in front of me trying to keep Lucy at a reasonable pace and my left arm was stretched out behind me, trying to encourage Rooney to keep up. I'm sure my neighbors enjoyed a chuckle as they passed me on their way to work.

There was no bonding, so we were back to taking turns in the kitchen. Whoever was loose wore the diaper. I was hoping some kind of truce would be declared soon. Meanwhile, I hung out a lot in the puppy room. Obie was the best kind of company. A puppy doth soothe the soul of a war-weary foster mom.

Lucy was a bit of a redneck, propelled by an intense appetite. She had no qualms about stealing food off the counter or licking abandoned plates at the table. She also didn't hesitate to pee on our living room carpet. To be fair, she wasn't the first dog to do it, and the large brown carpet probably smelled like a giant puppy pad. One night, I was mopping up her latest mess and shoved her out on the screened porch because Rooney was in the kitchen. Nick was on the porch reading. When I came out to get Lucy, he said, "At some point, this is going to stop, isn't it?"

"What?" I asked, hoping he was referring to the peeing in the house and not the fostering. He'd grown tired of the three-ring circus I was currently running with Rooney and Lucy battling, Oberyn trapped in puppy quarantine, and Gracie not getting along with any of them.

"They're ruining the floor," he said, nodding at the scratched-up cedar floor of the porch. I shooed Lucy off the screened porch onto the deck.

"That's not just the foster dogs," I countered. I knew Gracie was just as guilty of scratching up the floor with her nails as any of our guests.

"I'm not going to keep doing this," he said.

I looked at him in disbelief. I knew he'd been frustrated with the work and the mess lately. I'd abandoned him with it more than once as I traveled to promote *Girls' Weekend*. His own work was stressing him out of late, but I didn't dare mention it. He had a right to be upset about the dogs and it wouldn't be fair to blame it on his work.

"Obie will be out of quarantine soon. And Rooney already has an adopter," I said, trying to ignore his comment, pretend he hadn't just said what I thought he'd said.

"I can't work from home with Lucy here."

Lucy, being a hound dog, was very vocal. She had an uncanny knack for starting up every time Nick's conference calls commenced.

"Maybe you should just go to the office more, then." As much as it sounded idyllic for the two of us to work from home together, it had been anything but. What's that they say about too much of a good thing?

"Holy shit!" yelled Nick, jumping out of his seat and racing out on the deck where Lucy was now pooping. It should probably be pointed out that Nick built both our deck and our screened porch and feels a bit proprietary about them. I watched him drag Lucy down the stairs out into the yard. "I mean it!" he yelled back at me. "I'm not going to keep doing this."

Later, once all the dogs were in their crates, I joined Nick on the porch, hoping he'd cooled down.

"I've had enough," he said calmly when I sat down.

"Of what?"

"The dogs. It has to stop. You've done enough."

"But I haven't," I said. "I'm not finished."

"Well, I am."

"Are you telling me I have to decide between you and the dogs?"

He didn't say anything. He closed his book, got up and went inside. I hoped he didn't mean it. I love my husband, but the fostering had become about a lot more than enjoying the company of dogs. It was my mission. I was writing a book about it. *Would I give it up for Nick? Was it fair for him to ask?*

If I picked him over the dogs, I'd be angry with him for the rest of our lives. If I picked the dogs over him, well, what did that say about me? About our marriage?

When I finally went to bed, Nick was already asleep. I lay there wide awake. It was wrong for me to even consider dogs over my husband. What kind of person was I? I watched him in the dark. How could he just go to sleep after asking something like this? Didn't he understand how important fostering was to me?

As the night wore on, my anger and fear refused to let me sleep. I got up and wrote in my journal. I said the things I couldn't say to Nick. *How dare you ask me to choose between you and the dogs? I choose the dogs!* I got back in bed and stewed more, building my resentment at his unfair demand.

The next day Nick didn't mention his ultimatum and Lucy didn't have any accidents in the house or on the deck. I waited for Nick to bring it up, but he didn't. The week wore on. Lucy and Rooney made their peace; I waited for Nick and me to do the same. We tiptoed around each other, being impeccably polite.

I did my part to lessen the dog-strain on Nick. I located an outdoor kennel from another foster and installed it on the opposite side of the house far from Nick's work-from-home desk. I put Lucy in it while he was on conference calls, and instead of Nick's coworkers, the neighbors were treated to her lovely songs. I took her for long walks around the pasture. There were no more accidents in the house.

Eventually, we were able to joke about the ultimatum over a beer.

"I figured there wasn't a contest, you'd pick the dogs over me," he said.

"Never!" I said. "Okay, maybe."

As the topic of Nick versus the foster dogs faded, I promised myself that I would be very careful not to push him so far again. I wouldn't take my husband's help with the dogs for granted. I needed him. But more than that, I loved him.

Free from his quarantine, Obie became a source of great joy. He bounded around the yard and spent hours chewing on a stuffed pumpkin that came in his foster bag, making it *squeak-squeak-squeak.* At an adoption event, I mentioned it to another foster and she said, "You know why they like that sound, don't you?"

I shook my head.

"Because it sounds like a baby bunny dying."

She was absolutely right! I heard that sound nearly every night all spring as the cats disposed of all the new bunnies. Now, as I listened to Obie squeaking the pumpkin over and over, I thought, *He's too little and sweet to be a killer.*[*]

Both Rooney and Obie were adopted as soon as their holds were up, but Lucy lingered on with no adoption applications. I updated my kennel record,[†] and noticed that the next foster we took in would be number fifty!

Fifty dogs! Was it really possible we'd saved fifty dogs?

---

[*] A few weeks later, his adopter would email me to say that Oberyn found a nest of baby mice in his new home and killed every one of them. It did, indeed, sound like the pumpkin squeaking.

[†] We did finally have our kennel inspection (and passed!), so I was diligent about updating our records, especially now that we would easily surpass the twenty-five dogs-per-year mark.

TWENTY-THREE

Fiftieth Time's the Charm

There wasn't another transport scheduled for two weeks, but I was itching to find number fifty. A post popped up on the OPH Facebook feed. *Pregnant black Lab.*

I studied the picture. It was taken from above, so the dog's nose looked very long, but her belly didn't look so big. She looked like a real Lab, though, not just a BLM. I commented, "I'd like to take her, but I would have to move Lucy."

That was all it took to set things in motion. I felt a little guilty that I was trying to pawn Lucy off on another foster so that I could take this pregnant mama. Was I giving up on her? No! That wasn't it. But maybe someone else would do a better job helping her find her forever home, I reasoned as I watched her examine the same patch of grass for the eightieth time and not pee.

Later that week, we dropped Brady off for his second year at Susquehanna. As we moved him into his dorm room in a stately old building with pillars and brick, I felt like an old pro. We met his new roommate, an equally smart, nerdy guy with a bright smile and a positive attitude. His mom was a horse person and a writer, so we hit it off immediately. Nick rolled his eyes as we stood in the cramped room bonding over horse stories.

When the unpacking was finished, we took Brady to lunch at our favorite little pub that made wonderful craft beer. Brady was happy to eat with us, but it was clear that he was excited to get back to his dorm and reenter his college world, so we said goodbye and headed home.

This time my tears were minimal as we drove away. It seemed like it was only yesterday my own parents left me at my dorm in Virginia. It was also a traditional old brick dorm building, but not in nearly the excellent condition of Brady's new dorm. There was no air-conditioning and only cranky radiator heat on Bottom Davenport, where I lived for three of my four years at school. The old wood floors had dips and swells and you could pick holes in the plaster walls with their inch-thick layers of paint. I remember the rush of freedom that swept over me when I was finally alone in my new room. Life seemed so possible back then. Not that it isn't possible now, just, I don't think my life has been anything like I imagined it to be. It's been better.

I glanced at my husband. I have been blessed to have a partner like him. Even if he can irritate me at times with his Eeyore attitude and his need to explain details. Someone once told me that you should look for a person who brings out the best version of you. Most of the times, that is the case with Nick. His constant support for all my endeavors—writing, organic gardening, horses, and now dogs, has given me freedom to try almost anything because I know no matter how much trouble I get myself into, he'll be there to fix anything I break, clean up my messes, or pour me a glass of wine of congratulations or consolation. I really should tell him more often. I wondered, though, did I bring out the best in him? Who would he be if he'd never met me twenty years ago?

"We're lucky," I said and reached for his hand.

"We are," he agreed.

My phone lit up with a text from Ian and my nostalgic, romantic moment was gone.

When will you be home?

I was certain his real question was, *When's dinner?* but he was being polite.

"I wonder where we'll be driving Addie this time next year," mused Nick.

I shook my head. "I can't even begin to guess, but I hope it's Virginia."

Addie was considering Shenandoah University and I had my fingers crossed that it would be her first choice, and that they would offer some scholarship help, two very long shots.

"It's happening so fast," I said.

"The nest will be empty before you know it," smiled Nick. "But then you'll just fill it up with more dogs."

I laughed, but as we drove I wondered if he was right. Was I taking in more and more dogs to fill the empty places created by kids who no longer needed me? And what if I was? Was that such a bad thing? If I was honest, I'd admit that there were moments when I longed for a quiet house where only Nick and I lived. We'd never really had that. We met in February, started dating seriously in June, got engaged in October, and married the following November. Then I got pregnant with Brady three months after we'd married, so we had very little couple time that wasn't clouded by new love, wedding plans, or baby plans. It might be nice to just be us for a while. Well, us with a few dogs.

The dogs weren't replacing the kids, I decided. They were just giving me somewhere to aim the excess caregiving I found myself saddled with now that my kids had only occasional use for it.

The next day we hosted a gathering of OPH fosters and volunteers for a cookout. It was a last-minute affair, thrown together pot-luck style. Usually I only saw these people when we were "working" at adoption events, transport, or in my driveway or theirs handing off dogs or supplies, so it was a treat to see them for the simple purpose of being together. I discovered I enjoyed their company even when there wasn't a dog involved. Juanita observed Lucy, who was lapping up the attention and occasional dropped treats, and said, "I can take her. She'll fit right in."

"You're serious?" I asked. At that point, we hadn't found a replacement foster for Lucy, and I worried we wouldn't. Juanita's house was like dog paradise. Lucy would love it there. She'd quickly forget about me and my insistence that she pee outside and not bark so much.

True to her word, Juanita picked up Lucy on Thursday, which gave me two days to prepare for foster number fifty. I'd named the mama dog Edith Wharton, in honor of the first woman to win the Pulitzer Prize for fiction. It was a busy week as Nick was in France for most of it, so I was solo-parenting it. Addie was buzzing with the news that she got the part of Black Stache in the school's production of *Peter and the Starcatcher*. And before you ask, yes, Black Stache is normally a male role, but as I've pointed out before, my daughter absolutely breaks the norm on a regular basis.

All week as I went about my business, I painted a lovely romantic picture in my mind of Edith Wharton giving birth to a handful of puppies in our kitchen as we all watched the miracle. What a great experience for our milestone foster. I was so ready. I told everyone I met—"We're getting our fiftieth foster dog and she's pregnant!"

I borrowed a whelping box from Chris and Mary, my vet and his wife, who breed Gordon setters. Chris had built the box. It was large and spacious and too big for the puppy room, so we set it up in the kitchen. When Nick got home he ran to the hardware store and bought foam pipe insulators to cover the top edges so Edith wouldn't rub her heavy belly on it when she climbed in. I set down a layer of puppy pads and soft towels in preparation.

I looked through my calendar for the next week or so, making sure I could be home if necessary, already preparing my excuse ("Sorry, you're on your own. Gotta go. There's a dog giving birth in my kitchen . . .")

I read about puppy whelping and even watched a few badly made YouTube videos. I got advice from Mary and gathered all the supplies I'd need. Edith was due to arrive in less than twenty-four hours!

And then I checked my email.

Apparently, Edith was not made aware of my preparations and my whelping box. She'd given birth to the puppies at the shelter that morning.

I was disappointed and a little bit relieved. But then I read the rest of the story—Edith Wharton had TWELVE puppies. *Twelve?* I said to Gracie, who gave me a confused look and thumped her tail. *Where will we put twelve puppies?* Nine puppies pretty much maxed out the puppy pen last spring. Ah well, that was a problem for another day, because now I had to spend an entire evening worrying about Ms. Wharton traveling all night on a transport van in a crate with her TWELVE just-born puppies.

Nick and I were to meet the transport van at 6:15 the next morning. I barely slept. I'd stayed up too late drinking too much wine catching up with a dear friend I rarely saw who stopped by after book club. And then I lay in bed worrying that my alarm wouldn't go off and wondering if Edith would be a friendly sort of dog or would she say, "No, you may not touch my puppies and get out of my crate," when I reached in to move them to our car in only A FEW HOURS. Best not to sleep, just in case the alarm doesn't go off . . .

As we drove to the meeting place in the dark, I rattled on to Nick about how I was worried Edith wouldn't want me to touch the puppies and then how would we move them to the crate in our car and oh-my-gosh, why does this rescue trust me with things like this? He said, "She had *twelve* puppies. I think she'll be like, please, take a few."

Nick was more or less right, but only in the sense that Edith was fine with me touching her puppies. She still wanted to stay close to them, and fretted as I took her for a quick pee break while Nick moved the puppies. When Edith first climbed out of her crate, she brought tears to my eyes. She was SO skinny. Not skinny in like, she could use a sandwich, but skinny as in all of her bones were sticking out. I could count her individual ribs and her hip bones looked like horns on her back. The truly miraculous thing about this, beyond the fact that this girl was alive, was that she had grown TWELVE puppies and clearly, it had taken everything she had.

When we got home, Edith climbed in the whelping box and lay down with the puppies, and that's pretty much all she did for three days. The puppies nursed 24/7. They all had little fat bellies and were growing steadily. I fed Edith every hour—really good dog food, fresh eggs, vanilla ice cream, and a powerful fat/protein recipe another foster sent me called Satin Balls.*

I monitored the pups constantly, checking that everyone was breathing, and moving the two tiny ones to the better milk fountains. I started thinking about their names. Like their mom, I wanted to name the pups after famous writers. There were so many great names to choose from—Twain, Dickens, Fitzgerald. I had some girl names picked out too—Eudora Welty, Jane Austen, Louisa May Alcott.

I asked Chris, my unofficial OPH mentor, to come over to verify that everyone looked good and help me weigh the pups so I would be able to tell if they were all growing. I picked up each pup and described it to Chris, who wrote down my descriptions. Then I put a different color whelping collar on each pup so we'd be able tell them apart. Other than the fact that there were five yellow and seven black pups, they looked a lot alike. I picked up the first one—*girl*! The next one—*girl*! The next one—*girl*! If I hadn't been putting on whelping collars as I went, I'd have thought I was repeatedly picking up the same pup. It turned out that Edith gave birth to eleven girls and just one boy.

The puppies' eyes and ears were still closed and they couldn't support their weight, so they swam around on the towels in the box like seals on land or fat snakes with appendages. It was hard to tell if they weren't aware that their siblings were also puppies or if they simply didn't care, but they dragged themselves right over top of each other, stepping on heads or bellies and using whatever pup was handy for a pillow. If they woke up all alone, they'd begin mewling and blindly swimming around the box in their own version of newborn-pup Marco Polo until they found another soft body or the grand-prize—mama!

---

* Which Addie and I kept calling SATAN BALLS for some unknown reason.

I posted pictures on the Facebook group I'd started for readers of my blog and past or potential adopters. The pups had many admirers and already several of them had adoption applications.

As the pups grew, the noises coming from the puppy box ranged from an eerily accurate R2-D2 imitation to a rap DJ scratching a record to rubber sneakers on a gym floor. There was also a lot of grunting and snuffling, and honestly, they reminded me of the sounds my own kids made while nursing. Sweetness. Puppies, puppies, puppies . . . there were no bad days when twelve newborn puppies lived in your kitchen.

And then there was Edith. She was simply beautiful, which boded well for the funny-looking, noodle-limbed guinea pigs that adored her. They were "cute" now in the way that all odd-looking, helpless babies are, but if they grew up to be half as pretty as Edith, we'd be in good shape. Edith had gained a small amount of weight, enough that it didn't feel cruel to pet her, but not enough to make her look like she had any right to be nursing twelve puppies. Watching her care for them, nursing them, and giving them everything she should have been keeping for her own survival, was painful. So I tried to do everything I could to make it easier for her. I kept a thick layer of towels covering the thin carpeting that lined the box to make it softer on her bony body. I fed her five meals a day—concocting rich dishes of fat and protein to entice her to eat even more. I carried the water bowl to her whenever she was lying in an upright position so she didn't have to climb out of the box for a drink. We walked very, very slowly around the yard for potty breaks.

There were signs that Edith was feeling better. On the fourth day, she began leaving the box for reasons other than necessities. "What do you need doll?" I asked, offering food, water, and opening the door. She sighed and lay down near me. She just wanted my company.

Edith thumped her tail when any of us came near the box, whacking whichever puppies were in the vicinity in the process. She loved her "satan balls" so much that whenever I opened the fridge, she lifted her head and gave me her full attention, hoping I was going to pull out the magic container that held them.

Edith was doing better, the puppies were thriving, and it all seemed too good to be true. Because it was. I received news that Edith Wharton was heartworm positive. Unprotected dogs (those not on a heartworm preventative) can be infected with heartworms via a mosquito bite. These worms can grow to be a foot long and lodge themselves in the heart and lungs. Without the difficult, painful, and costly treatment, the situation progresses and the dog will die. Edith's heartworm numbers were high. She was exhibiting clinical signs. That soft little cough I thought was a cold was caused by the exertion on her compromised lungs. I watched her pant heavily whenever she was hot or with any exertion (nursing, walking around the yard) and my heart sank. Her body was incredibly thin for reasons other than growing twelve puppies, she was also hosting heaven knew how many dangerous worms.

I emailed the heartworm coordinator for OPH and asked about treatment. I was told that once the pups had weaned, Edith would have to wait a month to be spayed.* And then after that she would have her heartworm treatment†—a brutal, painful experience that I wasn't looking forward to, and at the same time I was because when it was over it would mean that we had truly saved her. Because if OPH hadn't stepped in and rescued Edith, nursing all those pups with little nutrition, the shelter's euthanasia list, or the heartworms, would have certainly killed her. Edith, I realized, was my biggest rescue.

I rubbed her sweet head and told her, "By Christmas you'll have a whole new world and this will just be a bad memory. No more puppies, no more heartworms, no more nobody caring about you. I promise."

---

* Dogs can't undergo anesthesia for at least six months after their heartworm treatment, so Edith would be spayed before her treatment to prevent another unwanted pregnancy.

† If left untreated, heartworms will eventually kill a dog, but the treatment can also sometimes kill a dog. Post-treatment, the dog must be kept as still and quiet as possible to make it less likely that as the worms break up they don't create a life-threatening clot.

My only niece (I have seven nephews!) and her adorable husband came for a visit from California when the pups were just two weeks old. Mary was a diligent nursery supervisor, always making sure that the two runts—Eudora Welty and George Eliot,* got their share. We managed to leave the puppies long enough for a trail ride through the early-autumn countryside and a visit to York's Central Market, one of the oldest and longest-running markets in the country. Mary and Daniel weren't the only visitors we had that fall. Our home became a destination for lots of people in need of puppy therapy, and the puppies worked their magic on everyone—especially me.

---

* George Eliot is a famous woman writer (look her up) but naming her George led to several mixups as adopters and adoption coordinators assumed she was the boy pup (that was Hemingway).

TWENTY-FOUR

Happy Endings

Lucy was doing well at Juanita's, but still had no adoption applications. We traded regular messages about her quirks and habits and sweetness. Juanita works nights as a nurse, so getting Lucy to one of the many adoption events held on the weekends proved difficult.

I spent one Saturday at the New Freedom Fest, a festival celebrating our little town that draws thousands of people. OPH's booth always does well and I'd committed to being there, so I dragged myself away from the puppies to help out. I brought along some of my books to sell and sign to benefit the rescue. Lots of people stopped by the booth looking at our adoptable dogs, not that many were interested in the *famous author*. Again and again I thought, "If only Lucy were here. She might find her family."

When I handed Lucy off to Juanita, I'd felt like I had failed her. It had been a long six weeks from the crazy pickup in Hagerstown to the faux-pregnancy and that awful flea allergy, plus the spay and the endless cone of shame–wearing. Add to that the challenge of teaching her how to live indoors without alienating all the people who lived there. Lucy wore me out physically and emotionally. When you put a lot of time and effort into a dog, as we had with Lucy, the payoff was seeing her find her forever home. I was bummed I wouldn't get that ending. But I was distracted by Edith and her dozen.

Driving back from the fest, I decided Lucy couldn't sit home again and miss the adoption event scheduled for the next day. I would go to Juanita's and pick up Lucy and take her to the event in a nearby town. It was high time she found her family. I owed it to her to help.

I've mentioned the adoption juju before, right? How sometimes dogs hang around and hang around and you just don't understand why they haven't been adopted, and later it all becomes clear? During the six weeks we'd had Lucy, she'd never had even one application. It didn't make sense to me—there was so much good about Lucy. Sure, she was a hound. In fact, she was ALL hound, but surely someone out there wanted a houndish hound. There had to be *someone* who wasn't put off by the food obsession and the busy chewing, who enjoyed the songs that hounds sing.

On Sunday morning, Lucy and I joined the OPH crew under the canopy outside the PetSmart. Shortly after we got there, a young couple and their little boy approached the tent and asked, "Is that Lucy?" as if Lucy were some kind of rock star. Having taken Lucy to four adoption events, I could honestly say that no one had ever referred to Lucy in that tone. Most people were there to see the Labs or the tiny dogs, and plenty of dads would stop and say, "Oh, look at the hound dog," but no one had ever been that delighted to see Lucy.

When I told them that yes, this was Lucy, they were overjoyed, even teary, and cried, "I can't believe she's here!"

Sarah and Tim had found Lucy on OPH's site, and just the day before had decided that she was the dog they wanted. They'd emailed OPH, but it being a Saturday, hadn't heard anything yet. They were so excited about the idea of finally finding their dog that they'd come to PetSmart to pick up a few items. I'm not sure they even knew that OPH would be there. Their little boy looked at Lucy and said, "She's gonna be my sister!" He bounced around like only a five-year-old who's getting his first dog can.

I warned them about her hound-dog habits—the food, the nose, the howl. They smiled and nodded. They knew about hounds. They'd had hounds before. Lucy leaned into her new dad and wagged all over. She seemed as sure as they were.

We learned that they had already applied and been approved, and had just been waiting to find the right dog. And here she was! They hadn't expected to see her and couldn't take her home right then because they still needed to get supplies and send a picture of their non-bully breed dog to their landlord.*

I gave them the leash and they took Lucy inside to pick out toys and be fitted for a harness. I watched Lucy with this family with whom she already seemed to belong. I got my happy ending, but more importantly, Lucy got hers.

Over the next month, the puppies grew, morphing from wiggling lumps to barking, whining, adorable little butterballs. I fed and fed Edith, but she barely gained an ounce. The puppies on the other hand were now all nearly five pounds. It was time to start feeding them puppy food and less Edith food.

I soaked puppy kibble in milk-replacer and then fired up my Cuisinart to turn it all to a pale gray mush. Then I filled three small plates and set them out in the puppy box. Edith and I watched from the side. In moments, the pups realized that this new item in the box was not for walking on, but for eating!†

It was getting pretty cramped in the box for twelve puppies, so I prepared our puppy room, which had been sitting idle since Oberyn

---

* Their landlord had his own BSL (breed specific legislation) prohibiting his tenants from owning *bully* breeds like pit bulls and rottweilers.

† Well, sometimes it was for walking on *and* eating.

left. Standing in the doorway, studying the space, I still couldn't figure out how we would keep twelve puppies in there for four more weeks. The Hamilton puppies had been a tight squeeze and this crew was even bigger. Laying an extra sheet of vinyl flooring on one end extended the space a few feet. If I could talk Nick into taking the door off its hinges and replacing it with a baby gate, that would buy us a little more room. Bottom line—the space was too small. But it was my only option, so we would make it work. I figured if I could get them outside as much as possible to wear them out, this space could be for sleeping. Best-laid plans. I've got tons of them.

The puppies moved into their new space and I began limiting Edith's time with them. I wanted the puppies weaned so we could start the work of saving her life. At five weeks, they were old enough to stop nursing. Each day I took away another feeding session with Edith until we were down to only once a day and then I shortened that session until we stopped altogether. I emailed the heartworm coordinator and medical director for OPH. Now what?

Cheryl, the heartworm coordinator, laid out a schedule for Edith. In three weeks she would start her pretreatment meds. In four weeks she would be spayed. In six weeks she would go to the vet for her heartworm treatment. Six more weeks of worms growing. I looked at her sleek coat and her growing waistline as signs that she would win this battle, but it didn't erase the little ball of terror niggling at the back of my mind—*what if?*

Nancy, Edith's adopter, was coming by regularly to visit with Edith and take pictures of the pups. I'd known Nancy peripherally in our small town. We were friends on Facebook, but I didn't know her well. Her youngest son had been in school with Brady. Nancy was a photographer and had regularly shot the shows Addie performed in, kindly sharing pictures with me after the events. It didn't take long for us to bond over our mutual affection for Edith and the pups. Very soon she felt like an old friend.

Nancy was in love with Edith and already imagining their future together. I started a fundraising page online and dozens of people donated to help pay for Edith's heartworm treatment and were following her story. And me, well, I adored this girl. If she didn't survive treatment, which was an unlikely but real possibility given the advanced stage of the worms and her high energy level that we were only getting a glimpse of now, well . . . well, a lot of hearts would be broken. Not the least of which was Edith's. She deserved a happy future.

Puppy adopters, blog readers, friends who stopped by all asked me where Edith came from. I didn't have a real answer. Obviously, someone had loved this dog at some point in her life. She couldn't have such a generous and friendly demeanor if she hadn't experienced love already. I wanted to think that her previous owner was just ignorant. She didn't know to give heartworm meds. She didn't realize how important it was to spay your dog. She never considered microchipping her. And Edith got lost. That's the best-case scenario, but it was still a scenario that sucked. The bottom line was someone, somewhere in South Carolina didn't love this dog enough to do the right thing again and again and again.

Edith's story is all too common, but she was a lucky dog. Nine out of ten dogs in her situation never left the shelter. Pregnant *and* heartworm-positive—very few rescues will take that on. Once again, I was proud to be part of OPH.

By the time the puppies were six weeks old, they each had an adopter. The adopter visits were constant and I could barely keep track of who was adopting who. The countdown began and I prepared the adopters for what was coming. *Get a crate. Find a trainer. Clear your schedule.* These puppies were big and smart and could easily takeover a life. *Beware.*

"We're running low on puppies," said Ian after he'd poked his head in the puppy room one Sunday and noticed there were only three puppies left to be picked up by their adopters. The quiet in our house was remarkable. The silence rang like it did when the baby finally stopped crying and fell asleep all those long nights a decade or two ago when we were young parents.

Isn't it hard to give them away?

If you foster dogs, this is a question tossed at you on a regular basis. Yes, it is hard to give them away. Every time. Sometimes it's harder than others.

I wouldn't miss cleaning up after twelve puppies, but I would miss each of these precious pups who I'd come to know and love. I would miss George's impish ways and Zora's constant need for hugs. I would miss Louisa May's soft, soft coat, and the quiet way Eudora leaned in to me, wanting my attention but not demanding it like the others. I would miss all these pups. Just like I missed all the dogs and puppies that came before them.

In the beginning, fostering for us was about having fun with a new dog, trying each one out as if it could be our own. Each adoption was a decision for me—*should we keep this one*? And each time when the decision was made to let a dog leave, I felt sad, guilty even. Somewhere along the line, though, I'd stopped thinking of the dogs as mine. It didn't hurt less, but it was easier. I didn't imagine any of them staying. I had an important job here. It was to prepare the dogs for their new home. If I did my job right and OPH's adoption coordinator team did their job right, there was a very good chance that the next home these dogs moved to would be their last. So when each dog left it wasn't because I'd decided not to keep it, it was because I'd helped it find its home, and now we could save another good dog.

Three weeks after the last puppy left, Edith went to the vet for her heartworm treatment. Driving home after leaving her for her overnight stay, I sent up silent prayers. It was cold and miserable and being the jinx-paranoid, sign-seeking person that I am, I worried this was a bad omen. Heartworm treatment is brutal but necessary. Without it the worms would basically consume Edith's heart and lungs. I tried not to picture the physical reality of the worms being killed by the treatment and how they would get out of Edith's body. The danger of a clot would hang over Edith for months. She wouldn't be truly heartworm free for six months, maybe more. It would be up to me and eventually, Nancy, to keep her quiet and unstressed to reduce the possibility of a life-threatening clot.

The next day, when the receptionist from the vet's office called to tell me Edith was doing well, and I could pick her up, she teased, "And if you don't pick her up, I would be happy to take her home." Seems Edith had stolen more than a few hearts in her short time at their office.

Over the next two weeks, I kept Edith as quiet as possible. True to form, she was an excellent patient, but near the end of her enforced quiet time she began to grow restless, and her eyes took on a new shine. She stopped backing down from Gracie, claiming the Frank bed for herself and stealing Gracie's food when she wasn't looking. She shocked us with her accomplished counter-surfing abilities and nearly ate a piece of the thousand-piece puzzle I'd almost completed. I fished the pieces out of her mouth and scolded her for the first time in her three-month stay with us.

Two weeks later, Nancy took Edith home to start her life. She wouldn't get the all-clear on heartworms for six months, but it was time for her to start her much-deserved happily ever after. And it was time for our next fosters to arrive—three puppies named Dusty, Russell, and Hershey.

"More puppies?" everyone asked. "Don't you need a break?"

No, I didn't need a break. I needed another good dog.

Epilogue

A nd what about my dog? The one I was going to find by fostering all these dogs. Time and again, I tried to envision what my life would be like if I kept Carla or Frank or Lily or Lafayette. I did want a dog that was truly my dog. But what stopped me from keeping any of them was Gracie. If I've learned anything in this adventure it's that I don't really know what any dog is thinking, and yet I'm convinced that keeping any of our foster dogs would have broken Gracie's heart.

Gracie may not be perfect, but she's the dog I chose seven years ago when I met her as a puppy in the apartment of a foster who had stepped up to rescue her litter. You never know what you're getting when you adopt any dog, not really. But you make a commitment when you decide to adopt. I made a commitment to Gracie, and maybe if I stopped wanting her to be something she wasn't I'd be happy with the dog she was—*my dog*. Fostering couldn't have been easy on her, and yet she'd accepted foster dog after foster dog, sometimes grumbling, but never getting angry. Perhaps having always been second banana to Lucy made it easier for her to share us with so many other dogs. Maybe we'd unknowingly trained her for this important job of fostering foster dogs. I watched her roll on the brown carpet, leaving a fresh coat of white hair. Maybe, just maybe, Gracie was perfect—for us.

Another foster, Juanita, and I were talking about me writing this book, and I said, "But I don't know what the ending is. I started fostering because I was looking for a dog to replace Lucy, but I haven't found her, and I don't think I will."

"Did you ever think that maybe you're getting what you're looking for with the foster dogs?" Juanita asked.

"What do you mean?"

"The dogs give us love and challenges and fun and companionship and a sense of purpose. Maybe those are the things you were looking for in a dog, and maybe you're getting them now. Maybe your dog is all these foster dogs."

I thought about Juanita's words long after she left. And I think she's right. I think that my dog *is* all these foster dogs. All those years ago, we rescued Lucy. And she gave us love and loyalty. She was our faithful companion and protector as we raised our babies. She was my best friend when I was lonely in a new town and my personal trainer, helping me discover my passion for running. But now what do I want from a dog?

Love. The unconditional, undeserved, and unending love that a dog offers. I'm getting that in spades again and again from foster dogs who have rarely experienced it themselves.

I used to think that "dog people," much like "horse people," were slightly *askew.** I can't say that by getting to know so many of them, that observation has changed, but then again, as I've gotten older I've realized that most of the really interesting people in this world are a little askew.

For years, I was involved in local politics and issues. I wrote a little column for the paper whenever I was fired up and had an opinion to push—charter schools, local elections, irresponsible growth, etc. I was a PTO president and served on our local political committee, working the polls, knocking on doors, carting voter registration cards around with me.

---

* That's my polite way of saying, *nuts.*

I found myself sad and frustrated by my efforts again and again. Disappointed in people, politics, and what I saw as hateful attitudes, outright stupidity, and unfair policies, I finally realized that all I was doing was expending my own emotional effort and precious time on issues and people and problems that I had no hope of changing.

So, I pulled back. I escaped into my fiction writing—a much more controllable world. And I fostered dogs. Fifty of them.

I've gotten to know the nutso dog people, the fosters, volunteers, shelter workers, and adopter after adopter who made their way up my driveway. I'm quite certain that many of them hold very different political viewpoints than I do. We most likely don't agree about gun control, funding education, abortion rights, the environment, or international business. We may have very different religious views, shop in different stores, eat at different restaurants, and enjoy completely different forms of entertainment.

And yet we have one thing in common—we love dogs. Through this joint passion we connect. We offer our respect, our stories, our mutual admiration for the canine in question. It makes me wonder if we all focused on something we have in common—like our commitment to rescue dogs—if we couldn't build a foundation for friendship that might be strong enough to allow us to hear each other on other issues.

I hope someday there will be no need for dog rescue. I hope we will all have to find a breeder to buy our next dog because there are no shelters and no homeless dogs.

As I worked to end this book, I couldn't figure out where I should stop. There is still too much work to be done. So maybe the place to end is with an invitation.

Join me.

Rescue. Foster. Adopt.

YOU Can Foster Too!

I know the problem of unwanted dogs in this country is complicated, but **it is a fixable problem**. It is a matter of changing perceptions and educating people about spay/neuter and proper immunizations. We can do this, and I believe we will, but meanwhile, what we need beyond finances, awareness, adopters, and education, is foster homes—people who are willing to open their doors and their hearts to shelter a pet, to give that animal a safe place, just long enough for its forever family to find it. Fostering is a magical opportunity to offer grace in a world with so little of it.

Approximately 3.9 million dogs enter shelters each year. Of those dogs, about 1.4 million are adopted, and somewhere around 542,000 are lost dogs returned to their owners. You can do the math and figure out how many dogs that leaves to be euthanized each year. Shelters can only house a set number of dogs. They are not the bad guys. I'm willing to bet that there isn't a shelter worker anywhere who enjoys making the hard decisions about which dogs will live and which will die. They simply don't have the resources to care for every single dog that comes through their doors until it is adopted. This is where foster homes can make the difference.

Foster homes offer the only chance for dogs (and cats!) who have otherwise run out of time. And beyond that, a dog adopted out of a foster home has a better chance of a successful adoption. A foster parent can give a more accurate description of their foster dog's habits, quirks, and needs than an overwhelmed shelter can, which will lead to a better match for adopter and dog.

I know you've got a really good reason why you could never foster. Or maybe you've thought about fostering but aren't sure you're ready. Let me tell you something—you're never ready. None of us are.

Luckily, the dogs are pretty understanding and more than patient with us. We offer them stability, food, safe shelter, medical treatment, and most of all—love. That's five things they may have never experienced in their lives.

And here's what they offer in return:

1. **Unconditional and many times overly enthusiastic love.** This can't be overstated. Time and again, I've been overwhelmed by the affection and devotion my foster dogs shower on me, often within hours of their arrival. It does seem they are grateful even if the experts might dispute that dogs understand the concept of gratitude.

2. **A chance to make a difference not only in a dog's life, but in the lives of its adopters.** Helping people is healing. I've discovered that when I am most down, the quickest way to get happy is to focus on others. Fostering dogs offers plenty of opportunity to touch the lives of others—both canine and human. We've placed over one hundred dogs and puppies now, which means I have at least one hundred new friends. I always thank them for choosing to rescue, and I can't count the number of times I get a message a few days later from the adopter explaining that he or she is the one who's been rescued.

3. **Exercise and inspiration!** There have been more than a few mornings, when I didn't want to go for a walk or

run, but many of those days I had a foster dog in residence who needed a walk or run. Fostering could be an excellent fitness plan for anyone.

4. **Entertainment!** Welcoming new dogs into your home on a regular basis means you'll have a steady stream of entertainment. The antics, quirks, silliness, and fun vary with every dog. It's also been one of the few things our family can do together. While some members are more enthusiastic than others, I'm pretty sure they're all glad we do it—even my daughter, who doesn't always appreciate their messy affections.

5. **A whole new network of friends who quickly become like family.** The rescue world is special. We are all on the same mission. Others who foster or volunteer are quick to reach out with help and support, whether it's showing up to help you give your first vaccine, drop off additional supplies, offer suggestions for how to handle housetraining issues, or simply cheer you on. Being welcomed into the OPH family was a huge benefit I never considered when I was making my decision to foster, but it's probably one of the reasons I can't ever imagine quitting.

I can hear you now, coming up with all your excuses, so let me address a few of the most common:

I don't know what I'm doing. True, you don't. As you've just read, I've made (and continue to make!) plenty of mistakes. OPH and rescues like it have plenty of resources—both on paper, online, and in person, plus conference calls and near-constant online support. No, you may not know what you're doing, but a good rescue does and you will too, soon enough.

What if I get a difficult dog? I'm lucky because OPH does a good job of screening dogs and doesn't knowingly bring in aggressive dogs.

That said, if you foster enough dogs you're going to run into an issue eventually. We've fostered over one hundred dogs,* and with no exceptions I could have kept every one of them. The toughest to deal with were Hadley, because she was the most traumatized, and Foo Foo, who about drove me crazy with her inability to understand the concept of peeing outside. Carla couldn't stay off the beds, John Coffey escaped a time or two, Whoopi's drool was disgusting, and Lucy's constant baying about broke me. But other than the damage to the living room carpet, our home is more or less unscathed. I can't say the same for many pairs of shoes and personal items that were not put away where they belong, and there is not a stuffed animal left stuffed anywhere in the house.

I know that more challenging dogs are on our horizon, but I also know that this organization will not abandon me, or any dog, so I'm ready.

I might get stuck with a dog long-term. We've been more than amazed that all of our dogs have been adopted pretty quickly (longest was Carla at four months and shortest was Tweety at twenty-four hours). The only way you get stuck with a dog is if you choose to foster fail.

It will cost money. I will tell you that it won't, but then it might. We've spent plenty of our own money, but we've done so willingly. Nearly everything we need is supplied through the rescue and donations, but sometimes it's just easier to go grab a few items ourselves. Mostly I remember to save receipts for the tax write-off, but in the end, sure, we spend some money. But who doesn't spend money on something they love?

I work full-time and the dog will be alone all day. I work from home, so many of my fosters can hang out with me as I work. Their company is welcome. But the majority of fosters I know crate their foster dog during the hours they are away. At first I thought, *poor dogs,* but then it

---

* As of this writing.

was pointed out to me that dogs sleep anywhere from twelve to twenty hours a day.* More than that, many, if not most dogs will be crated during the day while their owners work. As a foster, I can prepare my dog for this by crating it during the day so that it can learn to enjoy that quiet time.

My personal dog, Gracie, chooses to spend a good portion of time every day in her crate. We never close her in unless someone is visiting,† and still she chooses to sleep in her open crate easily twelve to twenty hours a day. Working full-time out of the house doesn't mean you can't foster dogs.

The biggest reason people don't want to foster is that they are afraid they won't be able to give the dog up or that it will hurt too much when they do. I'm not going to lie and say it doesn't hurt. It does. Sometimes more than others. But what I tell myself every time is that my pain is a small sacrifice I can make in order to save more dogs. It also helps immensely that most adopters stay in touch and regularly let me know how my dogs are doing with pictures and updates. "It will make me sad," really doesn't hold up when you consider the number of dogs our country euthanizes every year. *That* should make you sad.

Ready to get involved? There are quite literally thousands of dogs in need of foster homes right now. Consider opening your home and your heart to a foster dog. It's awesome, messy, fun, and occasionally stressful, but the bottom line is you will get so much more than you will ever give.

---

* This must be where the term "lucky dog" comes from!

† She is still learning how NOT to jump on the people she likes, and NOT to bite the people that frighten her.

Acknowledgments

I have to first thank Nick, Brady, Addie, and Ian for joining me on this adventure. I know you had no idea what we were getting into, but I hope it has been at least half as fun and rewarding for you as it has been for me. Thanks for indulging my mission—walking countless dogs, not grumbling about the baby gates, and tolerating the occasional ruined shoe without too much fuss. Fussing is understandable.

Thanks to my tireless agent, Carly Watters, for believing in this book and for reminding me (again and again), it only takes one "Yes!" Thanks also to Jessica Case and the fabulous people at Pegasus for making this beautiful book and for supporting its mission.

Thanks to early readers who said, "Why yes, this could be a book," and then gave me encouragement and instruction—Susan Robinson, Nick Achterberg, Lou Aronica, Margot Tillitson, and Pat Hazlebeck.

Special thanks to Kim Kavin, a fabulously talented writer and dog-hearted person whose writing inspires me and who generously offered to read an early draft of this manuscript.

There are so many people (and dogs) to thank for helping me on the journey chronicled in this book. My very first OPH contacts, Mindy Young, Erica Weaver, and Gina Pilsucki—thanks for holding my hand, patiently explaining, and stifling your laughter. Thanks to my PA OPH sisters—Chris DeHaan, Juanita Conroy, Deb Landers, Susan Alban, Nancy Slattery, and Karen Roland for your support, ideas, and ready presence. You make the work easier.

OPH founder, Jen Dodge, and current director, Laurie Landers, your professional and passionate ways set the tone for this outstanding organization. Thanks for your availability, honesty, and unfailing support, but mostly, thanks for always putting the dogs first.

To all the adopters I've met through the dogs in this book and the ones who have come after, THANK YOU FOR CHOOSING TO RESCUE. Despite the spotted carpet, chewed chair rungs, and sleepless nights, it has been my greatest privilege to offer your dog a safe place on its journey to you.

And to my entire OPH family—thank you for your work, your stories, your support, and your big dog-loving hearts. We are making a difference and I am so very proud to be a part of this family. *Together we rescue.*